The Rocky Road to the Great War

THE ROCKY ROAD TO THE GREAT WAR

The Evolution of Trench Warfare to 1914

NICHOLAS MURRAY

FOREWORD BY HEW STRACHAN

Potomac Books | Washington, D.C.

Potomac Books is an imprint of the
University of Nebraska Press.

Library of Congress Cataloging-in-
Publication Data
Murray, Nicholas, 1966–
The rocky road to the Great War: the
evolution of trench warfare to 1914 /
Nicholas Murray; foreword by Hew
Strachan. — First Edition
pages cm
Includes bibliographical references
and index.
ISBN 978-1-59797-553-7 (hardcover:
alk. paper) — ISBN 978-1-61234-
105-7 (electronic) 1. Fortification,
Field—History. 2. Intrenchments—History. 3. Military art and
science—History. I. Title.
UG403.M87 2013
355.4'4—dc23
2013008396

Printed in the United States of
America on acid-free paper that meets
the American National Standards
Institute z39-48 Standard.

Potomac Books
22841 Quicksilver Drive
Dulles, Virginia 20166

First Edition

10 9 8 7 6 5 4 3 2 1

Contents

Illustrations

Foreword

The trenches of the First World War have a bad reputation. Smelly and muddy, rat and lice infested, they do not rate among the most beautiful of military constructions. Nor, unlike the castles of the Middle Ages or the fortifications of Vauban, have they lasted well. They defined not only the western front but also the war as a whole and what it meant for a generation. Yet, a hundred years later, we need to look carefully if we are to detect where they once were.

Their notoriety is undeserved. They saved lives; without them the war would have been even more destructive than it was. In the half century before 1914, a revolution in firepower transformed the battlefield, creating a beaten zone swept by machine-gun fire and quick-firing artillery. Tactically, the attack became much harder to execute and its demands of human endurance even greater—at least in the minds of the general staffs that had to find a solution to the problem. One answer, and the one for which they have been most often castigated, was to stress the importance of morale and the need, in the final rush, to press home the offensive, "cost what it will." But this was neither the solution most regularly adopted in the First World War nor the only one to which military minds were bent before it. An alternative was to develop field fortifications, to think through how to fight the defensive battle, and to devise ways of making it strategically effective as well as tactically sensible. That is the story—a neglected one but one without which we cannot understand twentieth-century warfare—that Nicholas Murray tells in his important book.

In the aftermath of the Napoleonic wars, permanent fortification, built of masonry and stone, came to be seen as a specialist matter, separated from the conduct of campaigns of maneuver, and studied by a separate and self-contained part of the army. It was a subject for geeks, and it also cost a lot of money. The latter was a serious consideration when the technical advances in artillery, permitting heavier calibers to take the field and enabling them to fire with greater precision and consistency, presented fixed defenses with continuous obsolescence. Those built by France in the decade after the Franco-Prussian War were out of date ten years later, with adoption of smokeless powder and reinforced concrete.

Field fortification was cheaper than permanent structures, and defenses made of earth, reinforced with materials like wood, could be constructed more quickly and in locations where they were actively needed. It was not just price and materials that made field fortification attractive. It also fulfilled one of the cardinal principles of war, that of economy of force, and it did so in at least three ways. The first has already been mentioned: that of saving lives. Second, mass armies, made up of short-service conscripts, often with low levels of discipline and training, promised to be both easier to control and more effective if placed in defensive positions. At their most basic, they made desertion more difficult. And, third, a fortified position could be held defensively with fewer men, releasing others for operations elsewhere, including the offensive. In other words, field fortification could enable maneuver, as well as retard it.

Extraordinarily, no scholar has told before the story that Nicholas Murray tells here. Perhaps its importance has been too obvious; more probably, as he suggests himself, the determination to criticize the military thinkers who flourished in Europe between the ending of the Franco-Prussian War and the outbreak of the First World War, has prompted historians to deny such an obvious manifestation of common sense and pragmatism. Contained within it are the histories of five wars, the Russo-Turkish War of 1877–1878, the South African War of 1899–1902, the Russo-Japanese War of 1904–1905, and the two Balkan Wars of 1912–1913. All five were fundamentally shaped by field fortification and its application on the battlefield, and all were, in that sense and others, precursors of the First World War. Some of these conflicts themselves qualify for the epithet "neglected," and for all of them the role of field fortification has long demanded that they be examined not only in their own right but also for their contribution to changes in the conduct of war as the latter absorbed the impact of industrialization. Nicholas Murray has carried out research in archives in London, Paris, Vienna, and the United States, and he has ransacked the professional literature of a reflective and deeply committed generation of soldiers. He has filled a massive gap in the history of war. All those who study it are in his debt.

Hew Strachan
Chichele Professor of the History of War
University of Oxford

Preface

Between 1877 and 1914 the use of field fortification became increasingly important, and its construction evolved from primarily above- to belowground. These changes explain the landscape of the First World War, yet they have remained largely unstudied. This book defines, examines, and tests the theories and construction of field fortification between 1877 and 1914 for the first time.

The changes that took place in constructing field fortifications reflected the technological developments then occurring and the changing priorities of the forces' reasons for constructing them. Those reasons included preventing desertion, protecting troops, multiplying forces, reinforcing tactical points, providing a secure base, and achieving domination of an area. Field fortification theory and practice changed not solely at the whim of improving firepower or technology but rather through a combination of those factors as well as societal ones.

The primary sources of information for the case studies are the reports of military attachés who observed the conflicts. Frequently the observers witnessed events in person or were in a position to interview recent combatants. They were also military men with an understanding of the nature of war and, consequently, of much of what they witnessed. Many of their reports were disseminated around the armed forces of their respective countries in the form of histories or campaign reports. The other main source material is taken from contemporary technical manuals, which provide an exact idea of what was going on at a specific moment in time. The exception is for the chapter on the Second Anglo-Boer War of 1899–

1902. The attachés in this war were at the front only a limited time, and most of them went home as soon as the major fighting ended. Thus, they largely missed seeing the prolonged guerrilla war and the extensive use of fortifications later in the conflict. In addition, as Britain was one of the combatants during the war and did not have any attachés to speak of, I have chosen to include a number of personal accounts with their firsthand eyewitness descriptions of events to supplement the reports of the French, Austrian, and American attachés. I have also used the official history rather more for this chapter than is the case in the other wars examined. This solution is not perfect, but it does allow the reader to study the war with some level of detail.

The conflicts examined for the case studies are the Russo-Turkish War of 1877–1878, the Second Anglo-Boer War of 1899–1902, the Russo-Japanese War of 1904–1905, and the Balkan Wars of 1912–1913. These wars witnessed the evolution of the construction of field fortification, as well as a change in the importance of the various ideas about their use, with protecting the troops becoming more critical while preventing their desertion became less so. By 1914 artillery had become the dominant weapon, along with the combination of machine guns, barbed wire, and trenches. The evolution in the use of these fortifications and weapons set the scene for the western front, and during these wars the prevailing ideas about the role of offensive spirit were reinforced through the repeated success of the operational and strategic aggressors in each case.

Some words are in order on the matter of transliteration and dates. Throughout this book I have adhered to the most common spelling of both place and personal names as found in the sources. Owing to the complexity of all the different languages involved, the spelling might not always reflect the most modern form. On the matter of dates, I have followed the Gregorian calendar for the ease of the reader. The Julian calendar, however, remained in use in Bulgaria, Romania, Russia, Greece, and Turkey after the period covered by this book.

Regarding the names of individuals mentioned in this book, I have provided the first names when they are known. Otherwise, I have included the initials of the first names if the information was available. If the first name or initials were not available, I have listed as much information as possible about the person.

Acknowledgments

It is an honor for me to recognize the assistance I have received in completing this book. In this respect I would like to thank my doctoral supervisor, Professor Hew Strachan, who, as Chichele Professor of the History of War at All Souls College, provided much needed patience, guidance, insight, and impetus to my research. I would also like to thank Christopher Pringle, who sparked my interest in the Russo-Turkish War of 1877–1878 and has given greatly of his time, as well as access to his collection of books.

Professor Andrew Lambert of the War Studies Department at King's College in London helped me form my initial ideas on the subject, and for that assistance I am especially grateful. I would also like to thank Dr. Bruce Gudmundsson for help with papers and books, as well as stimulating conversations that sparked some helpful ideas. In addition, Kathleen Gudmundsson has been of great assistance with research in both the French and Austrian archives. Dr. Bruce Menning was kind enough to read through the manuscript and make some suggestions. Dr. Daniel Marston was very helpful with the chapter on the Second Anglo-Boer War, and Dr. John Kuehn with the one on the state of military thinking in 1914.

Institutions that provided help include the National Archives, Kew; the Royal Engineers Library, Chatham; the Library of Congress; the U.S. National Archives; le Service Historique de la

Défense; la bibliothèque de l'École Militaire; Österreicherisches, Kriegsarchiv, Wien; the Library of the United States Marine Corps; the Library of the U.S. Army Command and General Staff College; the U.S. Army Military History Institute; the National Army Museum in London; and the Oxford University Library Services.

Any flaws contained herein are my own.

The Rocky Road to the Great War

1

The Theory of Field Fortification, 1740–1914

The First World War was one of almost unimaginable destruction, bringing with it nearly ten million deaths and enormous social upheaval. The very savagery of the fighting and its great scale largely had not been predicted before the war, except by a few writers and theorists. The war itself is symbolized by its trenches, yet the reasons for the emergence of modern trench warfare have not fully been examined. Focus instead, and perhaps understandably, has been placed on other elements: the sheer human cost; the technological developments of tanks, gas, and machine guns; the experience of ordinary people during the war, unfortunately with an overemphasis on antiwar poets; arguments about the skill of the generals; and so on. We cannot fully understand the main causes of the four-year-long relative deadlock on the western front without studying the theory and practice of trench warfare prior to the conflict. This book seeks to fill this hole in the writing and thinking about the war—if the reader will forgive the bad pun—and illuminate an important aspect of the tactical and operational thinking that dominated the entire war.

This introduction examines the theory of field fortification from 1740 to 1914, a period chosen to emphasize the consistency of the ideas involved, particularly when set in the context of the enormous changes in the conduct of war over almost two centuries. This broad setting is used to better place, in context, the specific changes that took place between 1877 and 1914—the period covered by the case studies following this chapter and that is the main focus of this book. Though a single coherently expressed theory of field fortification does not exist, a number of themes run through the literature on the subject that could provide one. These themes are brought together here, as a whole, for the first time. Also examined are the technical changes that took place in the digging of fortifications, primarily from above- to belowground, which eventually led to the landscape of the First World War. These technical changes developed in response to the massive increase in firepower that occurred in the latter half of the nineteenth century and particularly to that of artillery, which benefited enormously from the emergence of the modern chemical industry during the second wave of the Industrial Revolution. (Improvements in metallurgy and chemistry largely allowed much heavier and more powerful shells to be fired with greater range and accuracy than previously had been possible.)

All of these innovations provided an unprecedented level of relatively mobile firepower, a leap that had not been witnessed since the emergence of effective and mobile gunpowder artillery at the end of the fifteenth century. Thus, the need to dig in more deeply and spread out over the battlefield created an increased demand for ever more plentiful and heavy artillery to blast men out of their positions. More heavy artillery meant digging in still further and so on and so forth, ultimately leading to the shape of the western front of late 1914. All of the technological changes in firepower, when combined with field fortifications, provided tremendous strength to the defense. In turn this shift pushed the idea that the offensive in war had become impossible and that the military men of the early 1900s ignored the evidence presented to them in the wars before 1914–1918. Simply put, this premise is not so. The lessons from the wars before 1914 were that the offensive could be successful if enough men, matériel, and moral strength were expended in gaining the objective, but the attacker must expect very heavy casualties. Thus, much of the postwar criticism of the pre-1914 officer corps on this subject is somewhat harsh.

The period 1740–1914 witnessed a great deal of change in the way Western wars were fought, as well as in the nations that fought them. At the start of the period being examined, Europe was a system of states with many disputed borders that needed protecting through the use of fortification. Generally speaking, Europe's wars were conducted by relatively professional armed forces recruited from all over the Continent and commanded by an almost equally international set of officers. This style of war fighting was transformed by nearly twenty-five years of almost uninterrupted warfare, from 1792 until 1815, between revolutionary France and its neighbors.[1] The first half of the period in question, from 1740 to 1792, witnessed the perfection of the old style of warfare, in which the general in charge would directly command the whole army both during the campaigns and on the fields of battle. Furthermore, sieges and positional warfare dominated the campaigns, with major battles being relatively infrequent. The period 1792–1815 culminated in the emergence of more mobile forces, frequent battles, and mass armies, and this newer style of warfare, to a certain extent, was followed until 1945. When combined with the two outstanding inventions of the first half of the nineteenth century, the percussion cap and the Minié bullet, the changes to the way wars were fought revolutionized infantry tactics. The first invention allowed the musket to be used in wet weather, while the second made the rifle the deadliest weapon of the century.[2] These factors, along with the increased industrialization of European societies, especially after the Napoleonic wars, accelerated the rate at which development occurred both in the societies in general and in warfare in particular. However, field fortification theories did not undergo any significant changes. Despite this stagnation, the technical nature of field fortification construction did begin to change in the latter half of the nineteenth century.

Field fortification came to play an increasingly important role from 1815 to 1914. Initially its use had been primarily confined to sieges, fortified camps, and only occasionally the battlefield. Its use on the field of battle was restricted because the only kind of field fortification of real value to a defender was a strong obstacle to enemy movement of some sort or one large enough to protect against artillery fire. The power and range of musketry were still limited, and thus men had no real need to protect themselves against it. Indeed, it was not normally advantageous for men behind a breastwork to receive enemy attackers in hand-to-hand combat. They were disadvantaged in a melee through being denied any impetus from countercharging and, by virtue of standing in the hole they had dug, being physically lower than their attacker. As constructing large works and obstacles that would be beneficial to the defender at this time was normally difficult and time-consuming, their use was limited. Thus, they were rarely employed on the battlefield unless there were enough time, men, tools, and material to construct them.

The widespread introduction of rifled firearms in the middle part of the nineteenth century changed this dynamic. Their increased accuracy and range meant that troops could no longer remain stationary in the open on the battlefield within effective range of the enemy's rifle fire. The lessons of fighting in the Crimean War (1853–1856) and the American Civil War (1861–1865) indicated that an effective answer to the increasing firepower available to armies of the mid- to late nineteenth century lay with the use of field fortifications.

That being said, the role and use of field fortifications had not greatly changed in warfare in Europe by 1872, yet the military schools of Britain, France, Germany, Austria, the United States, and Russia all had lectures and classes on the use of field fortification in their core courses of instruction.[3] Thus, the various military forces were noting the increasing importance of field fortification even if they were not consistently practicing what they preached.[4]

The tactical development of the large-scale use of field fortifications was demonstrated to the European public in 1877 when for six months the Turks heroically defended Plevna in Bulgaria against much larger Russian and Romanian Armies advancing toward Constantinople. The extensive use of field fortifications over a large area enabled the defense. The use of modern-style trenches with top cover at Plevna, and elsewhere during the war, directly led the Russian Army to introduce a 6-inch M1885 field mortar and to examine the concept of indirect fire (the Germans also started to study it more closely from 1892).[5] By the turn of the twentieth century, armies were beginning to set the scene for the First World War in their routine use of field fortifications. Certainly, the Second Anglo-Boer War of 1899–1902 demonstrated the effectiveness of well-dug-in and camouflaged infantry armed with small-bore magazine rifles, though it must be remembered that Britain did win the war. The Russo-Japanese War of 1904–1905 witnessed an increasing use of field fortification as the war went on. By the end of that war, short lines of entrenchments had given way to lengthy multilayered defensive systems that were very difficult to break down. However, despite their intrinsic strength, the sheer moral courage and numbers of the Japanese troops breached these systems, thus pointing to the logic of the Great War offensives on the western front in particular. The Balkan Wars of 1912–1913 witnessed the developments of the previous wars and added more modern weapons and tactics. Combatants routinely used field fortification combined effectively with barbed wire and machine guns to form formidable defensive obstacles that were reliably conquered only after using large amounts of powerful and heavy artillery fire, thus setting the scene for the wars that followed.

The use of field fortification and its corresponding theory—described by Nicolas-Joseph Cugnot, an eighteenth-century French military engineer, as "one of the principal parts of the art of war"[6]—played an increasingly important role in warfare. Yet historians have largely neglected its study, choosing instead to examine other technological, tactical, operational, and strategic changes occurring between 1740 and 1914.

Definition of Field Fortification

What then is field fortification? A working definition is provided in order to better understand its theory, which usually is divided into two main spheres—temporary/field and permanent. Sébastien Le Prestre de Vauban, marshal of France and fortress designer, defined fortification as "an art, which teaches men to fortify themselves with Ramparts, Moats, Covered ways and Glacis's [sic], to the end the enemy may not be able to attack any part without great loss of his men; and that the small number of soldiers which defend the place may be thereof [sic] able to hold out for some time."[7] Vauban was talking primarily about permanent fortifications, but his words were equally applicable to the role of field fortification.

In the middle of the nineteenth century, Dennis Hart Mahan, lecturer and curriculum designer at the United States Military Academy, provided the following definition:

> 1. ALL dispositions made to enable an armed force to resist, with advantage, the attack of one superior to it in numbers, belong to the ART OF FORTIFICATION. 2. The means used to strengthen a position, may be either those presented by nature, as precipes [sic], woods, rivers, &c., or those formed by art, as shelters of earth, stone, wood, &c. 3. If the artificial obstacles are of a durable character, and the position is to be permanently occupied, the works receive the name of *Permanent Fortification*; but when the position is to be occupied only for a short period, or during the operations of a campaign, perishable materials, as earth and wood, are most commonly used, and the works are denominated *Temporary* or *Field Fortification*.[8]

Col. Gustave J. Fiebeger, who was a lecturer and curriculum designer at the United States Military Academy at the beginning of the twentieth century, described the difference between permanent and field fortification thus:

> *Permanent fortification* deals with the defensive works constructed by a state to secure permanent possession of important strategic positions within its territory. . . . The works are usually constructed during time of peace, when the military engineer has at his command all the resources of the state. They are made sufficiently strong to resist all ordinary attacks of a field army. A position protected by permanent fortifications and properly garrisoned should yield only after a protracted siege. *Field fortification* deals with all defensive works of a temporary character which are constructed during a war, and which will lose their military value at its close. The works may be constructed by the field army with the tools which form part of its equipment, or by the reserve army utilizing all the resources of labor and material afforded by the surrounding country.[9]

These definitions were chosen because of their clarity and because they covered much of the period 1740–1914, with which this chapter is concerned. Taking them into account, the following definition will be used in this book:

> *Field fortification* covers the use of works of a temporary character, where those works are only to be occupied for the period of the campaign. This term excludes permanent fortifications but allows the inclusion of temporary supplementary works that support or increase the security of a permanent fortress, e.g., the temporary field fortifications added to the defense of Kars, Turkey, in 1877–1878 and those added to the fortifications at Port Arthur, China, in 1904–1905.

Technical Construction and Concealment

The main styles of construction examined are entrenchments, which evolved into trenches, redoubts, and obstacles. The issue of concealment will also be studied, as will other types of field fortification in order to present as full a picture as possible.

Entrenchments were the most familiar form of field fortification utilized from 1740 to 1914. They were constructed by throwing the earth dug up to one side, thus creating a bank at the top of the hole being dug. The entrenchments constructed using this method were roughly half above and half below the level of the ground, were normally about chest high, and were referred to as a breastwork (see figure 1.1). Indeed, for the purpose of this book, the use of the term "breastwork" is interchangeable with that of "entrenchment" when speaking of this type of fortification. Such fortifications had the advantage that they could be thrown up quickly if troops were issued the correct tools. Locally found resources, such as trees, brush, rocks, walls, fences, hedges, and so forth, could also be utilized in their construction. During the American Civil War, with the abundance of forest and lumber, felled trees frequently were laid out and covered in earth to provide a solid foundation, to speed up the process of construction, and to improve the field of fire. Fortifications of this type and based on this method of con-

Standard Breastwork with Trench

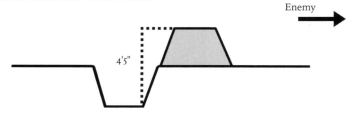

Standard Breastwork with Ditch

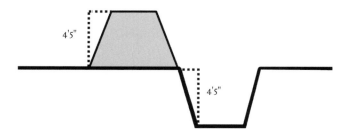

Typical Bomb-proof

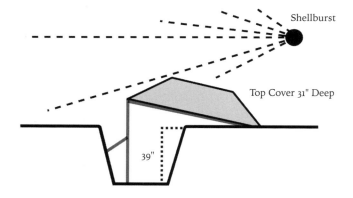

FIGURE 1.1. Typical field fortifications from the period leading up to and including the Russo-Turkish War of 1877–1878. The dominant form was clearly still the breastwork. Based on A. Brialmont, *Manuel de Fortification de Campagne* (Bruxelles: E. Guyot, 1879).

struction were used across the world, from the Maoris in New Zealand and the Sikhs in India to the two sides in the Russo-Turkish wars. Such fortifications were in use during other wars of the eighteenth and nineteenth centuries, though their use on the battlefield was by no means systematic. However, fortifications of this type possessed several disadvantages: they presented a raised profile to enemy fire, they were difficult to conceal in open ground, and they were vulnerable to artillery fire and to the increasing power of rifle fire toward the end of the nineteenth century. Indeed, the heightened power, range, and accuracy of artillery fire toward the end of the nineteenth century and before the start of the First World War hold the greatest significance.

The solution to these problems was found during the Russo-Turkish War of 1877–1878. At the battles and siege of Plevna, what came to be called trenches were utilized extensively at least in part because the heavy clay soil around the town facilitated their creation. Trenches were different from breastworks in both their construction and their profile. Rather than building earth up and creating a barrier that was both half aboveground and half belowground, a trench was dug almost entirely into the ground with the earth thrown up only high enough to protect a soldier's head. The earth was flung out far enough and just high enough to create a bulletproof barrier, while leaving only a low profile. (The trenches at Plevna bore greater similarity to those shown in figure 1.4 than they did to the breastworks depicted in figure 1.2; note too the changes in profile shown in figures 1.1 through 1.6.) Thus, the trenches were deep, they presented almost no target to enemy fire, and they were more difficult to observe when care was taken to camouflage them. The increasing range and effectiveness of rifle and artillery fire brought an increasing need to provide positions that were difficult to observe and to hit. The high velocity of rifle bullets and cannon shells combined with their flat trajectories dictated that aboveground entrenchments had become largely obsolete, because the rounds from modern firearms could penetrate the thin, tall barrier provided by a simple breastwork. Moreover, the barrier itself all too often could easily be seen and physically hit. Trenches provided the answer to this problem,

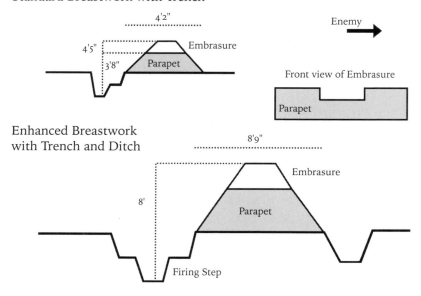

Standard Breastwork with Trench

4'2"

Enemy →

Embrasure

4'5"

3'8" Parapet

Front view of Embrasure

Parapet

Enhanced Breastwork
with Trench and Ditch

8'9"

Embrasure

8'

Parapet

Firing Step

FIGURE 1.2. Field fortifications by 1890. Very little real change had occurred. Based on *Handbuch für den Unterofficier des K. und K. Pionnier-Regiments* (Vienna: Verlag des K. u. K. Pionnier-Regiments, Drück von Rudolf Brzezowsky & Söhne, 1890).

and this type of field fortification became increasingly common in the years following the Russo-Turkish War of 1877–1878.

Unlike the American Civil War, the Russo-Turkish War was fought between European powers, albeit peripheral ones a decade later. This point is important because the Civil War was not a European war, and as such in the European military academies, the lessons from it took second place to the study of wars in Europe.[10] Furthermore, the Russo-Turkish War of 1877–1878 witnessed the widespread use, by both sides, of breech-loading artillery and efficient breech-loading rifles, weapons that were not available to both sides in large number during the American Civil War. The trenches and top cover that were extensively used during the Russo-Turkish War of 1877–1878 also drove the need for heavier artillery and the use of indirect fire, both of which played an increasingly important role

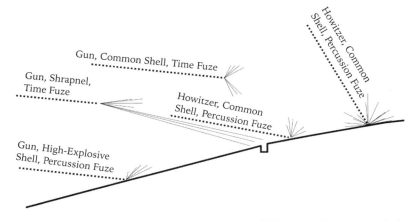

FIGURE 1.3. An artillery attack showing how different shells impacted the battlefield.

Fire Trench

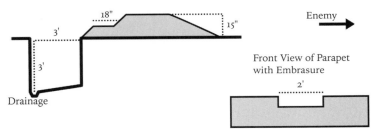

Reinforced Fire Trench

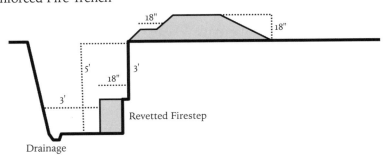

FIGURE 1.4. Field fortifications demonstrated obvious changes in the style of construction by 1902. Note the lower profile of these frontline trenches. Based on War Office, General Staff, *Instruction in Military Engineering: Part 1, Field Defences* (London: War Office, 1902).

Typical Bomb-proof

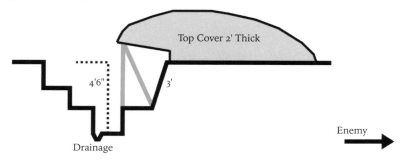

Top Cover 2' Thick

4'6" 3'

Drainage

Enemy →

Typical Bomb-proof

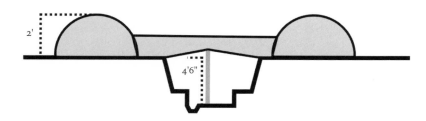

2'

4'6"

Communications Trench

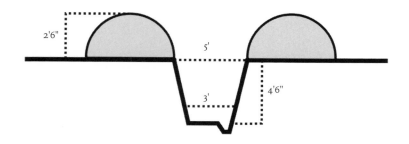

2'6"

5'

3'

4'6"

FIGURE 1.5. Additional 1902 field fortifications. A very low profile was not necessary for trenches situated to the rear. Based on War Office, General Staff, *Instruction in Military Engineering: Part 1, Field Defences* (London: War Office, 1902).

at this time and became essential during the 1914–1918 conflict.[11] Thus, the Russo-Turkish War of 1877–1878 offers an excellent starting point for the changes in fortification discussed.

Redoubts were the other main form of field fortification. As opposed to breastworks, redoubts overcame the problem of vulnerability to enemy fire through their sheer size — specifically the thickness of their earthen walls — which made them largely immune to anything but the heaviest shot. Military historian Maj. Gen. B. P. Hughes noted that a redoubt was virtually "impervious" even to enemy field artillery fire, and any embrasure provided only a "very small target."[12] Even with the widespread use of shell ammunition, redoubts remained nearly invulnerable until the introduction of more powerful artillery and high explosives on the battlefield.

The invention of improved propellants, such as poudre B in France in 1884 (cordite was the equivalent invention in England in 1889), allowed for greater accuracy and range. In addition, the French invention of the high-explosive melinite in 1885 (the English equivalent was lyddite) intensified the blasting power of artillery. Improvements in metallurgy and the expansion of steel production (facilitated by the Bessemer process of 1855) allowed for larger-caliber pieces for the same weight, thus increasing the firepower of an artillery piece for the equivalent level of mobility and weight of an older model. This improvement brought larger and more powerful artillery onto the battlefield.[13] Furthermore, this greater firepower was now more mobile than ever before and was sustainable, assuming modern transport links were available.

Redoubts also provided a difficult physical barrier for the enemy to cross. Essentially they are small earthen forts with high, steep walls constructed to provide both cover to their defenders and a physical barrier to the enemy. They were often also surrounded by a ditch, which was made when removing the earth to construct the redoubts' walls. This large physical mass not only assisted in protecting the defenders of a redoubt from the worst effects of enemy fire but also increased their protection against assault. To storm a redoubt, attacking troops would often need to bring such equipment as scaling ladders or fascines to fill ditches, thus encumber-

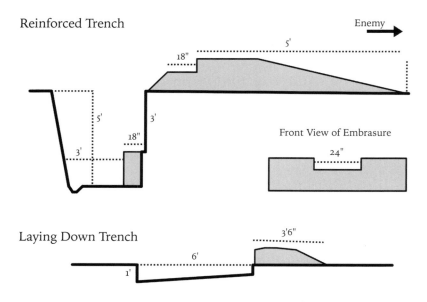

Reinforced Trench

Enemy

Front View of Embrasure

Laying Down Trench

FIGURE 1.6. By 1911 the trench is slightly deeper, and the manual recommended that if there was a good field of fire, no parapet should be provided. Based on War Office, General Staff, *Manual of Field Engineering* (London: HMSO, 1911).

ing them for the assault. This requirement, when combined with the obstacle itself, slowed attackers down and helped to provide an easier target for defensive fire. Thus, redoubts fulfilled a dual purpose in that they both protected the troops manning them and provided a formidable physical barrier to the enemy.

However, the very size of a redoubt, almost all of which was aboveground, presented a large target to the enemy. It was also difficult, though not impossible, to conceal as the Romanian and Russian soldiers discovered to their cost when they accidentally stumbled across Grivitza Redoubt No. 1 in a field of tall corn at the Third Battle of Plevna on 7–12 September 1877. Furthermore, redoubts required much time and labor to construct, thus limiting their potential use to a more static situation. As artillery fire increased in power, the redoubt's design also changed and followed the example of infantry trenches. Redoubt design developed a lower profile, which was easier to conceal from enemy observation, and had thicker walls (similar to large mounds) in order to withstand the more modern ammunition and artillery. They also shrank in tactical depth, which in this context means the distance from the front to the rear of the redoubt. Over time, this distance reduced in relation to the width of the side facing the enemy, hurting the enemy's ability to hit it physically with plunging fire, at the cost of the corresponding loss in flanking defensive fire. This deficit was quickly resolved with the deployment of machine guns.

Obstacles were also used to fortify ground. They served one main purpose: to delay or stop the enemy, thus prolonging the time he was under effective defensive fire. Typical obstacles included ditches, stakes, caltrops, or more elaborate devices. They might thus be military pits with stakes in the bottom or abatis formed from felled trees placed side by side with the branches pointing toward the enemy. These last obstacles proved to be very difficult for an enemy to move through or counter, thus significantly delaying him and greatly benefiting the defender. In addition, they were difficult to destroy with artillery fire, a problem that would recur later following the introduction and use of barbed wire. These types of obstacles were used from 1740 to 1914. However, the more elaborate ones were time-consuming to construct and could, if improperly sited, provide a hindrance to the defense if the obstacles themselves blocked the line of fire of the defender or provided cover for the attacker. If the defender had limited time available, a palisade or a barricade might also be used with the same effect. This barrier could be as simple as a wall of gabions or even mealie bags, which were used to great effect at Rorke's Drift in 1879. Against a non-rifle-armed enemy who relied on shock action, a physical barrier was the most effective form of field fortification. However, the ground, the time, and the material available to the troops constructing the obstacle normally limited the possibilities. In addition, with the modern firearms of the late nineteenth century, a force could relatively easily counter non-rifle-armed enemies in open country with few obvious exceptions.

One aspect of the construction of obstacles that changed between 1740 and 1914 was the increasing importance of maintaining a clear field of fire for the defenders. When firearms were of only limited power and range, a long field of fire was not that important; with the increasing range and power of firearms, it became invaluable. To exploit the maximum benefit of their modern firearms, the defenders had to create obstacles to delay the enemy's approach. This way they could engage their assailants to the maximum effective range of their weaponry. It was also important not to erect any obstacles that could provide cover to advancing enemies that would allow them to gain shelter to regroup. Furthermore, any obstacles built by the defenders reduced the amount of time and material available for the construction of suitable trenches or redoubts for their own protection. The increasing firepower available meant that ensuring protection was of greater importance to the defender than building obstacles that might delay the attacker. In addition, protection from the increased deadly fire action of the enemy superseded the earlier need to be able to countercharge and engage in hand-to-hand combat with the attacker. Because of these problems, the use of obstacles declined in importance until the introduction of the small-bore magazine rifle and machine gun.

These last two developments meant that troops could no longer remain stationary and in the open in daylight for more than a brief period because of the sheer volume and accuracy of fire that could be deployed against them. As Colonel Fiebeger put it when talking about modern breech-loading rifles, "No troops can remain stationary *in daylight* without cover within the limits of its [breech-loading rifles'] accurate fire."[14] This increased firepower led in turn to the greater importance, at least in theory, of the use of night for providing cover. Attacks at night made using obstacles once again necessary, both to delay the attacker and to warn the defender of his approach.[15]

The usefulness of obstacles on the battlefield, when combined with the problems that were often inherent in their use, indicates the immense importance of the introduction of wire entanglements. They held great advantages: they were fairly quick to construct, they allowed an unobstructed field of view, and they were difficult for attacking troops to surmount. Thus, wire provided an obstacle while simultaneously removing the main reasons for not construct-ing one—time and the obstruction of the field of fire. Furthermore, wire obstacles were difficult to destroy, a problem that would become a prominent issue during the First World War.

Concealment on the field of battle had always been a useful tool for attaining surprise and for avoiding enemy fire. Lowering the pro-file of field fortifications helped conceal them. The lower the pro-file, the less there was of the fortifications to see and the easier they were to camouflage. Before the introduction of smokeless powder in 1884, however careful a defender might have been in concealing his positions, they often became visible once the troops manning them opened fire. The increasing lethality and accuracy of modern weap-ons meant that once positions were observed, they could usually be brought under effective fire. Concealment thus helped reduce the risk of receiving enemy fire but still enhanced the element of sur-prise, which was most useful in action. The introduction of smoke-less powder made the use of concealment ever more important, as it allowed troops to open fire from concealed positions with less possibility of giving themselves away to the enemy. In 1904, mili-tary historian and former director of instruction in the Indian Army Maj. Gen. Henry Hutchinson noted that "concealment is even of more value than the material protection afforded by trenches. If a trench is clearly visible to the enemy it may, however well made, be found out by an occasional howitzer shell; and it will certainly be subjected to an accurate fire of shrapnel."[16] Thus, General Hutchin-son correctly predicted what the likely outcome would be when a position was located. When sufficient heavy artillery was available, a defensive position, once located, could be destroyed.

Better concealment also enhanced the effect of the "empty bat-tlefield" that had been commented upon regarding the American Civil War. During that war the restricted lines of sight for much of the forested terrain made it often difficult to see very far and thus to know if an enemy was in the immediate vicinity. In addition, sound did not travel as far as in an open area, thus providing the illusion that the battlefield was empty. In these circumstances, field fortification was effective at reducing the consequences of surprise.

In contrast more open battlefields, such as the more intensely farmed areas of western Europe, might have a clear line of sight for several thousand yards. Thus, often it was difficult to gain surprise and made the use of fortification in this context initially less useful until the developments in firepower rendered their use essential and concealment necessary. With the introduction of breech-loading rifles and smokeless powder, well-concealed troops could open fire and remain confident that their location would not easily be discovered. They could inflict casualties on the enemy to the full extent of the range of their weapons with relative impunity. This situation provides, perhaps, a better explanation of the meaning of the term "empty battlefield" than the context of the Civil War in which it is often used.

In addition to these changes, another important modification in the construction of field fortifications during the 1740–1914 period was the increased use of top cover, or, literally, overhead protection for field fortifications. Until 1877, the use of top cover in field fortification construction was normally reserved for protecting ammunition or artillery rather than for directly protecting ordinary troops in the positions themselves. During the battles and siege of Plevna, top cover was extensively provided for ordinary infantry both inside redoubts and in the trenches themselves at most of the key tactical points to improve protection from the effects of enemy artillery fire. Using top cover became increasingly necessary as shell fire and shrapnel became more widely used and effective. Previously an artillery round had to physically hit its target to cause damage. Both of the newer weapons burst and sent out a blast wave and shower of metal, thus rendering troops sheltering beneath the blast vulnerable.

The development of more powerful battlefield artillery in the latter part of the nineteenth century created more problems for troops under fire, especially following the introduction in 1897 of an effective hydraulic recoil mechanism in the French 75mm quick-firing cannon. Not only could more powerful high-explosive and shrapnel shells be used, they could also be fired much more quickly, thus compounding the problems of troops on the receiving end.[17] The increased use of top cover evolved into digging deeper and providing a thicker overhead barrier for the troops' added protection. This development was significant because field artillery seldom had the ability to damage troops dug deeply into the earth, driving the need for heavier guns. The same logic can be easily applied to using improved infantry firearms such as the small-bore magazine rifle and machine gun, thus indicating why these design improvements to field fortifications occurred. As these weapons became more accurate and powerful, troops had to dig deeper into the ground for protection or at least put ever more earth between them and the enemy's fire.

With the evolution in field fortification design, it is interesting to note that permanent fortification underwent similar changes in its construction, from as early as the sixteenth century, with the development of the *trace italienne*, or star fort. This change from a high to a low profile occurred in direct response to the increasing use of ever more powerful artillery in siege warfare. Thus, the changed techniques used in permanent fortification construction were mirrored, much later, in field fortification construction. One thus can surmise that battlefield firepower took some time to catch up with the firepower available to an army conducting a siege. After all, heavy artillery pieces had been rarely deployed on the field of battle because they lacked mobility, and so protection against them was largely redundant. Using lighter and stronger metals to construct artillery led to more powerful and mobile guns; thus, troops manning field fortifications required increased protection, as they were more likely to encounter these same weapons in the battle space.

Other techniques of field fortification were often used to improve existing cover. The latter normally took the form of hedges, walls, roads, embankments, sunken roads, and so on. The improvements could be as simple as providing loopholes in a wall or chopping down some trees to provide logs for cover. However, time permitting, the improvements usually involved constructing breastworks, trenches, or even a redoubt in the cover itself or more fully fortifying the cover to provide more protection. Increased fortification of cover had been less necessary when weaponry was less powerful; as weapons technology improved, improving preexisting cover to defend against the effects of enemy fire became essential.

One final point on the construction of field fortifications: only an industrialized country had the capacity to provide the requisite field fortification equipment for a large citizen army. Previously, only engineers, pioneers, or specially equipped troops had the capability to construct field fortifications on any kind of large scale. With the improvements in manufacturing efficiency brought about by the Industrial Revolution, equipping ordinary troops of the line with the entrenching tools that they increasingly needed for modern warfare became possible. Without these improvements in manufacturing, the requisite number of tools would not have been available, and much of the field fortification construction would have been rudimentary at best, severely limiting the extent of field fortification construction at any given time. Further, extensive digging was really only required to counter a modern enemy army. Less sophisticated enemy forces largely could be countered with the increased firepower that had become available.

Terrain and Soil

The type of soil to be entrenched also affected the type of fortifications used. Hard ground made the job of digging fortifications that much more difficult. Given sufficient time and material, troops with the right training and equipment could construct virtually any type of appropriate protection. However, time is precious in war, and the time needed to construct field fortifications was a factor in the decision-making process.

In 1909 Capt. James Woodruff of the U.S. Corps of Engineers described the amount of time taken to construct field fortifications thus: "*The capacity of the average untrained man* [italics in original] for continuous digging does not much exceed 80 cubic feet for easy soil, 60 cubic feet for medium, and 40 cubic feet for hard soil. He will do three-eighths of this in the first hour, five-eighths in the first two hours, and the other three-eighths in the other two hours."[18] Time-pressed troops seeking to fortify ground consisting of hard soil had reduced options compared with troops constructing field fortifications in easier soil. Thus, they might have time to construct only the most rudimentary protection.

Hard ground not only made the construction of field fortifications more problematic but also could even contribute to casualties. Troops positioned on hard ground could be more vulnerable to enemy fire: when a missile struck stone or rock, splinters often broke off that could wound or kill soldiers. Furthermore, if the ground was too hard, field fortifications were impossible to dig. During British operations on the northwest frontier of India in the late nineteenth century, for example, the ground was so rocky that aboveground positions called *sangars* were the norm,[19] with all the problems of concealment and raised profile that they entailed. Hard ground might consist of sunbaked mud, frozen ground, rock, and so on. The problems of hard ground might be geological — bedrock in a desert, for example — or caused by drought or a period of sustained cold. Thus, it could be difficult to surmount the problems that a lack of constructable cover posed unless sufficient material was available to build something aboveground.

At the other end of the scale was soil that was too soft, which presented its own difficulties. Constructing trenches or even steep-sided holes in extremely soft or sandy soil required supports to keep the soil in place; otherwise, the work was prone to subside or collapse. Support for fortifications in this sort of ground usually came in the form of wood supports, wicker panels, or gabions. If these materials were not available, then belowground construction was quite difficult. To overcome this problem, very soft soil or sand was piled up in a heap, like a breastwork, or made into sandbags and so forth. While this type of soil was useful, works constructed in it normally required a great deal of maintenance even without the effects of enemy action.

Other environmental factors could also play a role. A high water table might render any dug fortifications prone to flooding. Thus, much like those in rocky soil, these fortifications would have to be established aboveground, increasing the importance of camouflage and mass for protection. Even really heavy rain might have the same effect, rendering fortifications in such an area unusable or, at the very least, difficult to construct and maintain.

Winter posed its own problems. The Russian Army experimented with entrenchments constructed with piled-up snow. However, their walls needed to be at least six feet thick in order to withstand a bullet from a Berdan rifle (a black-powder breechloader), and it is unlikely that they would have stopped more modern small-bore rifle bullets as easily.[20] Thus, geographic and environmental factors often dictated what types of fortifications might be constructed in a particular area and how effective they were in protecting the troops manning them.

Field Fortification Theory

As mentioned previously, several main themes run through the literature on field fortification theory. These themes are relatively constant, despite the huge changes taking place in the nature of warfare during the eighteenth, nineteenth, and early twentieth centuries. The six main elements of this theory are field fortifications were used to help prevent desertion from the armies of the day; they provided actual protection for the troops manning them; they acted as a force multiplier, allowing fewer troops to engage larger numbers of the enemy or poorer quality troops to be committed to action; they provided, and reinforced, key tactical points on the battlefield; they provided a secure base and secure lines of operations anywhere; and they were used to cover or dominate an area. The following discussion reviews these theories regarding the use of field fortification, as well as the reasons for these ideas and examples of their use, to explain more fully the logic behind the decision-making process.

Preventing Desertion

The practical problem of dealing with the loss of soldiers through desertion runs through the writings up to the end of the Napoleonic wars. Noted German historian Hans Delbrück touched on the problems that eighteenth-century armies faced when he discussed the army of Frederick the Great: "From a list of the year 1744 that has survived by chance, we can deduce that in a company of the Rettburg Regiment, of 111 foreigners, 65 'had already served other potentates,' that is, had deserted. . . . There was hardly any military document of the king that did not concern itself with the prevention of desertion."[21] Further, British Gen. John Burgoyne is quoted as saying that the Prussian Army of 1765 "is more harassed with precautionary guards against their own soldiers deserting than against the enemy, and, after an unsuccessful action, the number missing usually trebles the number to be accounted for by death or capture."[22]

The armies' reasons for needing to prevent desertion in these circumstances had as much to do with the soldiers' harsh environment as with the quality of most soldiers of the time. Jacques Antoine Hippolyte Comte de Guibert described them as "discontented and coming from the most vile and pitiful classes."[23] Fortifications checked desertion by restricting the access routes into and out of a fortified camp. Small openings acting as exits and entrances in a fortified camp could be easily guarded and monitored, thus making desertion physically difficult. Furthermore, field fortifications were most likely used in close proximity to the enemy, making desertion a much more difficult and riskier proposition for the troops contemplating it. Frederick himself noted, "We Prussians intrench our camps as the Romans did earlier to avoid not only the enterprises of the enemy light troops, which are very numerous, but also to prevent desertion. For I have always observed that when our redans are linked together by lines all around the camp there is less desertion than when this precaution is neglected."[24] The French engineer Louis Clairac also raised the question of camp security, in 1750: "When there are reasons for keeping a large body of troops together, their camp is intrenched, for greater security. The *Greeks*, the *Romans*, and most other nations, seldom make any stay in a place, without fortifying themselves in it."[25]

This theme recurred well into the Napoleonic wars and afterward. Author and historian Paddy Griffith asserts that in France, fortification featured prominently in the "tactical doctrines in the Revolution's field forces" and that these practices bore great resemblance to those of the armies in the early phase of the American Civil War. The field fortifications that the armies dug to protect their camps served two goals — they provided all of the usual benefits of protection, and they allowed large numbers of men to be kept securely in a place from which they could not easily desert.[26] This observation is significant because, despite its still being an issue, desertion was mentioned in connection with field fortification far less often following the Napoleonic wars.

With the rise of more reliable citizen armies, desertion became a less important factor in deciding whether to utilize field fortifications. For one, these new citizen armies provided men in abundance, so an individual's deserting had less impact on the mission. And the men were cheap when contrasted with the routine problems that the more "professional" armies of the eighteenth century found in recruiting enough men and in affording their sheer cost. In these circumstances, where the risk of desertion was minimal and not likely to be costly, taking the trouble of constructing field fortifications to prevent desertion was both time-consuming and a waste of resources, making their use less relevant. However, the preceding explanation is not entirely satisfactory. Simply because troops were citizens did not make them braver or less susceptible to combat stress, homesickness, or all the other myriad reasons that led soldiers to desert their posts. Much more logical and likely, the increasingly commonplace use of field fortification for other reasons outlined later in this chapter reduced the level of desertion precisely because deserting from fortified areas was more difficult and dangerous. Desertion was especially so when fortifications were in the proximity of the enemy, and leaving would almost certainly expose the deserter to the hazards of enemy fire. As the range, firepower, and accuracy of the weapons available to armies of the late nineteenth century improved, any kind of exposure to enemy fire was likely to be deadly. Thus, the protection provided by a fieldwork was much more appealing than exposure to enemy fire and the almost certain death that would result. Indeed, officers became increasingly concerned that their men would not want to leave the shelter they provided and were in danger of losing some of their élan.[27] Gen. Ulysses S. Grant of the Union forces commented on this problem when discussing why the Army of Northern Virginia increased its use of field fortifications in 1864: "Lee's Army is really whipped."[28] Later in the Austrian *Feldbefestigungsvorschrift* (*Field Regulations*) of 1908, the idea was put forward that "the first and highest principle of each use of field fortifications is that the troops manning them must at each instant be ready to abandon them, in order to carry combat forwards, if this should be favorable to the fight. Consequently, fortifications are to be always created in such a way that they are not a nuisance to the troops' own offensive urge."[29]

Only when circumstances dictated that field fortifications had to be constructed and events proved that soldiers could be persuaded to launch attacks from their safe positions were these fears overcome. Thus, digging trenches presented a twofold problem—they protected the men, but their use risked diminishing the men's martial spirit. It is important to remember it was thought that only through offensive action could a war be won. The dilemma military men faced meant that in order to prevent defeat, they had to dig in, and such action could make taking future offensive action to win the war impossible.

Desertion was not a big problem for the Turkish troops fortified at Plevna in 1877, nor for the armies in the trenches of the Great War, almost certainly for these very reasons. As a result, the issue of desertion as a reason for constructing field fortification became largely redundant. That is not to say that desertion became an irrelevant factor as time went on—witness the problems of the Confederate forces in 1864–1865—it simply became less of a factor in the decision-making process. Other reasons for using field fortification gained more relevance for war fighting.

Providing Physical Protection

In addition to providing a useful tool for preventing desertion, field fortifications physically protected the troops themselves usually by having a barrier of some sort. This obstacle might take the form of an earthen mound such as a redoubt, wooden logs, a stone wall, a trench, or anything that acted as a physical barrier to protect the troops behind it. The battle of Talavera on 27–28 June 1809 provided an excellent example: its "unfinished" redoubt protected the guns of Lawson's battery of the Royal Artillery, and they were able to continue firing with great effect throughout the action and despite the close proximity of the enemy. It normally would not have been possible to keep the guns in action at this close range, and the earthworks allowed them to play an important part in defeating a French attack.[30]

Prussian staff officer and theorist Carl von Clausewitz also covered the use of field fortification to provide protection while defending a position: "To keep our troops covered as long as possible. Since we are always open to attack, except when we are ourselves attacking, we must at every instant be on the defensive and thus should place our forces as much under cover as possible."[31] He developed this idea of protection further when he stated that the object of defense was "preservation" and that the concept of defense was "parrying the blow." Preserving one's forces and parrying the enemy's blows allowed the defender to strike back at the attacker better and demonstrated that the *defensive form of warfare is intrinsically stronger than the offensive* [italics in original]."[32] He was putting forward the idea not of a passive defense but rather one where the defender eventually seized the initiative in order to attack and fully defeat the enemy. Clausewitz saw that using fortification to protect forces ultimately would fulfill a broader purpose.

Following the Napoleonic wars, the need to protect soldiers who were more likely to be citizens also drove the increased use of field fortifications. Professor Mahan theorized,

> But were not these reasons in themselves sufficient, others of greater cogency could be adduced, in favor of intrenched positions for militia. Its ranks are filled with all that is most valuable in society. The farmer, the mechanic, the merchant, the members of the learned professions, must all quit their peaceful avocations to meet the foe. The father of the family jeopards its future prosperity, the son exposes his widowed mother to the chances of an old age of penury, to bear their breasts to a mercenary band, without other home, without other ties, than the camp affords. Surely nothing but a reckless disregard for the best interests of society could urge men, under such circumstances, to forgo advantages of every possible conservative means.[33]

This idea was significant because it was the first time that a theorist discussing the benefits of the use of field fortification specifically addressed the social needs of the nation from which the army drew its troops rather than applied a strictly military rationale to his theory. It is also important to recognize that an American officer, serving in a liberal democratic state, wrote this piece. Thus, despite its significance, the influence that this idea would have had on military forces elsewhere in the world was, perhaps, somewhat limited.

The theme of utilizing field fortifications to provide cover from enemy fire continued through the nineteenth century. Alexis Henri Brialmont, the Belgian military engineer, argued, "The wars of 1866 and 1870 have furnished a new argument in favour of hasty intrenchements, by proving how formidable musketry has become in consequence of the progress it has made as regards range, accuracy, flatness of trajectory, and rapidity of fire. As the difficulty of keeping troops beyond the range of projectiles increases every day, the necessity of concealing them becomes more and more evident."[34] This shielding could be done physically by protecting them, by hiding them, or, ideally, by both. In 1880 British officer Maj. William Kemmis stated in his Royal Artillery Institution prize–winning essay: "The main object of the universal use of entrenchments on the field of battle is to obtain cover from the enemy's fire; the latter, under modern conditions, being so effective and therefore so deciding in the fight."[35]

Again, the use of field fortifications to provide cover, in this context, could be taken as providing both concealment and protection. The theme of protection is repeated in the Ministry of War's revised *Instruction Pratique sur les Travaux de Campagne à l'Usage des Troupes d'Infanterie* for the French Army of 1911: "Field fortification's essential aim is to supply the soldier with the means to protect himself against the blows of the enemy."[36] Here the French Ministry of War in its manual echoed Clausewitz when he stated the need to provide as much cover as possible for troops, and it further demonstrates the constant nature of the theme. Thus, it became increasingly important to protect troops from enemy fire, primarily for military effectiveness but also for civil reasons in a country such as the United States, and the best method for doing so was through the use of field fortifications.

Enhancing Fighting Power

The physical protection provided by fortifications gave the troops manning them increased confidence in their ability to survive enemy action. This conviction in turn allowed troops to operate their weapons with greater confidence and efficiency. Field fortifications therefore acted as a force multiplier, another common theme running through the theories dealing with the subject. Fortifications effectively took the place of soldiers on the defense and provided a substitute for manpower, or a good replacement, because of its efficiency. Griffith pointed out that the ancien régime in France understood that poor-quality troops performed best when protected by some form of fortification.[37] Many different writers and theorists echo these ideas. Napoleon Bonaparte noted that "with mediocre troops one must shift much soil,"[38] and he meant that they should have their confidence reinforced by placing them in field fortifications. He also applied this idea to isolated detachments: "It is a principle of war that all detached corps should entrench, and it is one of the first steps that one should take on the occupation of a position."[39] The logic was that detached corps were more vulnerable to enemy action and needed the additional protection that field fortification could provide. This barrier in turn, through the multiplication of their fighting power, would increase their ability to resist.

From the Revolutionary and Napoleonic wars, Clausewitz drew on his observations and experience fighting in them: "From all this it follows that we should use such obstacles on one flank to put up a relatively strong resistance with few troops, while executing our planned offensive on the other flank. It is very advantageous to combine the use of entrenchments with such natural obstacles, because then, if the enemy should pass the obstacle, the fire from these entrenchments will protect our weak troops against too great superiority and sudden rout."[40] He went on at length: "We adopt a strategic defensive mainly when the enemy is superior. Fortresses and intrenched camps, which constitute the chief preparations for a theatre of war, afford, of course, great advantages, to which may be added the knowledge of the terrain and the possession of good maps. A smaller army, or an army which is based on a state with more limited resources, will be better able to withstand the enemy WITH these advantages than without them."[41]

Clearly Clausewitz was putting forward the idea that using field fortification would enhance the fighting power of the troops manning them. This idea fit in well with the previous comments on his later thinking that the defensive, being the stronger form of war, was useful only in that it would eventually allow the offensive to be taken in more favorable circumstances. Therefore, not only was an individual soldier's fighting power enhanced by the use of fortifications but also an army as a whole was able to gain a more advantageous position through their use.

Later in the nineteenth century, Lt. Henry Yule of the Bengal Engineers affirmed this idea: "[Field fortification] is the art of economizing force in war—the art which gives strength to a military position by a right expenditure of labour, and so enables a body of troops which occupies that position to resist a more powerful force."[42] Mahan expanded on the theme:

> To suppose irregular forces [militia] capable of coping on equal terms with disciplined troops, is to reason, not only against all probability, but against a vast weight of testimony to the contrary. . . . But place the militia soldier on his natural field of battle, behind a breastwork, and an equilibrium between him and his more disciplined enemy is immediately established; with a feeling of security in his position, his confidence in his own exertions is restored; with a full certainty that his enemy cannot close upon him, before he can retire beyond his reach, he does his duty coolly, and with an execution so terrible, as to have placed the achievements of our militia, from the day of Bunker Hill, to the closing of our last war at New Orleans, on a line with the most brilliant exploits of the best disciplined troops in the world.[43]

By choosing an example from almost seventy-five years before he wrote that passage, Mahan confirmed that this theme was applicable across a broad span of history despite the revolutionary changes in warfare that had occurred since the events described.

The impact of field fortifications acting as a force multiplier was also evident in fortifications' effect on the morale of the troops manning them. In 1872 Brialmont wrote,

> Fortifications on the field of battle have a favourable moral effect on the troops defending them, and an unfavourable one on the attacking forces. They increase the difficulties and the losses of the assailant; and he, being taken unawares, and sometimes not even knowing of their existence at the commencement of the action, cannot form a correct opinion of their importance or take steps in time to avoid or outflank them. On this account hasty intrenchements [sic], formed unknown to the enemy, will often be of greater use than redoubts and forts executed at leisure and with great care.[44]

This last point echoed one that Hutchinson made earlier on the importance of using concealment, which adds to the fighting power of those concealed through the denial of visible targets to the enemy, as well as providing the benefit of surprise. Of course, the preceding reasons outlining why concealment is important in the defense also apply to the offense.

Summing up these ideas, in 1875, Royal Military Academy instructor Maj. E. D. C. O'Brien wrote that "good defensive works undoubtedly enable a small force to fight a much larger one on tolerably equal terms, and, moreover, a less amount of training and organisation is necessary to enable troops to defend fortifications than would be required for manoeuvring in the field."[45] Similarly H. Turner of the Royal Artillery answered the question as to the utility of fortification by arguing that strengthening the position that troops are to defend against an enemy enables "a small force to repulse a stronger one."[46] The *Instruction Pratique sur les Travaux de Campagne* of 1911 also cited force multiplication as a reason for using field fortification: "Such fortification constitutes a direct factor in the economy of force, and diminishes by the very protection it provides, the waste of employed troops."[47] This last point clearly emphasizes one of the most important reasons that the increasing use of field fortification so appealed to commanders: it also allowed part of a force more efficiently to hold an important position while giving the rest of the force the ability to maneuver.

Reinforcing Key Tactical Points

That concept of force multiplication ties in with the idea that field fortification can provide, or reinforce, key tactical points on the battlefield, thus enhancing the ability of the army on the defensive to resist. This use of fortifications could take many forms: from the fortification of buildings to the placing of wire entanglements through to the construction of a redoubt at a key point where there might not have been time to fortify a larger area. The effect would be to make an attacker's job physically more difficult with the use of obstacles, such as ditches or wire entanglements. These obstacles would slow down an attacker or break up his formations as he advanced, increasing the time he would spend under fire and disrupting his ability to fight as effectively. A redoubt or fortified building both provided an excellent physical barrier to the attacker and also gave the defender the benefits of cover, protection, and some level of concealment. Instances of using field fortification in this manner occurred frequently, and even when time was pressing, small key positions could be strengthened to better enable the defense to resist. So rather than fortifying the whole line, a commander might choose to focus on a hilltop, village, or other "prominent feature" to improve the defense. This use of field fortification had the further benefit of allowing their utilization as a "hinging point" on which success is based. They also could restrict the space available to an attacker, limiting his options. Examples can found in the fortification of Hougoumont and La Haye Sainte in 1815, at Fontenoy in 1745, and at Pultava in 1709.[48] At the battle of Borodino too, in 1812, the redoubts acted as key tactical points. This battle was dominated by artillery fire combined with the use of field entrenchments, and tactical offensives in this case were very costly.[49] Indeed, the tactical attacks that took place during the battle of Borodino were as bloody as many that occurred much later in the century, and the latter had to face more advanced weaponry and tactics.

During the Crimean War of 1853–1856, many examples of field fortifications were used for this very purpose, such as the Great Redoubt at the battle of the Alma (1854) and the Turkish redoubts on the Woronstov heights at the battle of Balaclava (1854). The Royal Engineers, in *Instruction in Field Engineering, Field Defences,* stated that

> the advantage sought to be obtained by standing on the defensive, and receiving the attack of the enemy in a chosen position, is the infliction of severe loss on him by the fire of troops posted in such a manner as to see him as far as may be at every step of his advance, whilst themselves more or less protected from his fire, and hidden from his view; so that finally he will be forced to retire from sheer loss or demoralisation, or the defenders will be enabled to close with him on more equal or even superior terms. To help bring about this result the enemy is subjected to every possible disadvantage, both from the nature of the ground (such as ascending heights, and so on), and from artificial obstacles placed in his way for the purpose of detaining him under fire, or limiting his movements to ground favourable to the defenders.[50]

The fortification of key positions also provided the ability to use them as a point for tactical and possibly strategic (if used on a large enough scale) maneuver. The fortified position could act as a pivot for an army, the better and safer to maneuver in the face of the enemy. This use of field fortification, combined with the efficiency of it, could free a part of the army for more mobile warfare on the tactical level, as the part of the army protected by such a position was better able to resist enemy actions. Alternatively the whole force could move by denying the key tactical point to the enemy through flooding, mining, or extensively barricading the area. Therefore, a defensive measure of this sort gave increased tactical, and sometimes operational, flexibility to the army employing it. During the siege of Paris, in the Franco-Prussian War of 1870–1871, Capt. Albrecht von Boguslawski noted that the Prussians used blockhouses (redoubts) to support the fire trenches and to secure the more "extreme advanced posts." They also fulfilled the function of sheltering sentries when off duty, and they provided a secure place for launching sorties.[51]

At the strategic level the same principles applied, as a fortified position could be used as a point of maneuver for an army or as means to deny a key strategic point to an enemy. Traditionally a permanent fortress performed this role, but field fortifications gave an army commander a much greater degree of flexibility as to where and when he chose to maneuver. It also made the enemy's planning more difficult because a temporary fortress could be thrown up at short notice, such as happened at Plevna in 1877 (presenting the Russian Army with an immense, and unforeseen, problem).

Providing a Secure Base

The use of field fortifications as a tool for reinforcing key tactical points leads into the next theme of providing a secure base. This fortified site could be used as either a base of operations or a means of protecting supply routes. Small isolated posts could be made relatively safe from enemy action through the use of field fortification, which allowed an army to detach forces in order to help maintain lines of supply and communications more effectively. Fortifications could also be used in this context physically to protect the supplies as well through providing some type of protected storage. Armies required a continuous flow of food, fodder, and ammunition as they moved through hostile country, all of which needed to be protected from the threat of enemy raids and the increasingly long range of artillery. In 1877 Maj. Gen. Henry Schaw of the Royal Engineers wrote, "A question frequently arises in defensive as in offensive warfare how to secure depots of provisions &co. by a small guard from a sudden attack. The long ranges of modern artillery make this problem extremely difficult. There are only two ways, in which it can be solved, viz.: by keeping the enemy at such distance that his artillery fire cannot effectively reach the point to be protected, or by placing the stores under bomb proof cover."[52]

Schaw was making clear that field fortification was an excellent method for securing bases, supplies, and so on, extremely cost effectively. Admittedly, he was discussing the protection of a base in the tactical sense, yet his words are relevant because a secure tactical base of operations was important to the local commander.

This issue became more significant with the expanding size of armed forces, which demanded a corresponding increase in the quantity of supplies that needed to be moved in order to support the troops, as their ability to sustain themselves through forage was very unlikely. Increased firepower too, particularly the ability to fire more ammunition more quickly, demanded an ever-increasing supply of ammunition. By the end of the nineteenth century, when modern industrial technology and mass armies were combined, soldiers required unprecedented levels of material support in order to fight. No campaign could start until sufficient supplies had been accumulated for the army, and the rate at which an army could advance was limited not only by the distances that troops could be expected to march but also by the rate at which magazines and supply dumps could be built up along the lines of communication. Movement was further limited by the amount of time that supply convoys took to move from the base to the front. Railways helped, as they allowed great strategic mobility and facilitated the movement of an increasingly large volume of men, matériel, and firepower. However, troops often were limited to operating within a short distance of the railhead largely because localities lacked forms of transport more modern than the horse and railways were very vulnerable, as was demonstrated repeatedly in the American Civil War. The tactical and operational response to these problems was the use of fortified posts.

In 1761, when the Russian and Austrian armies had succeeded in joining forces against Frederick the Great in Silesia, his army was saved by the protection of the field fortifications it had constructed at Bunzelwitz.[53] Later in the eighteenth century, Dietrich von Bülow's book *The Spirit of the Modern System of War* gave us such expressions as "base," "flanks," "lines of communication," "interior lines," and "exterior lines" and the idea of securing them against enemy aggression.[54] Most military theory of the time viewed field and permanent fortifications as efficient ways of providing a secure base of operations and lines of communication for the army. Paraphrasing Bülow in a long analysis of Bülow's writing General de Malortie stated, "If the country conquered have no fortress, the first thing to be done is to consider the means of entrenching the towns, villages, and posts, which may best secure the magazines and lines of operation, as well as the communications of the army acting offensively."[55] This work was not solely for defensive reasons. It was also to facilitate the safety of the lines of communication and to free more of the army for offensive purposes.

Napoleon understood the role of field fortifications to protect his base of operations and lines of communication. His words are especially significant given that his army is credited with feeding itself on the march and prospering by maneuver. Historians seeking to emphasize the mobility of his armies often overlook Napoleon's attention to logistic detail and ignore the fact that by securing his lines of communication through the use of fortifications, frequently he allowed his armies the freedom of maneuver his enemies often lacked. It also gave the army the possibility of resupply if foraging failed, though of course this effort was not foolproof, as the 1812 campaign demonstrated. When field fortifications were used as a base of operations, they could also be used as a secure point of maneuver, thus enabling the army's greater freedom of movement. Napoleon described the use of field fortifications in that manner when he discussed his invasion of Russia:

> In 1812, Danzig, Thorn, Modlin, and Prague were my fortified cities on the Vistula; Pillau, Kovno, Bialystoc, and Grodno on the Niemen; Vilna and Minsk on the Dnieper, and Smolensk were my great fortified depots for my movement against Moscow. In this operation I had a fortified base every eight or ten days' march. All post houses were loopholed and intrenched; they were held only by one company and a single gun, which protected the postal service so effectively that throughout the entire campaign not a single courier (there were several each day) or convoy was intercepted. . . . Even in the retreat, except for four days where Admiral Tchitchakof was repulsed beyond

the Berezina, the army constantly maintained free communications with its fortified depots.[56]

He went on to say that

> in the last century the question was asked whether fortifications were of any utility. It is the sovereigns who have judged them useless and who would consequently have dismantled their fortresses. As for me, I would reverse the question and ask if it is possible to plan war without them? The answer must be no. Without fortified depots it is impossible to establish good plans of campaign, and without fortified towns — which I call field depots [*places de campagne*] — in other words fortifications safe even from hussars and detachments, one cannot wage offensive war.[57]

Clausewitz's thinking resembled these ideas about the need for a secure base: "Even under the most favourable circumstances and with greatest moral and physical superiority, the aggressor should foresee a possibility of great disaster. He therefore must organize on his lines of operation strong points to which he can retreat with a defeated army. Such are fortresses with fortified camps or simply fortified camps."[58] Thus, he harked back to Frederick the Great's use of field fortification in the eighteenth century. It is also worth noting that in the Franco-Austrian War of 1859, the French fortified Vercelli, Palestro, and the bridgehead at Turbigo to provide secure bases for the offensive march and for their line of retreat in case of a reversal. In contrast, the Austrians made no use of field fortifications in their disastrous campaign, relying instead on a quadrilateral of permanent fortresses.[59]

The use of fortified supply lines and bases was also commonplace throughout the American Civil War. They were essential given the long lines of communication involved in supplying the Union Army's march into Confederate territory. However, the frequent overreliance on the use of field fortification in the role of semipermanent bases created a problem during the Civil War and had an impact in later wars, particularly if the troops manning a base became too attached to it and lost their mobility. The military historian Maj. James Edmonds (who later became Maj. Gen. Sir James Edmonds) of the Royal Engineers wrote that

> an attempt was next made to close the rivers [Red, Mississippi, Cumberland, and Tennessee rivers] to the Federal fleets by the construction of heavily armed works on their banks. But in this new departure a grave mistake was committed when these works were constructed on altogether too extensive a scale, so that they more nearly resembled entrenched camps, and required armies to hold them. Consequently when these fortresses were eventually forced to capitulate, the Confederacy suffered a loss in the men captured in them which it could ill afford.[60]

This point is important because it correlates with what happened at Plevna, Kars, Paardeberg, Port Arthur, Adrianopole, Janina, and Scutari. Where troops stayed in a fixed position, they gave up their mobility and were truly useful only so long as they tied up large numbers of the enemy. However, if the troops were militia or fortress troops, rather than regulars, their loss was of less importance as they unlikely would have been able to maneuver effectively in the field in the first place. If the enemy could successfully isolate them, frequently they were doomed, and while they remained in the proximity of large numbers of the enemy, they often lost their ability to take to the offensive. This possibility also helps to explain why generals were concerned about the loss of offensive spirit, which could easily move from a tactical to an operational problem, as these cases seem to indicate.

Osman Nuri Pasha created the field fortifications at Plevna to act as a base of operations in 1877, and he fortified his lines of supply in the same manner. In securing his base he had physically to protect the supplies in the town of Plevna itself, as much of the area occupied by the Turks was within range of the Russians' guns. With his base secure, Osman was able to launch attacks knowing that he had a safe place to fall back on if necessary. Further, his supplies were unlikely to be destroyed by a stray shell. Thus, he had free communication with the Ottoman headquarters for much of the campaign, though apart from the supplies and reinforcements he received, communicating with the senior Ottoman command does not seem to have been of particular help. Later, the Russians used small detachments based in field fortifications to protect their rail and communication lines into and out of Manchuria in 1904–1905 against bands of *hunghutze* (red beards) bandits.[61]

Theorists from the 1740–1914 period recognized that since Roman times, in establishing a base and lines of communication in both the tactical and strategic realm, the use of both field and permanent fortifications was an important, if not essential, part of the process of war fighting.

Dominating an Area

Traditionally the use of fortification to cover or dominate an area, operationally and strategically, was carried out by permanent fortification. This idea had been accepted for hundreds of years. The Romans had used extensive earthworks to cover large parts of their frontiers. For example, they constructed the Antonine Wall in Scotland, and in the Balkans some of their lines of earthworks were ninety-five kilometers in length.[62] In the mid-eighteenth century, Marshal Maurice de Saxe stated that field fortification "is to cover a Country; to oblige an enemy to attack it before they can pass it; to secure a Retreat for ones Troops; there to lodge them in Safety, there to form Magazines; and there to lay up in Stores, the Artillery, Ammunition, &c. during the winter."[63] Previously he had advocated that "it is more advantageous for a ruler to establish his strong points in localities aided by nature, and situated to cover the country, than to fortify cities at immense expense or to augment their fortifications. . . . A fortified place, located as I have proposed, could hold out for several months or even years, provided it can be supplied, because it is not encumbered with the civil population."[64] As early as 1750 Clairac had recognized that "an army, intrenched with judgment, produces, in many respects, the same effect as a fortress; for it covers a country, supplies the want of numbers, stops a superior enemy, or obliges him to engage at a disadvantage."[65]

One of the largest uses of field fortification to cover ground occurred in Portugal during the Napoleonic wars. The lines of Torres Vedras were constructed to cover the approaches to Lisbon and stop the French offensive in the summer of 1810. They also served a dual purpose for Arthur Wellesley, the Duke of Wellington — protecting his base of operations from French attack and allowing his army a secure place to gather its strength for the eventual march to attack the French. Though they resembled permanent fortifications, they largely lost their utility with the end of the campaign. The use of field fortification to cover ground occurred again in the Crimean War in 1854–1855. During that war a number of extended lines of fortifications to cover an area were built: the lines of Bulair in the Gallipoli Peninsular (and the Turks used them against the Bulgarians in 1912–1913), the Russian works thrown up to the south of Sevastopol, and the lines covering the allied rear from Inkerman to Balaclava.[66] In the American Civil War, field fortifications were used to cover the area around Richmond and Petersburg in Virginia, and in the Russo-Turkish War of 1877–1878 field fortifications were used to cover the strategically important Shipka Pass in the Balkan Mountains and most famously at Plevna. In the Second Anglo-Boer War, long lines of blockhouses were used in this way, and though they were more permanent they too largely lost their utility at the end of the conflict. During the Russo-Japanese War, the Russian Army dug long lines of field fortifications to dominate the main routes of the Japanese advance, such as those defended at Nanshan near Dalny. Field fortifications were again used on a large scale during the Balkan Wars of 1912–1913 and particularly during the fighting in Thrace. There, the Ottomans reinforced the lines of Tchataldja, covering the route to Constantinople with extensive field fortifications.

Conclusions

Although there was no single, coherent theory of field fortification, several dominant themes run through its study. Field fortification was used to prevent desertion, which had been a common problem before the middle of the nineteenth century; however, its construction for this particular reason declined in importance with time. Fortifications, of course, provided physical and moral protection to the troops occupying them, but the protection they were designed to provide changed with the type of enemy threat they were supposed to guard against. Providing a physical barrier remained important, especially for armies of countries with foreign empires, for their troops were likely to need a physical barrier to defend them against attacks by peoples without rifles or artillery. However, the changes witnessed from 1877 to 1914 more closely reflected the increasing importance of firepower in the late nineteenth century, in particular with heavier and more powerful artillery on the battlefield. The protection field fortifications provided also became more important as the numbers of citizens serving as soldiers grew and the attitudes to the value of their lives changed. Thus, as armies expanded in size, their need to entrench remained, but their reasons for doing so evolved. The greater use of citizens also further intensified the tension between the need to protect them in war and the need to put them at risk through offensive action.

Through this physical and moral protection, field fortification acted as a force multiplier. The protection provided to the soldiers gave them the confidence to use their fighting power fully. At the same time, the job of an attacker became that much more difficult, as killing or neutralizing the soldiers defending fortifications was harder. Thus, attacks against troops in field fortifications, as opposed to attacks against troops in the open, increasingly required much more time, effort, and preparation in order to be successful.

Field fortification also provided, and assisted in, the defense of key points on the battlefield, as well as allowing those positions to be used as points of maneuver. Securing a key position on the battlefield through denying the enemy his use of the ground—by flooding, for example—forced the enemy to maneuver in a more predictable pattern or to move where the army that had constructed such points desired it to go, making the enemy's action easier to counter. Fortifications constructed for this purpose did not necessarily need physically to protect the troops sheltered behind them from the effects of the enemy's fire in the way that a trench might; instead, they simply needed to be sufficient to carry out their purpose.

This physical and moral protection, as well as the effects of force multiplication, combined to make field fortifications extremely useful to armies seeking to secure bases and lines of operations. They allowed small groups of men to protect lines of communication cost effectively against all but a concerted effort by the enemy. In addition, these fortified posts themselves could be used as bases of operations in their own right.

Field fortifications were used also to protect or dominate an area. Tactically, this latter idea partly fits in with the fortification of a key point. However, as has been shown, this theme can be expanded to the larger operational or strategic area. Field fortifications built at strategic points on a communications network, for example, could effectively allow their possessor to dominate an area through securing control of traffic and movement. This case was especially so in parts of the world where the transport net was less well developed. Control of a large transport hub might well provide control over a whole region. Likewise, flooding on a large scale could deny the enemy the ability to use a particular route. Normally permanent fortresses carried out this role, but unless they were constructed to cover the enemy's entire potential approach route—an expensive endeavor—an enemy could circumvent them by choosing another avenue of advance. The advantage of field fortifications is that they could be constructed anywhere and at short notice given enough resources. Thus, they could more easily be adapted to a changing military situation.

The technical design of field fortifications remained largely unchanged until 1877, despite the background of monumental changes in warfare and its increasing lethality, indicating that the basic design of field fortifications had remained largely effective until that time. However, starting in 1877, the design of field fortifications underwent gradual change and came to resemble the defensive structures seen at the start of the First World War. Artillery became lighter and therefore more mobile, for the weight of its destructive power, thus facilitating its increased use on the battlefield. This development led to a corresponding buildup in the strength of the fortifications, which were designed to withstand the greater fire; consequently, more and heavier guns were needed to deal with them. Thus existed a clear link between improving field fortifications and the increasingly static nature of large-scale warfare. As heavier and heavier artillery was needed to shift troops in better-designed field fortifications, so the problems of moving these weapons returned to the fore.

Armies could transport these large weapons about on the rail lines, but it proved difficult to move them far from the place where they disembarked from the train without sufficiently large resources of muscle power, whether in horse or human form. A solution to this problem arrived with steam traction engines and petrol engines. However, though they might be capable of moving large guns, they still were limited by the quality of the road network. Moreover, being new technology, often petrol transport was not entirely reliable, so it was not used in large numbers until it became more dependable and more necessary.

If a defender could dig in effectively, the chances were that an attacker would have to wait until sufficient numbers of heavy artillery pieces had been brought up to break the defensive line. The troops manning the fortified lines would then have more time in which to fortify themselves and increase their ability to resist, thus compounding the problems for the attacker. Often this development forced the attacker to halt until heavier artillery could deploy, which might take some time, or he would have to try to find a flank to go around, envelop the enemy, and threaten the lines of supply, the favored solution. The latter part of the nineteenth and the early twentieth centuries clearly demonstrated these problems, which would occur in the First World War. There, armies were faced with an enemy whose very size, should he have dug in, meant that they could not easily outflank or break through his position without sufficient quantities of heavy artillery to do so. This level of firepower previously had been available only to armies conducting sieges, where there was adequate time to bring up and properly site the relatively immobile heavy artillery needed to breach the fortifications.

Though this next idea occurs only rarely in the literature, it is also important to remember that field fortifications could deter an attack as effectively as a permanent fortress if they were constructed well enough. Thus, they could be useful even when not actually put to use in combat. If the strength of a position is such that an attacker opts for another "less advantageous scheme," then the fortifications have "materially assisted in protecting the position" despite not being physically tested. The lines of Torres Vedras provided the most prominent example of a fortification's discouraging an enemy attack.[67] Thus, a clear link exists between the deterrent effects of field and permanent fortifications, a link that frequently is overlooked.

Field fortifications, through their inherent flexibility, were constructed to suit all levels of warfare, almost anywhere they were needed, and at short notice. Field fortification theory thus slowly began to impinge on areas where permanent fortifications previously had been viewed as the only viable solution. The great flexibility that field fortifications provided, especially when compared with permanent fortifications, saw their use expand dramatically in the late nineteenth century. They required vastly less of a country's time, money, and resources to construct. Thus, they appealed both to the military and to the taxpayer. These factors, combined with the increasing need for their use, led slowly and inexorably to the multilayered defensive systems of the First World War.

This chapter argues that the use of field fortification formed an important aspect of warfare. Clausewitz was correct when he asserted,

> It was once fashionable to belittle entrenchments and their effectiveness. The cordons on the French frontier which were pierced so often, the entrenched camp at Breslau where the Duke of Bevern was defeated, the battle of Torgau, and a number of other examples caused this prejudice. Moreover the victories that Frederick the Great won by mobility and aggressiveness had cast a shadow over defense as such, over all fixed positions and especially all entrenchments, which further increased this disdain. Certainly if a few thousand men are expected to defend several miles, or if entrenchments are nothing more than lateral communication trenches, entrenchments will not

be worth anything. Any confidence placed in them is dangerously misleading. But it must surely be a contradiction or even
nonsense when this opinion is extended to the very concept
of entrenchment. . . . What use would entrenchments be any-
how, if they did not help the defender? No, not only reason,
but hundreds and thousands of examples show that a well-
prepared, well-manned, and well-defended entrenchment *must
generally be considered as an impregnable point* [italics in original],
and is indeed regarded as such by the attacker. If we proceed
from this factor of the effectiveness of a single trench, we cannot really doubt that the assault on an entrenched camp is a
very difficult and usually an impossible task for the attacker.[68]

However, despite today being largely ignored, field fortification
proved its utility throughout the 1740–1914 period. Indeed, its theory and practice became an increasingly important part of warfare
particularly in the thirty or so years leading up to the First World
War, and this time frame is the main focus of the case studies in
this book. Field fortification's importance is reflected in how many
theorists and engineers wrote about, and promoted, its use. Field
fortification theory remained relevant, serviceable, and relatively
unchanged despite the massive technological and theoretical developments in warfare that had occurred. In contrast, the practice of
field fortification changed in response to increasing firepower, with
a move from aboveground to belowground fortification beginning
with the Russo-Turkish War of 1877–1878. Fortifications went deeper
and deeper until they resembled the trenches and strongpoints of
the First World War—with all of the bloody problems consequent
with that conflict.

2

The Russo-Turkish War and Plevna

The Russo-Turkish War of 1877–1878, during which the battles and siege of Plevna in Bulgaria occurred, is an important war in European history. The last war fought between major European powers before the First World War, it involved more than half a million troops fighting in two theaters on either side of the Black Sea. The war lasted longer than the Franco-Prussian War of 1870–1871 and utilized some of the most modern weaponry then available.[1] (The Italo-Turkish War of 1911–1912 was fought on a much smaller scale, with most of the fighting taking place outside Europe, and as such this war is ignored here.) Its result effectively ended Turkish, or Ottoman, rule in the Balkans, and the war emphasized the decline of both Turkey and, to a lesser extent, Russia as major powers.

The battles and siege that took place during this war highlighted the problems that the industrialization and modernization of warfare created. They also provide numerous excellent examples of the theory and practice of field fortification at the time. In particular, the battles and siege that took place at Plevna serve as the basis for an outstanding, and unique, case study because they repeatedly showed the human cost of attacking entrenchments defended by men armed with breech-loading rifles. This example is particularly important, as the Turkish forces had prepared all of their own defensive works with their normal field equipment.[2] It also encapsulates the idea that the fighting during the war in general, and in and around Plevna in particular, was significant as the area around Plevna witnessed four major actions. The first battle took place over relatively open ground. By the time of the second battle, the Turks had fortified the main points, and by the third all of the most important positions had been fortified based on their experience in the previous two actions. By the time of the attempted Ottoman breakout, the Russian Army, after its own experience in the previous battles, was fully dug in too. Col. John Formby, a British officer, claimed that the siege of Plevna provided an "almost unique" opportunity for "studying the relation of Field Works to Ground."[3] Though this opinion demonstrates a Eurocentric worldview, which was common in the armies of Europe of the time, it does have its validity.

Only a dozen years before the Russo-Turkish War of 1877–1878, the Americans had finished fighting a civil war in which both sides had used extensive field fortifications, particularly in the war's last two years. However, the Russo-Turkish War was different. During that war both Russia and Turkey made extensive use of field fortifications, breech-loading artillery, breech-loading infantry weapons, and Gatling guns, a forerunner of the modern machine gun; thus, the war cries out for greater modern study. The Ottomans brought in outside expertise, former soldiers from the United States in particular, on the Gatling guns' use.[4] The author himself saw more than twelve Gatling guns from the actual battles and siege, still in and around the Plevna battle site, during a visit in April 2002. Even taking into account the possibility that these guns were moved there from other areas of the campaign after the war, their presence does indicate their use in that theater of war.

Some of the Turkish Army's field fortifications constructed during this conflict, particularly the trenches at Plevna, would not have looked out of place in the First World War. The Russians too were quick to learn, despite the Russian military reformer Mikhail Dragomirov's prewar thinking that field fortifications sapped the offensive spirit of the attacker and that the best use of entrenchment was for creating obstacles to enemy movement.[5] The Russo-Turkish War of 1877–1878 also demonstrated that the Ottoman Army was widely versed in the use of field fortification and its construction well before German officers came to train and lead them.[6]

The reasons for the fortifications' construction mirror the main ideas previously outlined. Trained as both an engineering and artillery officer, the American military attaché to the Russian Army, Lt. Francis Vinton Greene, wrote that the field fortifications constructed during the war fulfilled three main purposes: they provided large entrenched camps, they facilitated the defense of strategic points, and they gave protection to troops in open ground.[7] French engineering officer Capt. J. Bornecque argued that there were five main reasons for their use during the war: for the defensive-offensive, for combat taking place over a period of time, for the cover of strategic positions, for the cover of communications, and for help with the investment of a place.[8] Their observations demonstrate that officers from other armed forces were watching this war and that the role of field fortification clearly was of interest to them.

Terrain and Soil in Bulgaria

Prior to the war nothing was remarkable about Plevna except for its location, straddling the main road between Sofia and the fortress city of Rustchuk (located on the Danube bordering Romania and part of the quadrilateral of Turkish fortresses in eastern Bulgaria). Rolling hills surround Plevna, and it is about three miles east of the River Vid, which flows north to the Danube. Much of the soil around the town is fertile, black, fairly heavy, and clay-like.[9] This last point is important because it allowed the easy construction of the fortifications around Plevna, particularly the trenches and bomb-proofs that were so important to the defenders.

Four main battles, as well as a number of smaller actions, occurred at Plevna, and the building of the town's fortifications will be examined chronologically to track the subsequent changes that took place in their construction. At the first battle of Plevna on 20 July 1877, the Ottomans had constructed only some rudimentary fortifications along the ridgeline of the Janik Bair, as well as some more on the heights east of the town itself.[10]

By the second battle, 30 July 1877, a small redoubt and some entrenchments had been built outside Opanetz, three miles northwest of Plevna. Directly north of Plevna were some entrenchments along the western end of the Janik Bair, as well as a redoubt south-east of Bukova. In addition, trenches ran along part of the middle of the Janik Bair ridgeline, and two further redoubts to the northwest of the village Grivitza guarded the flank of that ridgeline. To the east of Plevna were four of the redoubts of the "middle group" (see location 5 on map 2.1) that had been constructed along with some supporting entrenchments. Osman Pasha, the Ottoman commander at Plevna, described the entrenchments at that time as shelter trenches in his account of the battles and siege. He also reported that many of the redoubts were simple epaulements for the field artillery.[11] His account makes clear that the Turks had spent time fortifying their positions, but they had not had time to finish the process before the battle. Lieutenant Greene was correct when he asserted that the middle group of redoubts was located in an area dominated by the hills to the west and southwest, between the villages of Grivitza and Radischevo. This location was chosen because of the insufficient troops available for the defense of Plevna, thus denying full use of the best ground around the town for its defense. However, this poor location obviously was not a problem for the Turks because none of these well-constructed works was captured during the siege, and the shortage of Russian siege artillery meant that little damage could be done to them anyway.[12] To the south of the town were more entrenchments, but because these entrenchments and the redoubt covering the bridge over the River Vid on the Plevna–Sofia road west of Plevna played little part in the battle, they will not be discussed in any detail.

By the time of the third battle of Plevna on 7–12 September 1877 (these dates include the artillery bombardment and the general assault), the fortifications surrounding the town were largely complete and had become very sophisticated, providing multiple lines of fire for the defenders and top cover to protect against Russian and Romanian artillery fire. An additional redoubt had been added at Opanetz (see figure 2.1), and almost the entire ridgeline of the Janik Bair had been heavily fortified with both redoubts and supporting trenches. The middle group had expanded to include a much more extensive use of fortifications and five additional redoubts (locations 4, 5, and 6 on map 2.1). Also extensive fortifications were con-

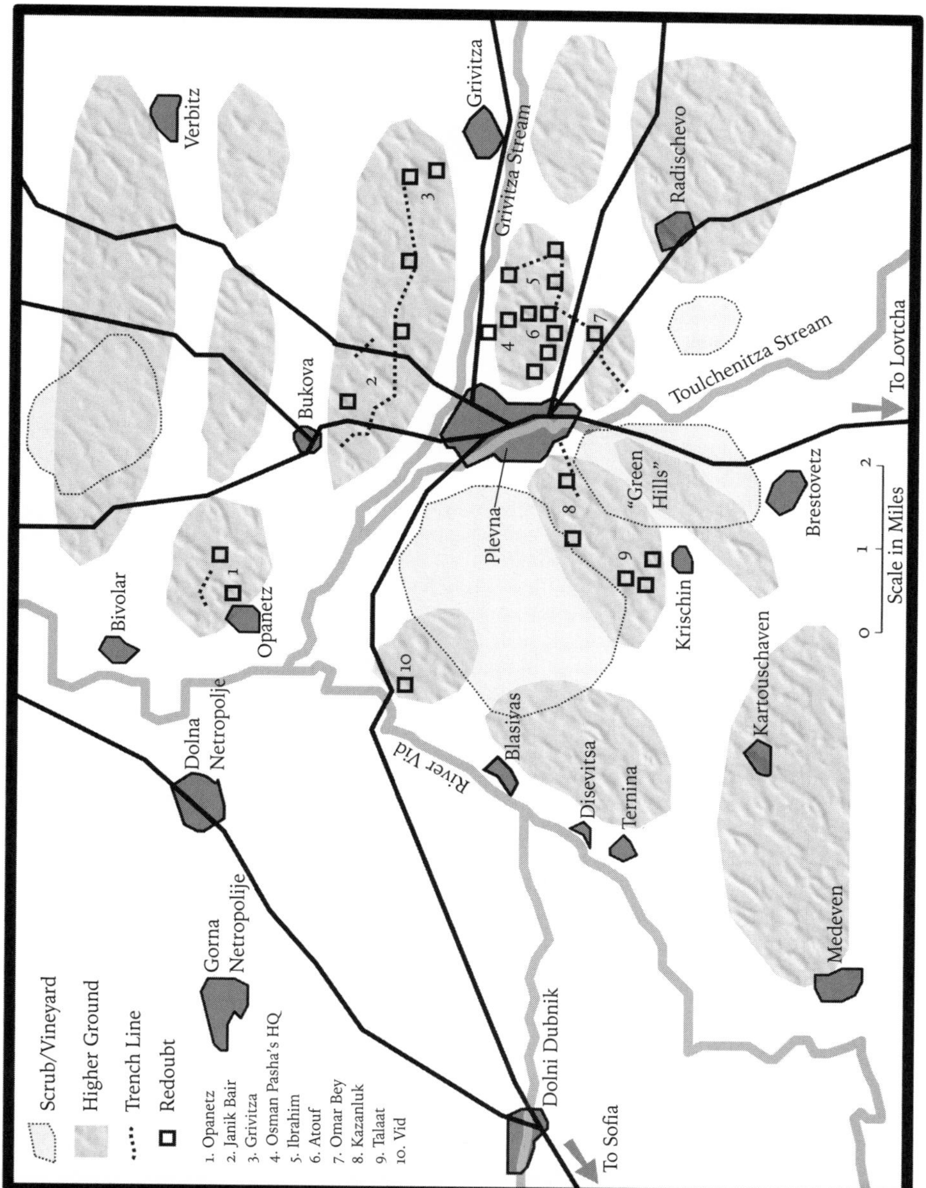
Scrub/Vineyard
Higher Ground
Trench Line
Redoubt
1. Opanetz
2. Janik Bair
3. Grivitza
4. Osman Pasha's HQ
5. Ibrahim
6. Atouf
7. Omar Bey
8. Kazanluk
9. Talaat
10. Vid
Verbitz
Grivitza
Grivitza Stream
Radischevo
Bukova
Bivolar
Opanetz
Plevna
"Green Hills"
Toulchenitza Stream
To Lovtcha
Brestovetz
Krischin
Scale in Miles
0
1
2
Kartouschaven
Dolna Netropolje
Blasiyas
River Vid
Disevitsa
Ternina
Gorna Netropolije
Medeven
Dolni Dubnik
To Sofia

MAP 2.1. Fortifications at the Third Battle of Plevna.[13]

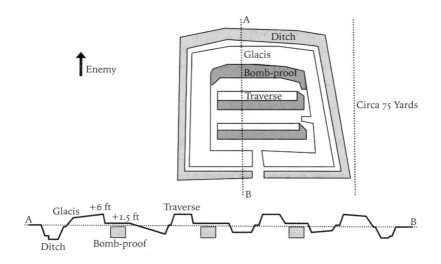

FIGURE 2.1. An Opanetz Group redoubt. Based on "Notes by a Russian Engineer on the Theatre of War in European Turkey," trans. Capt. J. W. Savage, *Professional Papers of the Corps of Royal Engineers* 9 (1883).

structed southwest of the town, where six redoubts and supporting trenches had been placed, guarding the axis of advance from the village of Krischin and across the area known as the Green Hills directly south of Plevna (locations 8 and 9 on map 2.1). This area of the defenses witnessed most of the heavy fighting on 11–12 September, during the ultimately unsuccessful Russian assault led by Gen. Mikhail Skobeleff's force.

Following the third battle of Plevna, the fortifications were continually improved, and the Russian investment witnessed large-scale construction that eventually completely encircled Plevna and the Turkish fortifications. Though both sides constructed fortifications right up until its fall on 10 December 1877, following the lessons learned during the series of battles there, the fortifications built after the third battle of Plevna were not fully tested in a large attack.

The War Begins

Following the Balkan crisis that erupted in 1875, fighting continued through 1876, eventually drawing Russia into war with Turkey on 24

April 1877. The Russian Army anticipated a quick campaign against a weak enemy, but the war dragged on for forty-seven weeks.[14] The opening phase of the war in Europe went well for the Russian Army. Its crossing of the Danube at Sistova proved to be a relatively easy affair, that it followed by securing Nikopol (see map 2.2). The advanced guard under Gen. Joseph Gourko boldly seized the main passes through the Balkan Mountains.[15] Russian operations then paused, and progress slowed. The British military attaché to the Russian Army, Col. Frederick Wellesley, described the situation to British foreign secretary Edward Stanley (Lord Derby) in a letter dated 27 July: "The progress of the Russians, since the capture of the Shipka Pass has been slow, and the delay is to be accounted for: 1stly by the Russian defeat at Plevna, 2ndly by the fact that great commands have been given to the Grand Dukes, 3rdly by the insufficiency of troops. The Turks are said to have entrenched themselves strongly outside Plevna, and it will doubtless cost the Russians many men to carry so formidable a position."[16]

The delays in the Russian advance had allowed Osman Pasha to rush troops to Plevna by 19 July, and as mentioned previously, they arrived in time to repel the first Russian assault. The Turkish forces under Osman Pasha were situated on the right flank of the Russian advance into Bulgaria, and the Russians decided that the menace that the force at Plevna posed must be eliminated quickly because of the threat to their lines of communication to the Balkan Mountains and in particular to their troops holding the Shipka Pass. Hence the second and almost equally hasty and ill-prepared Russian assault on Plevna occurred 30 July and ended in failure. Meanwhile, the Turkish forces at Plevna under Osman Pasha had been expecting an attack, and according to Dr. Charles Snodgrass Ryan, a medical doctor in service with the Turks, they had prepared accordingly: "Our men were working away as busily as bees fortifying outposts, digging entrenchments, and building redoubts on the cordon of hills that formed the natural rampart of the town."[17]

The second defeat of their forces at Plevna placed the Russian Army in a precarious position. Its advance into Bulgaria had stalled and still confronted a small but potentially powerful Turkish force.

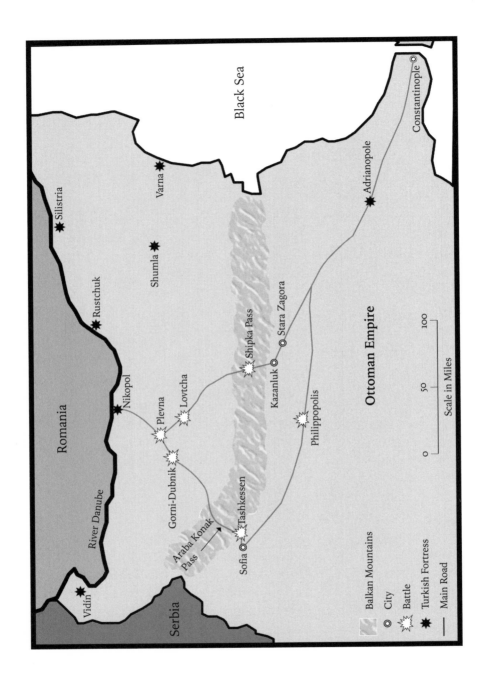

MAP 2.2. The Russo-Turkish War in Europe.

Osman's troops were battle hardened due to their experiences fighting the Serbs in 1876, and they threatened the Russian Army's flank and rear. Because of the tenuous situation in which the Russian Army in the Balkans now found itself, it had become politically, as well as militarily, necessary for Russia to hold on until Osman Pasha's strength had been crushed because further setbacks might easily have led to unrest in Russia itself. Thus, it had become extremely important to defeat the Turks at Plevna. A lull in the fighting followed, while the Russian Army, now supported by elements of the Romanian Army, prepared for another assault on the Ottoman positions at Plevna. However, the Ottomans also repelled this attempt on 11–12 September 1877, despite a four-day artillery bombardment of the Ottoman positions. This defeat sapped the Russian Army's morale and confidence and led to this response from Baron Jomini, the Russian minister for foreign affairs, who felt Plevna's fate was of great political significance: "What we want is the fall of Kars as well as that of Plevna, and should we be fortunate enough to take these two fortresses I've no reason why negotiations should not be commenced without at the same time [bringing] an end to military operations."[18]

The stalemate at Plevna had become a big political issue for the Russians, with Jomini clearly equating the conquest of the temporary fortifications at Plevna with the permanent ones at Kars in their importance to the war effort. The political significance of Plevna to Russia and the Ottoman Empire was in no small part owed to the scale of the defeat of the third Russian assault there. Colonel Wellesley informed Lord Derby in a letter, dated 21 September, of this matter:

> As your lordship is aware, I was present at the recent bombardment and final assault of the Turkish positions in the stronghold of Plevna. Although these military operations are regarded in a large portion of the English press as having terminated in a partial Russian success [due to the capture of a single Turkish redoubt, Grivitza No. 1], as a matter of fact the result was a disaster for the Russian armies, and the disas-

ter was accompanied by a loss of not less than 20,000 men, killed and wounded, inclusive of some 3,000 Roumanians.[19]

That the Russian and Romanian Armies had spent longer than a month making preparations, had deployed an attacking force more than three times greater than that of the defending Ottomans, and included four full days of preliminary bombardment using more than 400 guns heightened the impact of the heavy casualties. This battle's losses were in addition to the two previous failed assaults, which had cost the Russian Army 2,900 officers and men at the first attempt and another 7,500 at the second.[20]

Following the setback at the third battle of Plevna, Gen. Eduard Ivanovich Todleben of Crimean War fame was sent to take charge of operations around the town. He decided that after three failed assaults, an investment of the town was the best available system of attack.[21] The investment was a slow process as the Russian Army whittled down and cut Osman Pasha's lines of communication with the rest of the Ottoman Army in the Balkans, but Plevna eventually surrendered on 10 December after the Turks failed to break out. The Turks, by denying Osman Pasha the authority to remain mobile, effectively delivered up a considerable force to Russian arms. However, the Russian Army had been stalled in front of Plevna for six months by an Ottoman force that was about a third of its size. With Plevna taken, the Russians were able to renew their advance through the Balkans, forcing Turkey to sue for peace within three months.

The campaign in Asia had started on 25 April 1877, when the Russian Army of the Caucasus launched separate columns aimed at the fortresses of Batum, Ardahan, Kars, and Bayazid (see map 2.3). The Russian forces had as their objective taking Ardahan and Bayazid, as well as shielding the fortress at Kars in order to allow the army to continue its march to Erzeroum (modern-day Erzurum). On 28 April Russian troops under the command of General Tergukassoff took the fortress at Bayazid without a fight as the small Ottoman garrison fled upon sighting the Russian advanced guard.[22] In turn a combined Ottoman and irregular Kurdish force of more than 30,000

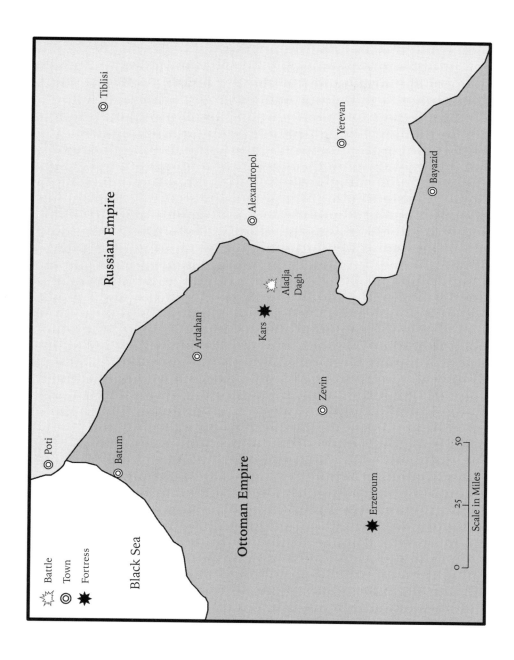

MAP 2.3. The Russo-Turkish War in Asia.

men led attacks on the 2,100-man Russian garrison and massacred much of the civilian population in the town itself on 18 June.[23] However, the Ottoman force possessed little artillery and, being unable to soften up the Russian defenders in the citadel effectively, had several attacks repulsed. The Russian garrison was thus besieged and in need of rescue. General Tergukassoff was forced to return to relieve Bayazid.

Meanwhile, Gen. Mikhail Loris-Melikoff, the Russian commander of the Alexandropol column marching against Kars, detached part of his force to assist in the attack on Ardahan. Loris-Melikoff himself drew up the plan for the assault on the fortress on 16–17 May, and it was successful in part owing to the demoralization of the Ottoman garrison and to a number of siege guns that had been brought up with the Russian troops (in spite of the poor roads and mountainous terrain). These guns both caused great losses among the defenders and covered the attack of the Russian troops. It is also reasonable to think that they undermined the confidence of the Turkish garrison, as the men might have thought that the Russians' ability to move powerful artillery into position and attack Ardahan so quickly when the roads and tracks were muddy and frequently snow covered was virtually impossible. Indeed, most of the Ottoman losses came from the well-handled Russian artillery.[24] General Loris-Melikoff then left a detachment to shield the fortress at Kars and continued his advance toward Erzeroum. He was stopped at Zevin by Moukhtar Pasha, the Ottoman commander in Armenia, who had selected and fortified a defensive position there in anticipation of the Russians' advance. Because they could no longer look to assistance from Tergukassoff's troops, the Russians also were compelled to retreat and pull back the troops shielding Kars.

Thus, at the beginning of July, the Russians were forced to halt their offensive in Armenia largely for the same reasons as they had in Bulgaria—a lack of troops and poor planning.[25] The Russians' advance on Batum had stalled; indeed, they had been forced to retreat, and the only notable success was the taking of the small fortress of Ardahan. As in the Balkans, the Turks were in a good position in Armenia, but they failed to capitalize on it.

In July, Loris-Melikoff received reinforcements, which allowed him to renew the Russian advance on Kars toward the end of the month. In the mountains and hills north and east of Kars, the Russian advance stalled, and a long period of skirmishing followed until an unsuccessful Russian attack on 2 October. Shortly after this battle, on the night of 8–9 October, Mouhktar Pasha abandoned the positions he had fought so hard to maintain. Almost certainly, he carried out this retreat after snow had already fallen because he felt the campaigning season was over and did not want the men to winter on the hills and mountains outside Kars. Loris-Melikoff had other ideas. He was determined to prosecute the campaign despite the onset of winter weather and prepared his force to deal a decisive blow to the enemy. On 15 October, the Russian forces attacked at Aladja Dagh and inflicted great losses on the Ottoman defenders. The Turks fled their trenches before the Russians charged home. Turkish morale collapsed, and part of the army surrendered, leaving the rest to flee toward Kars. In addition to the 7,000 men captured by the Russians, the Turks lost 4,000–5,000 men,[26] almost certainly owing to their exposure to shrapnel while retreating from their entrenched positions. General Heimann was dispatched to pursue Mouhktar Pasha to Erzeroum, defeating his forces in battle there on 4 November,[27] while the rest of the Russian Army under Loris-Melikoff set about the siege of Kars, which they eventually stormed on the night of 17–18 November.

The Russians finally had completely defeated the Ottoman troops in Armenia, much as they had done in the Balkans. The successful storming of Kars sealed the fate of the Ottoman forces, just as the war in the Balkans had turned on the outcome of the siege at Plevna. Not long after these events, the war was brought to a close.

Fortifications: Preventing Desertion

No direct evidence indicates that preventing desertion was an explicit motive for the fortifications' construction, but per the reasons outlined in chapter 1, the field fortifications did have that effect during the war. They did help prevent large-scale desertion even when the situation and conditions were bad for both sides, and large-scale desertion from the fortified areas around Plevna does not seem to have been an issue for either side. However, it had been a problem for the Turks at Kars and Erzeroum before the war was waged in earnest. In general, desertion was a problem for the Turkish Army because of the poor quality of its troops and the lack of supplies. Before the war had started, the Russian consul in Erzeroum, M. Obermüller, commented on morale among Turkish troops there: "Desertion from the ranks has commenced now the roads have begun to be free from snow, and competent persons assure me the ranks will be very seriously thinned as soon as the weather is sufficiently warm to permit of deserters living in the mountains."[28]

Accepting that Obermüller's report might have been making the most of the situation to encourage any potential Russian advance on the place, the British military attaché, Col. W. Lennox, found that it indicated a sufficiently credible problem and forwarded it to his superiors. When Russian troops approached Kars and Erzeroum during the war, the desertion of Turkish troops became less of an issue because those who had wished to desert or were more prone to desert had in all likelihood already done so. Further, it had become increasingly dangerous not only to be outside fortifications by the time the Russian Army had closed with the Ottoman positions but also to desert and make it out of the war zone after the enemy had invested these towns. The presence of Cossacks and Bashi-Bazouks roaming around the war zone, particularly given these troops' ferocious reputation (the massacre of civilians at Bayazid in Armenia being but one example), also must have had an impact on any potential deserters' willingness to risk leaving the relative safety of fortified positions. In a report written on the war in Asia, Lt. W. A. H. Hare of the Royal Engineers describes these irregulars as "hords [sic] of savage irregulars, thirsting for plunder and bloodshed, and over whom the Turkish Muchir had little or no control."[29]

The lack of much evidence regarding the issue of desertion indicates that it was not a primary reason for building field fortifications during the Russo-Turkish War of 1877–1878. However, it certainly had an impact when the two sides closed with each other and increased the risk to those troops foolhardy enough to venture outside of fortified positions, as witnessed during the Turkish retreat from Aladja Dagh.

Providing Physical Protection

British newspaper correspondent J. Drew Gay witnessed the benefits of physical protection that the entrenched positions provided at Plevna:

> Here the battle began, from a south-easterly direction, by the sudden opening of twenty-four guns upon a little battery in the very front of the position. I was not in that battery during the day, so I cannot detail the incidents which occurred there; but it will please the Russians to know that, though they fired nearly 500 shells into its confined area, and ploughed up every metre of ground in it, they only wounded one Turk and did some trifling damage—quickly repaired—to a gun carriage. Of the next battery I can speak from personal observation. Thirteen hours' fire, sometimes from thirty guns at once, carried no harm of any kind into that battery. Dr. Ryan, an Irishman, who was there in the medical service of the Turks, had not a single case.[30]

The reasons for the lack of damage are most likely the soft clay soil found around Plevna and the lack of sufficient numbers of large siege guns in the Russian artillery arsenal there. Indeed, the Russians did not fully rectify this problem at Plevna until after General Todleben assumed command and certainly not before the third battle of Plevna had taken place. Shortly afterward French military attaché to the Russian Army Col. L. Gaillard noted that the Russian forces at Plevna possessed only twenty siege guns, to supplement the field artillery,[31] and they had arrived at Plevna on 4 September 1877 only just in time for the third unsuccessful assault.[32] After visiting a Russian redoubt commander during the bombardment preceding the third battle of Plevna, Colonel Wellesley also noted the artillery fire's ineffectiveness on soldiers in entrenchments:

> Here I had the opportunity of asking him what his losses had been, and to my intense astonishment he replied that notwith-

standing the good practice made by the Turks he had not lost a man, nor had a gun been scratched. He held a book in his hand which registered the number and effect of each Turkish shell, and he pointed out that the last shell was the thirty-fifth that had burst inside his battery up to that moment. While we were there five more shells fell and burst right in the battery and to our rear, but no damage was done. The fact was that the parapets of the battery being enormously high, the trajectory of the Turkish fire was so curved that the projectiles plunged straight down into the ground, which, fortunately for all of us, was extremely soft, and buried themselves there, bursting upwards in the line of least resistance, instead of laterally, which would of course have wrought great havoc.[33]

Given that the Turks did not possess any siege guns at Plevna, the Russian commander's experience is not too surprising. Describing his own experience at Plevna, Todleben wrote in a letter to Brialmont that "the enemy was not slow in taking his own precautions; the garrisons of the redoubts were withdrawn, and placed in trenches a certain distance from the works; the deep and narrow ditches above were occupied by the Turks. It hardly need be mentioned that our Artillery was powerless against the trenches and ditches. As to the reserves, they were hidden in folds of the ground, or withdrawn out of range of our artillery."[34] Furthermore, in 1883 Lt. Col. Cornelius Clery noted in his work *Minor Tactics* that General Todleben had reckoned that "it took each Russian battery a whole day's firing to kill one Turk."[35]

The effectiveness of field fortifications is clearly borne out when examining the casualty figures of both sides during the three battles. At the first battle of Plevna, Russian casualties were 2,845 men and 74 officers, or close to a third of the Russian troops who fought that day.[36] The figures for the first battle compare well with those given by Colonel Gaillard, who gave Russian losses as 2,832 men and 66 officers killed and wounded. At the second battle, Russian casualties amounted to 7,338 men and around 170 officers, which represented a quarter of their strength.[37] In comparison, Turkish losses at the first battle, where they were not entrenched, were 2,000 men. At the second battle, when they were entrenched, Formby claims the Turks gave the figure of "1200, accounting for the greater difference because the Turks were behind cover and had a better rifle."[38] Even if we treat these figures with a reasonable degree of skepticism, they still represent a significant difference between the two sides. This contrast is striking when considering that the number of troops engaged on both sides — especially that of the Russians — increased between these two battles.

The third battle of Plevna witnessed Ottoman casualties of approximately 5,000 men. Of that total, roughly 4,000 men became casualties in the fighting with General Skobeleff (who led the section of the Russian assault aimed at the group of redoubts covering the Green Hills south of Plevna).[39] These particular losses occurred largely when the Ottoman force was exposed to enemy fire as it was forced out of the Kazanluk Redoubt during the attacks by Skobeleff's force. Many of these men likely fell during the several counterattacks made in the ultimately successful attempt to retake the Kazanluk Redoubt. Thus, approximately 1,000 casualties were taken on the remainder of the field where the men remained in their entrenchments. Especially interesting, a combined Russian and Romanian attack also forced the Turks out of the Grivitza Redoubt No. 1 (the more southerly of the two redoubts east of that town), and they were unable to retake it. It must be said that the Ottoman Turks did not make as much of an effort to retake this redoubt for several reasons: the Grivitza Redoubt No. 2 (immediately north of Grivitza Redoubt No. 1) dominated it and was still in Turkish hands, while Grivitza Redoubt No. 1, as opposed to the Kazanluk Redoubt and its supporting fortifications, was not crucial to the defense. In addition, Osman Pasha was probably wary of the massed artillery fire that the Russian and Romanian armies could deploy against his troops if they were to venture into the open. As Höhneysen, the Austro-Hungarian military attaché with the Russian Army, noted, "The attack on the Grivitza Redoubt was accompanied by the artillery fire of 250 guns (including 14 Romanian batteries)."[40]

His point emphasizes the fact that the Grivitza fortifications must have provided a significant protection in order for the defenders to withstand the massive Russian and Romanian onslaught for so long. Compared with the Turkish casualties, at the third battle of Plevna Russian losses almost certainly exceeded 20,000 men,[41] almost all of whom became casualties while out in the open and exposed to enemy fire. Later, on 20 October 1877, Höhneysen commented that a Romanian attack on Grivitza Redoubt No. 2, which had taken place the previous day, had failed. The attackers had to cross only three hundred meters of open ground and, in some cases, only forty-five meters from the closest Romanian parallel, but they incurred more than 1,000 casualties in the process.[42] (Turkish casualties are unknown, but almost certainly they were nowhere near this number. Interestingly, and tellingly, Osman Pasha devoted only a few lines to this attack in the book *Défense de Plevna*, where he mentioned that the impetuous attackers were forced to retire with great losses by both the fire of the Turkish infantry and grapeshot.[43]) This imbalance of casualties between troops caught in the open and entrenched troops is further reinforced when examining the previously discussed comments from Todleben and others on how ineffective the four-day artillery bombardment was.

So important was the issue that General Skobeleff wrote a letter to Prince Alexander Imeretinsky on 15 September 1877 about his experiences during the battle. The general argued that

> the importance of this question of preparing and entrenching fields of battle has assumed in actual warfare is my excuse for making some remarks on the subject. Infantry soldiers after any brisk action return for the most part without tools. A soldier of our Army, when he advances to the attack over difficult country, especially on a hot day, relieves himself first of all of the entrenching tool; he throws it away, his great coat follows, and, lastly, his bag of biscuits. Thus when the troops obtain a position they ought to hold, they have no longer the means of covering themselves from the enemy's fire, as infantry have often protected themselves in the War of Secession, during the

four sanguinary years of the Carlist war, and in this war also, where it is the regular practice of the Turks.[44]

Clearly, Skobeleff was referring to the lessons of the American Civil War as well as to the Third Carlist War of 1872–1876, where a number of battles involved assaults on fortified positions. He was also highlighting the difficulty of holding a position captured from the enemy without the proper means to fortify it. Furthermore, he argued that troops seeking to secure a position taken from an enemy would find the task almost impossible without field fortifications to protect them from the worst of the enemy's fire: "A weighty reason for the delays in the attack was the evident necessity of fortifying, by earthworks, the positions that had been carried; an operation which offered at once considerable difficulties owing to the lamentable insufficiency of intrenching tools at the immediate disposal of the troops, which has occurred through the campaign."[45]

In 1909, Gen. Hippolyte Langlois—a French officer, staff instructor, and one of the most influential officers of his time—similarly concluded that the indisputable effects of modern rifle fire meant that "even the assailant is forced to have recourse to field works."[46] All of these observations provide stark evidence that the battles and siege of Plevna demonstrated the need for protecting troops by field fortifications on the modern battlefield and that the theories about their use were correct. Field fortifications were felt to be beneficial both in defense and in attack, and the experiences were disseminated in military writing.

Enhancing Fighting Power

This theme regarding fortifications was of particular interest to the Ottoman Turks owing to their being on the strategic defensive, as well as frequently on the tactical defensive too. A number of reasons led to this situation, but it largely stemmed from the quality of the officers and men in much of their army. The problems the Turks faced are summed up in a report that Col. J. Zohrab, a consul in Erzeroum, wrote before the war: "With good officers and good pay regularly given, the Rediffs [sic][47] might be changed into good steady soldiers, but so long as they are commanded by ignorant, dishonest, and cowardly officers, so long as they receive a miserable pittance, either paid at irregular and long intervals, or not paid at all, so long will they prove useless for the defence of their country."[48]

Colonel Lennox reported on Turkish staff officers in a letter to Derby:

> There is a great deficiency of staff officers, the headquarter staff is very small, and regular divisional staffs can scarcely be said to exist. At Rustchuk there were 3 real staff officers for the whole force of 34 battalions; at Silistria, only 1 staff officer, at Totrokan, 1, with an untrained assistant; at Shumla there appears to be so great a dearth of staff officers, that they are even employing the Europeans in their service, which is, I understand, unusual. As to the efficiency of the staff officers, many of them are Turks of the old school, and others are inexperienced young men fresh from the military school. Altogether, I cannot say that I have formed a very high opinion of their capacities. I ought to add that, at a time when the staff officers' own duties ought to have been arduous enough, owing to the process of organization that was going on, they were expected also to perform those of engineer officers, in laying out and superintending the works for the defence of the places.[49]

Colonel Lennox also commented on the quality of the actual Turkish troops themselves and on their ability to take to the field:

> The men are, for the most part, fine, healthy men, and seem to possess the well-known admirable characteristics of the Turkish soldier. They are badly clothed and shod, but armed with the Martini-Henry rifle. They are reported to have all gone through a course of ball-practice, and to be good shots. As the practice is said to have taken place before the arrival of the battalions at the theatre of war, I have no means of verifying the statement, but imagine it can only be partially true. As regards the infantry officers, those for many of the Redif battalions are merely non-commissioned officers from the Nizam. . . . It is

not expected that many of them will possess the intelligence and amount of education requisite for the efficient discharge of many of their duties. I have been some time now with the Turkish troops, and without being able to give any good reason for it, an impression is growing on me that they do not intend to try the open field. . . . All these things combined, and the dispositions and characters of the Pashas, lead one to suppose that very probably the Turks will confine themselves to the defence of their fortified positions.[50]

Though Lennox's observations referred to the Turkish troops at Shumla, his comments were applicable to much of the Ottoman Army with few exceptions. They also were rather prescient regarding the behavior of much of the Turkish Army during this war. Consul Kirby Green also communicated impressions of the poor quality of Turkish troops in a letter to Lord Derby: "The men are under fed, ill clothed, and not properly sheltered from the inclemencies of the weather and the prospect of the commencement of hostilities is inspiring them with fears which will render them quite unable to meet an enemy."[51]

Given these descriptions of the conditions they endured, it is no wonder then that the Turkish Army chose to fight from fortified positions. The men were unlikely to be relied on in an open battle, and even if they could have been, the poor quality of much of their equipment, assuming they actually had it, meant realistically little could be expected of many of them. Again per Colonel Lennox:

The movement of the three battalions the other day to Totrokan from Silistria (one of the best appointed places the Turks apparently possess) makes one despair of the Turkish troops being in any way mobile. The small force at Totrokan is utterly unable to move; the six battalions have only 102 bat-animals [battalion animals] among them, the regulation number being about 468. When the artillery marched there their ammunition had to be carried in 35 country carts. Part of the troops are shod in very bad boots, instead of in the opankas, or country-made skin shoes, laced to the stocking or gaiter.[52]

Lennox highlights the lack of supplies and equipment, which was one of the main problems for the Turkish troops. Thus, even if they were willing to fight, they often had little choice but to stay put. The enemy's presence almost certainly exacerbated this situation.

Januarius MacGahan, an American freelance war correspondent who covered the war and was present at a number of engagements, described the benefits of field fortifications on Turkish troops:

> Put a Turk in a ditch, give him a gun, a sackful of cartridges, a loaf of bread, and a jug of water, he will remain there a week or a month under the most dreadful artillery fire that can be directed against him, without flinching. He can only be dislodged by the bayonet, and with the rapidity of fire of modern arms it is very difficult to reach him with the bayonet, as the Russians found to their cost at Plevna.[53]

MacGahan's implication was that the soldier in question would not fight so well in the open, away from the protection provided by field fortifications and the sense of security they engendered. Further, with modern weapons the soldier could be expected to exact a heavy toll of any troops that attempted to attack him. Thus, we see that the use of field fortification increased the soldier's effectiveness. By the time of the second battle at Plevna, the Turkish fortifications on the Janik Bair allowed a force of about 2,100 men with six pieces of artillery to hold off a Russian attack of roughly 5,000 men supported by forty pieces of artillery. The Turks were able to do so despite having to guard a front four kilometers long.[54] Indeed, the Ottoman Army's entire defense of Plevna demonstrates how field fortifications act as a force multiplier. Osman Pasha's Ottoman force held up a combined Russian and Romanian Army, three times its size, for almost six full months.

Reinforcing Key Tactical Points

How then did the idea of reinforcing key tactical points manifest itself during the war? Henry Thuillier, a captain in the British Army, described how it was put into effect at Plevna: "No attempt was made to occupy the whole of the widely extended line of defence, but only such hills as commanded the approaches in such a manner as to render their attack by the enemy a necessity. On these the works were so placed as to sweep with their fire the whole of the ground over which the enemy could advance."[55]

With three battles being fought over the same ground, the opportunity was afforded the Turks to improve the fortifications and to add new ones where needed. After his victory at the second battle of Plevna, Osman Pasha himself toured the battlefield, ordering entrenchments to be built or improved where they were needed and most valuable to the defensive. This work was carried out immediately as he feared, incorrectly, that the Russian Army would renew its attack the next day.[56] The position of Grivitza Redoubt No. 2 was such that it absolutely dominated all approaches to it, in what would otherwise be a completely featureless piece of ground, as did the redoubts situated to its west on the Janik Bair. Grivitza Redoubt No. 2 has further significance. Any cursory glance at a map of the area surrounding Plevna would demonstrate that had this redoubt fallen, the Turkish position on the Janik Bair would have been untenable, and the defense of the town would probably have collapsed.

The field fortifications at Plevna were utilized in a manner that perfectly supported the theories on the subject. Osman Pasha placed the redoubts where he felt they would be of most benefit to the defense, paying particular attention to the fields of fire from the various positions. Multiple lines of trenches were provided to maximize the Turkish troops' ability to generate firepower and aid the defense. Thus, if one line of trenches was taken, another could be used to resist the Russian attacks. Concealment of the defensive positions was beneficial but not essential, because artillery had not yet become powerful enough to destroy the fortifications constructed. Thus, the field fortifications could make full use of the terrain and of the field of fire, with the latter being so important given the modern breech-loading weapons of the period. As the Russian assaults highlighted the line's weaknesses, so the Turks placed redoubts and entrenchments to reinforce the key tactical points.

Providing a Secure Base

As both Lieutenant Greene and Captain Bornecque highlight in their reports, Osman Pasha also used field fortification to provide a secure base of operations.[57] His army entrenched not only its positions at Plevna but also those positions guarding its lines of communication with the rest of the Turkish Army. Had the Russians managed to establish a base of operations along the Plevna–Lovtcha line, they would have been able to separate the Ottoman force into two parts more easily. This effort would have been especially worthwhile with the Shipka and Sofia–Orkhanie roads, as a major part of Osman Pasha's reinforcements and supplies had to travel along them.[58]

However, it was primarily along the route to Sofia that Osman Pasha used field fortifications to defend his lines of communication. Valentine Baker Pacha, a British officer in Ottoman service during the war, commented, "In September the Russians had succeeded in cutting off the Turkish communications with Orkhanié, but no actual investment of the place had been attempted. Shefket Pacha, who had been entrusted with a considerable Turkish force, acting from Orkhanié, had been able early in October to throw into Plevna a large reinforcement, together with military stores and supplies."[59] Shefket Pacha had achieved this feat by using field fortifications as a secure base from which to operate. Ultimately, only when the Russians attacked and captured these entrenched positions did Osman Pasha's force have its lines of communication threatened and eventually cut, a process started only after the three defeats at Plevna had demonstrated the difficulty in attacking a large, dug-in force head-on. The process of reducing and capturing the works guarding Osman Pasha's line of communication from Plevna was slow, lasting from the Russian defeat at the third battle on 12 September until 24 October, since each position had to be dealt with individually. However, this action was still preferable to waging another large assault on Plevna itself, as each small set of fortifications could be tackled more easily. Of the end of this series of operations in which the Russian Army attacked the last of the entrenchments protecting Osman Pasha's communication, Greene wrote, "The result of the 24th of October was therefore the capture of the position of Gorni-Dubnik, by which Gourko got a firm footing in the center of the Turkish line of fortifications along the Sophia [*sic*] road. He immediately set to work to fortify his position, facing both ways on the road."[60]

Thus, the use of field fortification on the road to Sofia had helped to keep the Turkish lines of communication open from July 1877 to the end of October. When the Russian Army took the positions from the Turks, it used them as bases for its own operations against the Turks, as well as for its own communications. The use of field fortification at Plevna, and along Plevna's lines of communication, provides a clear example of its utility in providing a secure method of protecting those same lines of communication. Indeed, it forced the Russians to alter their plan, as the Russian Army abandoned all attempts at aggressively subduing the Turkish force and instead strengthened its defenses in preparation for a possible Turkish counterattack.[61] So disastrous for Russia was the third defeat at Plevna that when General Todleben was given the task of taking the town, he at once decided to deprive the Turks of supplies and to besiege it in a regular manner.[62] In this respect, Todleben treated Plevna in the same way as he would have treated a permanent fortification, a response that had parallels with what later occurred during the First World War on the western front, when warfare broke down into an effective state of siege. The Turkish forces at Plevna were relatively secure until the Russian Army made deliberate and sustained attacks on their lines of communication. These attacks against the isolated entrenched detachments eventually led Osman Pasha to surrender his force. Had Osman Pasha not entrenched his base and lines of communication, however, it is doubtful whether he would have held the town in the face of the furious Russian assaults for as long as he did. In fact, field fortifications allowed the commander a great deal of flexibility in where he could choose to make a stand against the enemy.

The inherent advantages that field fortifications had when used to protect lines of communication or to provide a secure base of operations are highlighted in a report from Consul Zohrab, in Kars, to Lord Derby:

> It is, however, doubtful if any attempt would be made against Kars. The fortress commands no pass or gorge through which an enemy must pass to invade this Province. An Army need not go within ten miles of it, and, therefore, could not place itself within range of its guns. Kars, though it has been turned into a powerful fortress, is, in reality, useful only as a fortified camp to give refuge to an Army in case of need, or to cover an inferior force which might harass the line of communication of an invading Army.[63]

This report indicates that the fortifications around the town of Kars were not strategically significant in themselves, but they were important to secure the base of operations and in the protection they provided to the Turkish lines of communication in Asia. Events eventually proved Zohrab's logic correct, for the Russians only shielded Kars on their first attempt to take Erzeroum before deciding to storm the fortress later in the campaign.

Dominating an Area

Although Plevna was not as strategically important as Lovtcha, it was a useful advanced position. It acted as an anvil against which the Russians "knocked their heads," as they had done at Tashkessen; there, they had lost an action against Baker Pacha, who had then withdrawn to his real position after having beaten the Russian's "handsomely."[64] The use of field fortification allowed Osman Pasha to dominate the area around the town, which was important because the route from Plevna and Lovtcha to Kazanluk crossed the strategically important Shipka Pass, and the one from Plevna to Sofia crossed the Araba Konak Pass. As these roads were two of the few good ones in the country,[65] and railways were scarce, Plevna was a key strategic and operational point. In addition, it was centrally located north of the Balkan Mountains and sat immediately to the side of the Russian right flank. When Osman Pasha encamped at Plevna and sent a force to Lovtcha, he enabled the Turks to dominate an important part of the Bulgarian road network and denied its use to the Russian Army.

Earthworks were also used to cover potential crossing points on the Danube River, fulfilling their role in reinforcing a key tactical point. Russian troops made use of such a set of fortifications, originally built by the Romans, to protect a bridge south of Galatz. So well made were the Roman fortifications that they required only a limited amount of digging to render them useful for the defense. Well placed on a plateau overlooking the mouth of the Sereth River, Russian artillery used them to thwart an attack by Turkish gunboats.[66] This effort also demonstrates that fortifications built centuries earlier were still, with some digging, capable of withstanding the artillery fire of 1860s and 1870s technology. Once more modern explosives and artillery were developed in the 1880s, it is doubtful whether these fortifications could have withstood a similar bombardment so effectively.

Improving Technical Construction

Two notable changes occurred in the technical construction of fieldworks during the war. First, top cover (overhead cover for sheltering troops) became essential with the increasing use of shell fire and shrapnel. As previously noted, both of these munitions burst, sending out a blast wave and shower of metal, thus rendering troops sheltering beneath the blast vulnerable, whereas previously an artillery round had to hit its target physically to cause damage. Top cover also provided protection against the worst effects of the weather, thus providing another reason for troops not to desert their fortifications. Staying put was particularly important in the rugged country of the Balkans and the Caucasus, especially in winter. If nothing else, protecting troops from the effects of bad weather lessened the likelihood of wastage through illness. Prior to the battles at Plevna, top cover in field fortification had been used primarily to protect ammunition supplies or other vital stores; however, the battles and siege of Plevna also witnessed its widespread use for providing cover for troops under enemy artillery bombardment. The military thinker Col. Charles Brackenbury discussed the issue at length:

Even long range infantry fire would cover the interior of the work. Some better means of protection than defilade is therefore required. This is found in the construction of a splinter-proof, "field casemates," as they are called. . . . These should be made whenever there is any probability of a lengthened occupation. In one form or another they have entered into all well-known defences of earthworks, as at Sebastopol and Plevna. They have the enormous advantage of preserving all men, not actually required at the moment, from that drain of nervous energy which the enemy desires to produce before attacking. We read of shaken and unshaken troops. The difference is that the former have had heavy calls made on their stock of nervous energy while the latter have not. It is impossible to exaggerate the importance of husbanding nervous energy to the last moment possible. After a fever or long fasting the bravest men are sometimes reduced to such nervous prostration as to start at the slightest noise and even weep at the merest trifles. Between that condition and a full stock of energy there are many stages. No troops can bear more than a certain amount of exposure to fire without suffering in moral force, which is but another word for one form of nervous energy. Northern races such as English, German, Russians, are cooler, and therefore do not expend nervous energy so fast as southern, but the best of us must yield at last. Economy of nervous energy is even more important than economy of food or ammunition. In the meantime we may recollect with advantage how completely the use of field casemates at Plevna prevented the Turks from being shaken by the long-sustained bombardments of the Russians. During the bombardments most of the Turks sought shelter. On the commencement of the assault, they poured out of the casemates entirely fresh and ready, behind their ordinary parapets and in various tiers of firing ranks, to shake the Russians, who, being in the open, were then exposed to the demoralizing influence of the fire from the works.[67]

Brackenbury's description clearly demonstrates the benefits of top cover, as well as being an early example of thinking about countering problems that would later be associated with "shell shock." Clearly, Brackenbury was concerned with the effects of prolonged exposure to artillery fire and its impact on the men sheltering from it. Thus, the action required against the increased power of artillery fire was to dig deeper; however, this action meant that men would have to endure ever larger and heavier bombardments for longer periods, leaving them vulnerable to demoralization. These bombardments would have to have been longer and heavier to provide the results that the attacking side would require in order to mount a successful assault in the first place. So digging deeper, the solution to heavier fire, better protected the men from physical harm but prolonged their exposure to the risk of psychological damage. The irony that the same fortifications protecting the men from physical harm was in all likelihood increasing their risk of mental harm should not be forgotten given what other troops endured in the Great War less than forty years later.

The second change in the practice of field fortification came with the construction of the infantry entrenchments. These fieldworks changed from being largely aboveground structures to being mostly below ground level. As British Maj. Gen. Sir John Frederick Maurice noted,

> Curiously enough one of the exceptions is the infantry shelter trenches used by the Turks. These were generally of the type which we to-day call "Boer trenches," that is to say they were deep, and narrow, with perpendicular sides. The stiff clay soil of the country around Plevna, which would stand at any slope, lends itself as well to this style of trench as does the soil of South Africa. The general principles on which the Turkish works were constructed are, however, worthy of note, as they are as applicable to warfare in this year of grace as they were in 1877. The greatest care was taken in the siting of all redoubts and shelter trenches. Uniformity was not attempted, in each case the nature of the ground was the ruling factor.

Protection from enfilade fire was everywhere provided, and whenever the ground admitted, arrangements were made for two or even three tiers of infantry fire. The reserves and supports were provided with overhead cover and approaches to the fire trenches. Overhead cover was also subsequently provided for troops in the firing line, and since it was impossible to make enough cover for these inside the works the gunners alone were provided with bombproof cover there, and that for the infantry firing line was made some distance in rear of the trenches and connected with them by means of covered ways. Rifle pits and short trenches for sharpshooters were constructed in advance of the main line of works. Lastly, every care was taken to improve and extend the already excellent system of communications inside the defences.[68]

These deep, narrow trenches were very difficult to see and even more difficult to hit, as they presented only a small profile to the enemy and could be easily hidden. Observing the fighting at Plevna, Wellesley commented,

These shelter trenches had been absolutely unobserved and unobservable until this withering fire opened from one trench after another on the advancing Russians, whose losses were terrific. Notwithstanding, they rushed gallantly over some three or four lines of trenches, until, coming within a moderate distance of the redoubt, they were suddenly checked by the most murderous fire of infantry and guns, the latter belching out grape and canister without cessation. The Turks had reserved their fire from the works until almost the last moment, and as the Russians reached the parapets, the whole redoubt appeared to be ablaze from the flashing of the guns and rifles, the smoke from which rose in a dense damp column to the sky.[69]

The great level of firepower was combined with protection for the infantry, creating a tremendous defensive combination.

Artillery proved virtually impotent when shelling troops sheltering in this style of trench even when they approached the relatively close range of one mile. Any closer and the artillerymen would be quickly wiped out.[70] A report by an unnamed Russian engineer illustrates this point:

> A closer inspection of the style of construction of the Turkish works shows the great value they attached to the power of their infantry fire, and their endeavours to make it as damaging as possible, whilst protecting themselves from fire. They attained the first of these objectives by successive tiers of fire, and the second by numerous traverses. In order to obtain several tiers of fire they generally placed along the brow of the slopes several rows of trenches, one behind another; they moreover provided for two tiers of infantry fire in their works, either by cutting out a banquette in the counter-scarp, or by having an advanced trench in front of the ditch.[71]

The multiple lines of fire and defense in depth described can only have magnified the murderous effects of modern breech-loading firearms and artillery and forced the attacker to prepare more thoroughly with heavier artillery capable of reducing the defense's ability to resist. Thus, when modern technology combined with these two improvements in field fortification, it marked the start of a new era in their technical construction, that is, the move from above- to belowground fortification. Permanent fortifications had to be adapted in the sixteenth and seventeenth centuries to the changes brought about when forces widely adopted the trace italienne to counter heavier and more powerful siege artillery. This shift in the style of permanent fortification mirrored what occurred in the late nineteenth and early twentieth centuries with field fortifications. Though overhead cover previously had been used, now its use had been restricted. Overhead cover and the deep, narrow trenches that the Ottoman soldiers dug were increasingly seen on the battlefield leading up to the First World War as they provided the best means of protecting the soldiers from the effects of the enemy's fire.

Using these deep, steep-sided trenches was made possible largely because the ground in Bulgaria facilitated their construction, and Russian artillery was sufficiently plentiful and powerful to make their virtue a necessity. In contrast, the fortifications surrounding the fortress city of Kars, and on the heights of Aladja Dagh overlooking the town, were largely aboveground because the rocky nature of the soil there precluded much digging. Thus, forces had to build up rather than dig down, including having to transport earth to the site in order to build the redoubts.[72] The difficulty in observing deep, narrow trenches also hints at new themes in warfare — namely, those of concealment — and a change in the meaning of the term "empty battlefield." This problem became an even greater one for the attacker after the emergence of smokeless powder and modern machine guns.

The issue of using field fortification as a physical barrier during the conflict largely has been neglected, as few of the observers and participants mention it. The only barriers that were constructed on a regular basis were the ditches and walls of redoubts. Thus, properly examining the issue with any authority is difficult, except to say that both sides cannot have placed a great deal of faith in using barriers as part of the defensive positions they constructed, a problem not really solved before the widespread production and use of barbed wire after the 1870s.

Conclusions

So important had the use of field fortifications become that the Russian Army raised its concerns regarding British engineering officers serving in the Turkish forces at Plevna with Colonel Wellesley, who received the following from the War Office: "War Office state that none of the officers mentioned in your Tel. of the 16th Oct. now belong to the British Army."[73] The Russians were probably aware of the official presence of British engineering officers with Turkish forces. In February 1877, nine British Army engineering officers had been serving in Turkey.[74] Russian concern followed earlier reports in the *Times* that "several American Army officers who served during the Civil War have been offered and accepted service under the Turkish Government, whose object was to obtain men acquainted with the use of American arms."[75] These officers would undoubtedly have provided assistance with American firearms, possibly even the Turks' use of Gatling guns, and they must have had an influence—even if only a small one—on the widespread use of field fortification by the Turkish armed forces, given its appreciation during the American Civil War.

Field fortifications provided very effective protection to the troops occupying them. This factor became more important in the nineteenth century as armies took increasing numbers of citizens to serve as soldiers and attitudes changed as to the value of their lives. However, the Russians' abolition of serfdom in 1861, followed later by their introduction of universal military service in 1874, was largely a product of the need to rework the Russian military at that time rather than one to transform Russian attitudes toward society.[76] Thus, countries such as Turkey and Russia, whose social attitudes were not as liberal as they were in Western Europe, still had to protect the lives of soldiers and preserve their morale under fire in order for the army to function to its maximum potential. Fortifications acted as force multipliers, and Austrian Col. Anton Springer, who traveled to the site of Plevna, noted, "Someone with circa 15,000 men and 30 to 50 guns in field-works covering a front of 5,000 paces, dared to face and halt an attacker, which against this put up, from the beginning, 200 to 300 guns and about 40,000 men, and eventually employed some 400 guns and 60–80,000 men, this is certainly greatly praiseworthy."[77]

Field fortifications helped provide a secure base and lines of operations. It was certainly true of Osman Pasha's operations in and around Plevna, which was fortified with the intent to use it as a base of operations to attack the flank of the advancing Russian Army. His communications, too, remained secure for several months through the digging in of troops along his army's lines of supply.

Fortifications also assisted in the defense of key points on the battlefield. The redoubts at Plevna anchored the line on the Janik Bair and covered all of the main routes of advance into the town. In the Shipka Pass, where their use protected and dominated the area tactically, operationally, and strategically, the fortifications effectively blocked movement through that important pass. The technical design of field fortifications remained largely unchanged prior to the battles and siege of Plevna, despite the immense modifications in warfare during the nineteenth century, indicating that their design remained effective throughout the period leading up to the Russo-Turkish War of 1877–1878. Following the actions at Plevna, however, warfare witnessed the increasing use of top cover and deep, narrow trenches as the role of physical protection came to the fore.

The quote that follows illustrates the timeless nature of field fortifications and the impact of their use in 1877 on military thinking. Maurice stated,

> There is a lesson in this which it is important for us Englishmen to mark and learn. It is commonly said that in these days, when the armies of the Continent number their conscript soldiers by the million, that any idea of intervention in a European campaign by our little Army is ridiculous. To admit this is at once to diminish the influence of England among the nations of the Continent. Fortunately the idea is far from ridiculous. In our unrivalled Fleet and Mercantile Marine we possess the power to transfer our land forces to almost any point washed by the sea. We have therefore in our hands the power of creating Plevnas of our own, and of exercising a decisive influence upon the fortunes of a campaign. It will not be disputed that it would, even with our present military organization, be possible for us to transport to and maintain upon the Continent an Army of 40,000 men. At Plevna we have seen such an Army neutralizing a force nearly three times its number, and the chief lesson of Plevna for us appears to me to be that, given that we possess the command of the sea, the power that the British Army can wield beyond the seas cannot be measured in terms of the number of men on its rolls.[78]

Thus, Maurice, in pointing to the study of this war because of its potential lessons for British strategy and planning, presaged the role of the British Expeditionary Force in 1914 and in Gallipoli in 1915. The Russo-Turkish War of 1877–1878 also highlighted some of the difficulties modern armies were to face in the First World War. The tactical offensive had become increasingly difficult to carry out successfully, particularly against troops in field fortifications armed with modern breechloaders and machine guns. Upon meeting an entrenched enemy, armies had to make preparations, and supplies and heavy guns had to be moved up if any potential assault were to have a chance of success. The start of the move from aboveground to belowground fortifications also signified a change to a more static form of warfare dominated by difficult large-scale set-piece assaults.

However, it was often overlooked that tactical offensives could be successful, as was demonstrated at Lovtcha, Gorni-Dubnik, and Kars and by General Skobeleff during the third battle of Plevna. Combine the effectiveness of properly prepared and led tactical offensives with the strategic success of the Russian Army, which was on the offensive both tactically and strategically, and the most important lesson of the war was clear: attacks could and did succeed despite the apparent evidence to the contrary and the changes in warfare of the time. Advancing technology, improved defensive tactics, and the increased use of field fortification made the attack more difficult, but an offensive operation could—and did—lead to victory. Lt. Francis Greene addressed this point: "The more the latter is studied [the battle of Aladja Dagh and the storming of Kars], and the stubbornness of the defense is considered, the more certain it appears that those who lay down as a proved principle of modern tactical warfare that fortifications defended by breech-loaders can not be carried in open assault, have made a hasty judgement."[79] This victory was achieved despite the formidable nature of the fortifications at Kars that French military attaché Gen. Philippe Roussel de Courcy described as a "fortified camp . . . a citadel with 12 detached forts."[80] These fortifications were successfully assaulted at night, because the Russian commander on the spot had deemed a daytime attack too risky. It was not the first night assault of the war. Suleyman Pasha had attempted a night attack, 16–17 September, to avoid the same problem—that is, attacking an entrenched enemy equipped with modern firearms in daylight.[81] This offensive demonstrated that the power of the defense might well have increased, but it could still be countered with planning, innovation, and motivated troops. Lieutenant Greene's observation was again demonstrated to the wider world in the Russo-Japanese War of 1904–1905, when attacks on an entrenched enemy could and did succeed.

3

The Second Anglo-Boer War

The Second Anglo-Boer War of 1899–1902 was an important war because it was the first major conflict, since the American Revolution, fought by a European colonial power against white settlers.[1] Its significance for warfare was that it was the first time that modern small-bore magazine rifles were used on a large scale. The Boers, in particular, were to demonstrate how devastating modern rifles were, even when placed in the hands of nonprofessional soldiers. The war showed that large numbers of militia and volunteers could do an awful lot of damage with modern weaponry. This lesson was worth noting owing to the sheer number of nonprofessionals who would later serve in the Great War. As the South African war dragged on and became more attritional in nature,[2] the importance of having highly trained professional soldiers diminished, offering yet another important lesson for the Great War. The Boer War also witnessed the large-scale use of field fortification, both in the form of modern-style trenches and in the use of fortified lines, hundreds of miles of which were constructed across southern Africa. In addition, many officers on both sides who saw service in South Africa went on to senior command in the Great War. Ian Hamilton led the ill-fated expedition to the Dardanelles (he also served as an attaché to the Russo-Japanese War of 1904–1905); John French led the British Expeditionary Force to France in 1914; Jan Christiaan Smuts and Louis Botha led troops in Africa and somewhat ironically fought on the British side in the First World War; Henry Rawlinson went on to command an army, as did Edmund Allenby and Herbert Plumer;

and Douglas Haig went on to become a field marshal. This list is not exhaustive but does show how the war influenced a generation of important officers.

Fighting began in a fashion that would have been familiar to students of warfare in the nineteenth century, with the British often moving troops in close order onto the field of battle. Once the British had defeated the Boers' main army, the war transitioned into a guerrilla conflict. The firepower available to both sides meant that bodies of troops in close order could not operate on the battlefield. The large and dense target they presented to the enemy resulted in such heavy casualties that units effectively often ceased to function, as with Maj. Gen. Fitzroy Hart's Fifth Irish Brigade at the battle of Colenso on 15 December 1899. This experience demonstrated the need for the increased use of open order, even when operating at a significant distance from the enemy and with the consequent difficulties of command this formation entailed.[3] As the war transitioned into a counterguerrilla fight for the British, small numbers of men were often left very much alone for long periods in small fortified posts.

As with the Russo-Turkish War (discussed in chapter 2), the military attachés saw a fair amount, though certainly not all, of the fighting. Both sides restricted the attachés' movements in the theater of war, and though their access was quite good, it was neither perfect nor equitable. For example, Capt. Stephen L'Hommedieu Slocum, an American military attaché with the British, noted that at Waterval Drift only two of them arrived in time to see anything of consequence.[4] Again, on 7 March 1900, the Boers captured both a Russian and a Dutch attaché who were away from the main group of attachés. At Sanna's Post, Dutch Indian Army attaché Lt. M. J. Nix was severely wounded while watching the fighting.[5] Meanwhile, his compatriot, the Dutch attaché Captain Ram, probably saw little of anything, as he suffered from a bout of typhoid in Pretoria. Thus, each attaché's experience was quite different. Further, on the British side of the war the attachés were limited to observing "the main course of operations along the main line of communication."[6] The British clearly opened the mail of at least one of the attachés.[7] This intrusion can have done little to build trust between them and their British hosts, and it leads the author to conclude that the attachés might have adjusted their reports in response. In comparison, reporting from the Boers' side of the war seems to have been less difficult, although Capt. Carl Reichmann, an American military attaché with the Boers, noted, "Much of the time [March 1900] the attachés could not find out what was going on or where any particular command was or what commands were in the field; the consequence was that we did not see much of the operations."[8] These comments seem to apply only to the period mentioned, as the rest of his report indicates his access to the war was quite good. Thus, short of providing all the various attachés' reports, the picture from the reports contained herein is consequently more of a snapshot when compared with the other cases examined in this book. While the attachés' reports are still helpful, some personal accounts of the war and those from British Maj. Gen. Sir Frederick Maurice's *History of the War in South Africa, 1899–1902* (which was the British official history of the war) have been included in order to provide a more complete picture of the conflict.

In addition to the attachés, a large number of journalists and amateur reporters covered the war. Frederic Unger, himself a journalist writing for the *Daily Express* (London), wrote that "there were possibly, altogether, two hundred newspaper men in South Africa, many of whom had gone there at their own expense, armed only with the necessary credentials. A number of officers acted as correspondents, while a few enlisted men were also doing work for home papers."[9] Therefore, multiple sources of information were available for the reader at home, and a great deal of information easily flowed back to Britain.

Terrain and Soil in South Africa

The enormous size of southern Africa, along with the lack of widespread road and rail infrastructure, had a significant bearing on the war. The geographical area itself is more than 425,000 square miles,[10] though, admittedly, not all of it saw fighting. The main lines of operations of the British forces largely followed the rail lines, owing to the difficulties involved in moving large bodies of troops away from efficient logistical support. The sheer scale of the operational area makes it difficult to characterize the typical physical geography of the war, in the same way as the northern plain of Bulgaria or parts of Manchuria have been elsewhere in this book. However, a broad description of the country is useful in understanding how the conflict evolved (see map 3.1).

Roughly parallel to the eastern coast runs a series of high mountains culminating in the Drakensberg range, which ends about fifty miles to the southwest of Ladysmith. These mountains largely separate the interior from the coastal regions, where most British settlement occurred. The Boer republics themselves, the Orange Free State and the Transvaal, were to the north and east of this series of mountains.

The territory of both Boer republics largely was semiarid veld. Despite heavy rains in the spring and summer months, the dry ground does not easily absorb the moisture, which runs off very quickly, swelling streams and rivers with fast-flowing water. The veld was interspersed with occasional hills, or kopjes, breaking the ground and providing excellent opportunities for long-range vision.

The southern part of the Orange Free State and the area on both sides of its border with Cape Colony was almost all karoo. This semidesert was very dry for much of the year, and, lacking water, most of the Boer farms in this area raised sheep rather than crops or cattle. The relatively arid nature of so much of the campaigning area had negative consequences for the British in particular, as they had to move everything needed to sustain their forces, including water.[11]

The War

British governmental policy toward the Boer republics over the period leading up to the war had effectively forced the Boers into a corner. War broke out on 11 October 1899 with the expiration of the Boer ultimatum to the British government calling on Britain to withdraw all of its troops from the border of the Transvaal. The war can reasonably be divided into four phases, starting with the

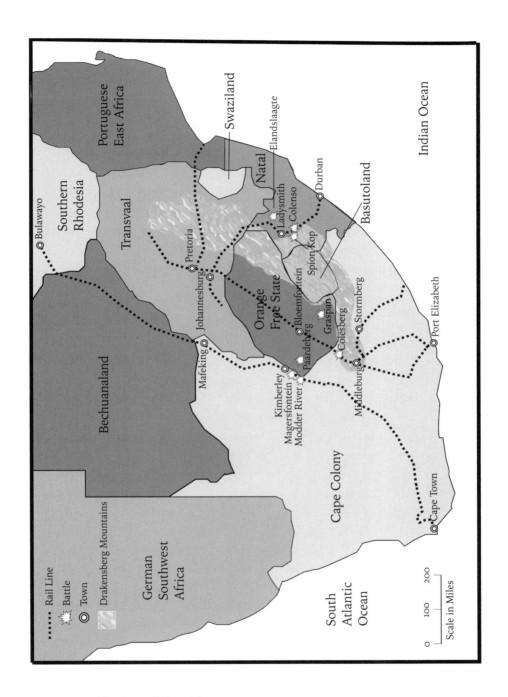

MAP 3.1. The Second Boer War.

Boer offensive. A failed British offensive followed. A second one was more successful: the British defeated the main Boer armies in the spring of 1900, then the war transformed into a prolonged guerrilla conflict during its final phase, which lasted until the spring of 1902. Boer forces crossed the frontier into Natal and Cape Colony,[12] and they quickly laid siege to Mafeking, Kimberley, and Ladysmith. Though the British gained tactical victories at the battles of Talana Hill on 20 October and Elandslaagte on 21 October 1899, they surrendered the initiative to the Boers, who consolidated their hold on the territory they had seized. However, the three sieges tied up a large number of the Boers in static operations, which restricted the ability of Boer forces to carry the war to the British.[13] Thus, the Boers were unable effectively to prosecute the war and, in turn, surrendered the initiative back to the British.

At the outbreak of war, the British, who expected conflict, had already begun reinforcing their South African colony, and they were soon in a position to launch a counteroffensive to the Boer offensive. Gen. Redvers Buller arrived in South Africa on 31 October and took command of British forces there. He had three main options open to him. The most obvious line of operation was to advance through the Orange Free State north along the rail line and through Bloemfontein, then into the Transvaal through Johannesburg, and into Pretoria, thereby capturing the three most important cities in the Boer territories. A second option was to advance up the western railway through Kimberley and on to Mafeking. The third was to advance along the railway from Durban to Ladysmith, which was the most easily reachable of the three besieged towns.[14] Buller chose to focus on the campaign in Natal and made the main effort there. With the bulk of Boer forces also there, it provided Buller the opportunity to deal with them decisively. In addition, operations in Natal also had the benefit of a relatively short line of communication with the coast. Lt. Gen. Paul Methuen was placed in command of the forces marching to relieve Kimberley, and Lt. Gen. Sir William Gatacre was tasked with repelling the Boers from Middleburg and Stormberg in Cape Colony. Given the large distances involved, with several hundred kilometers at least between General Buller and his subordinates, he had no real possibility of maintaining detailed coordination between the three operations.

General Methuen was the first seriously to engage the Boers, launching an attack on Belmont Kopje on 23 November. In this small and quite bloody affair, British infantry fought gallantly in pushing forward against a stubborn but sensible foe. The burghers (a common name often used to describe individual Boers) defending the kopje withdrew as soon as their position looked untenable, with losses of around a third of those of Methuen's force. He followed up this success at Graspan two days later, where the burghers were well dug in and achieved similar results. This pattern was oft to be repeated throughout the conflict: stubborn Boer defense turned to withdrawal as soon as the British could effectively threaten a flank or push home an assault with sufficient vigor. By withdrawing, the burghers managed to avoid being pinned down and destroyed by superior British numbers.[15] Methuen continued to push his troops forward, toward Kimberley, until he again engaged the Boers at Modder River on 28 November.

The battle at Modder River saw Boer Gen. Koos de la Rey skillfully deploy his men along the banks of the river itself. They were dug in, well hidden by scrub vegetation, and the nature of the ground meant they had some natural protection from artillery fire. They also had a good field of fire across which the British had to advance. Effectively engaging the Boers proved difficult. Maurice's official history repeatedly mentions the British troops' problems in properly identifying Boer positions because of their effective concealment; thus, simply suppressing the burghers' defensive fire was punishing.[16] Though Methuen's attack ultimately succeeded, again the casualty rate was rather pyrrhic: the Boers lost, roughly, 75 men against British losses of nearly 500. The British troops were not very well handled and suffered a lack of effective communication, while the Boers put up a skillful and brave defense before withdrawing.[17] This battle proved to be the last British victory in the west before "Black Week," when the British suffered a series of defeats between 10 and 15 December 1899.[18]

The British push under Gatacre (who pursued the first option), via the Boer-occupied towns of Stormberg and Colesberg, came to a halt during Black Week at the battle of Stormberg on 10 December. In this first of three disasters for the British, many of the same command problems that dogged the British at the battle of the Modder River were again evident.[19] Ultimately they led to the loss of almost an entire battalion of British troops. On the other side, Boer losses in this engagement were negligible. Similar problems also occurred on the other main axes of advance.

At the battle of Magersfontein on 11 December, more command failings contributed to a rather bloody setback for the British forces under General Methuen. After a nasty fight close under the Boer guns, Methuen withdrew his troops from contact largely because many of them already were retiring, and unusually, the Boers had stood their ground. The loss of almost 1,000 British casualties was for naught. Boer losses were roughly 250, and the ratio between the two sides is telling. This result, essentially, was repeated at Colenso on 15 December.

General Buller proved little better than Methuen or Gatacre. Buller's plan and control of the battle could have been more inept, but it is difficult to see how.[20] Despite immense displays of bravery on the part of the ordinary officers and men, the entire attack was a failure. In this third battle of a disastrous few days, the British forces experienced around 1,100 casualties to the Boers' 40. This result was a telling indictment of the British command, as well as of the difficulties that the relatively new combination of small-bore magazine rifles, trenches, and smokeless powder posed. General Buller estimated his army had faced 20,000 Boers who "had the advantage both in arms and in position."[21] In actuality, there were probably no more than 4,500 Boers, including 800 who were relatively isolated on the south side of the Tugela River.[22] This estimation of Buller's displays a George McClellan–style grasp of mathematics and rather sums up Buller's command of the battle. Unfortunately, this defeat also seems to have contributed to a temporary collapse of his moral courage.[23] A change in command was imminent.

The British government placed Field Marshal Lord Frederick Roberts in overall command on 16 December 1899.[24] In effect this change meant a lull in fighting on the British side, as he did not arrive in Cape Town until 10 January 1900. Further, given the sheer size of the area over which the war was being fought, exerting his full control once he arrived was not easy, and Buller retained command of those British forces trying to relieve Ladysmith. In the interim some intermittent and indecisive fighting continued, particularly in the area around Colesberg.

The Boers did not take the opportunity to launch a new offensive. They seemed transfixed upon the three besieged towns and left the British to resume their offensive as soon as Lord Roberts was ready. Roberts prioritized the relief of Kimberley. Buller however wanted to relieve Ladysmith now that he had received some reinforcements. Largely owing to poor roads and wet weather, his forces struck west at a snail's pace, which allowed the Boers time to counter his moves. Poor British reconnaissance contributed to the bloody failure of the next attempt to cross the River Tugela near Spion Kop on 24 January. Again, British casualties were disproportionately much heavier than those of the Boers, and this battle has become a prominent symbol of the conflict.[25] Despite his haste, Buller did not relieve Ladysmith until 28 February, after it had withstood more than four months of siege. Meanwhile, Roberts set out to relieve Kimberley on 11 February and had done so by the fifteenth. He concentrated an overwhelming force against the Boers and then used maneuver to winkle them out of their prepared potions. By 27 February, the British had also rounded up Boer Gen. Piet Cronjé at Paardeberg Drift, along with 4,500 of his men, and the war looked as though it was entering its final phase. The British captured Bloemfontein, capital of the Orange Free State, on 13 March and relieved Mafeking on 17 May, and Roberts captured the capital of the Transvaal, Pretoria, on 5 June. Despite the loss of their main cities and towns and the defeat of their field army, however, the Boers refused to surrender.

Instead, the Boers turned to guerrilla warfare. Southern Africa was well suited to this style of conflict given the British forces' lack of effective communications and the vast area over which they sought to exercise control. The British Army failed to deal with this change in Boer tactics, and the war dragged on for almost another two full years before the two sides signed a peace treaty at Vereeniging on 31 May 1902. It took the deployment of tens of thousands of extra troops, many operating as mounted infantry, as well as the construction of as many as 8,000 blockhouses,[26] along with thousands of miles of barbed-wire fences to obstruct the Boers, restrict their mobility, and pin them down for destruction (see map 3.2). Victory largely came through the attrition of the Boer forces' will to fight and the removal of its guerrilla support network following the roundup of the burghers' wives and children into concentration camps. This last point hints at new uses for temporary fortification—that of concentration and prisoner of war camps—in the years after 1902.

Fortifications: Preventing Desertion

In the literature of the war, desertion is mentioned quite a number of times; however, many comments are rather vague as to the reason for the desertion, the method, or the time. On the Boer side, this problem probably occurred because the Boer Army consisted of large numbers of militiamen who frequently seemed to come and go as they pleased. It was very difficult to discipline them effectively, and ascertaining an accurate count of unit numbers seems to have been the exception.[27] In those circumstances, determining if someone had popped home to check on a wife or a farm or even to switch sides would have been almost impossible. On the British side, desertion does not seem to have been a large-scale problem. In the great empty spaces that the troops frequently moved through, it is hard to imagine where the average British soldier considering desertion would go, particularly given the number of wild animals, the hostile locals, and the scarcity of water he would encounter. Further, large numbers of British troops were housed in thousands of small isolated garrisons, and making the choice to leave the relative security of a sheltered and fortified post for the open veld would not have been easy. Ultimately, this topic is difficult to pin down, and admittedly not much direct evidence ties the use of field fortification to the prevention of desertion. Thus, getting an accurate read on it is somewhat problematic. However, not all is lost.

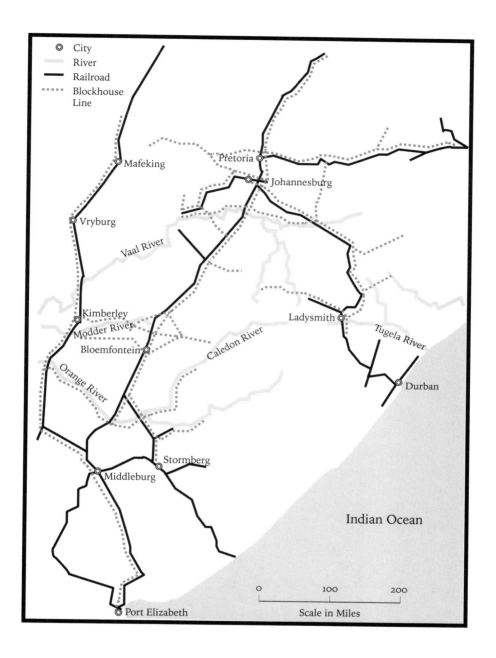

MAP 3.2. Blockhouse lines.

In the literature of the war, some commented about desertion, and their accounts are often similar in nature to those of the Boer Gen. Christiaan de Wet. He mentions deserters but, in his case, only in the context of Boers who deserted to aid the English.[28] Captain Reichmann, an American attaché with Boer forces, made a vague comment regarding Boer ranks "being thinned nightly by burghers who went home."[29] Though the Boers were retreating from Middleburg at the time of his comment, he does not make it clear if that proximity was the sole reason for the men's desertion. Most others' comments are similarly vague. However, given the great mobility of the war and the immense area over which it was fought, particularly in relation to the size of the forces involved, it was probably quite easy for a burgher to desert. In this sense, the Boer War resembled the final phases of the Russo-Japanese War of 1904–1905 and the early phases of the Balkan Wars of 1912–1913, where troops deserted more often when on the move than they did when in a static position. Thus, considering the nature of the war and the plentiful opportunities available, one might expect to see desertion being a major problem for both sides. It was not, presumably for the previously stated reasons.[30]

Providing Physical Protection

What was true in 1877 was still so in 1899. Protection on the battlefield was essential. Perhaps the biggest change between the Russo-Turkish War and the Boer War was the distance at which engagements took place. Whereas the infantry firefight during the former might have started at 600–800 yards, with really effective firing at about two-thirds of that distance, modern small arms meant that troops in the open during the Boer War could effectively be engaged at more than 2,000 yards. If artillery was available, shelling of enemy positions was often begun at 6,000–7,000 yards, or almost double the ranges possible in 1877–1878.[31] This expansion of the battle space coincided with an increase in the lethality of munitions. Thus, the area in which field fortification was necessary had massively expanded. Likewise, the area that small numbers of men could affect had also increased, significantly boosting the power of the defense.

Not only the ranges but also the velocity of the bullets fired had increased. For example, a Martini-Henry rifle, of the type that the Turks used in 1877–1878, had a muzzle velocity of around 1,200 feet per second and an effective range of 400 yards (it could kill a man at distances out to 1,000 yards, but it was not particularly accurate at that distance). By 1899, a modern 1895 model Mauser rifle, of the type used by the Boers, had a muzzle velocity of roughly 2,500 feet per second.[32] This capability increased the rifle's firing distance to more than 2,000 yards and enhanced its lethality and accuracy. Very accurate fire could be achieved at long ranges, particularly by experienced shooters. In addition, as this author can testify, without a cloud of black smoke,[33] the shooter did not have to reacquire his target after each shot, making for faster and more accurate firing. Furthermore, as each individual cartridge was lighter and smaller, men could easily carry greater numbers of them. These factors combined with the increased power of artillery forced the men to ensure that more earth (or some substitute) was between them and enemy fire if they were to survive. However, when properly dug in, troops were usually physically safe.

The nature of the ground in South Africa, where much of the soil on the hills was stony, often meant that the men had to construct aboveground positions. Christiaan de Wet had his men build *schanzes*, using boulders, for his two pieces of artillery to protect against expected heavy enemy fire.[34] Both guns survived the action. Deneys Reitz, a Boer, described the effects of British high-angle fire on his well-protected commando: "The casualties were few, owing to the height of the bank, and not one of the Pretoria men was hit."[35] During the fighting on the Tugela River, he again described the artillery fire's lack of effect on his unit:

> Our trench was shelled at intervals by a sixty pound naval gun [presumably a 4.7-inch cannon] standing at Chievely [just south of the line of the Tugela River], seven miles away, but, although some of the huge projectiles fell within a few feet of us, we suffered no damage. . . . I had read of its effect on the Dervishes at Omdurman, and the English newspapers

had predicted equally terrible results for us, but the men made light of it and dubbed the shells "little niggers" (klein Kafferkeis).[36]

The comparison with the fate of the Dervishes is interesting. It tells us that at least some Boers were far from the illiterate rustics that some elements of the British press portrayed them as being. It also provides a clear difference between the two wars. The Boers shot back and dug in, thus reducing the effectiveness of British fire. The Dervishes did not, and they were massacred. Of course, other factors were at play, but the essential truth stands: cover protects. The Austrian attaché Capt. Robert Trimmel noted in his final report on the war that despite the British deploying a hundred artillery pieces to conduct a nine-day bombardment of "excellently dug-in Boers" at Paardeberg, only around 150 Boers were wounded with a similar number killed.[37]

Of course, not everyone dug in, at least not at first. Henry Mackern, an American journalist, noted the absence of the use of cover:

From the way in which the British gunners work their guns, without any cover whatsoever and stand to them, you would imagine that they were merely on parade or firing salutes, until the grim truth is vividly impressed on the onlooker by seeing here and there a man drop, his place quickly to be filled by another.[38]

It is perhaps not surprising that the men changed this system relatively quickly and particularly after the battle of Colenso. The British there lost a number of guns to the Boers after most of their crews had been hit by rifle bullets rather than by counterbattery fire.

The men did not rely solely on trenches for cover. During the war, they made much use of semipermanent and permanent fortifications. As previously mentioned, the British constructed roughly 8,000 blockhouses to protect lines of communications. The cover they provided was very effective, particularly as the enemy had little or no artillery available once the major fighting ended in the summer of 1900. Lt. Alexander Kearsey, an officer in the York and Lancaster Regiment, described the effectiveness of both blockhouses and trenches:

> We were then holding Cork Post, and nearly all the men were in the blockhouses; but we soon turned out and manned the trenches until four in the morning. It was a horrible night with rain, sleet, and darkness. We could see nothing of the Boers save the flashes of their rifles, as they contented themselves with firing at us from a distance. We husbanded our ammunition during the night, expecting the enemy to come on at us at daybreak; but instead of that they retired just before dawn to the Witkopjes. The firing from the trenches round the hill was kept up all night: one blockhouse fired as many as 2,000, another 450 rounds [a typical blockhouse garrison was seven to eight men]. Luckily we had no casualties, though some of the blockhouses were very much peppered, and one of the Boers' bullets went through a loophole, striking a rifle that a man was in the act of firing off.[39]

These blockhouses were bulletproof, but they would not have withstood artillery fire. General de Wet described a successful Boer attack on an English blockhouse near Sanna's Post, where he had a piece of artillery available. This weapon proved crucial as the garrison promptly abandoned the place upon sighting the Boer cannon.[40] Thus, blockhouses were very much a product of their situation—that is, they were effective when used away from major combat and away from well-armed enemies.

Ultimately, perhaps the best evidence of the difference field fortification makes comes from the previously mentioned disparity in casualties between the British attacking forces, particularly early in the war, and those of the defending and well-protected Boers. This imbalance in casualties matches up well with the effects of fortification on the fighting power of the men.

Enhancing Fighting Power

The physical protection that fortification provided again was demonstrated in the Boer Wars. The Boers in particular were noted for their fondness of digging in. That they were familiar with the use of effective cover to enhance their numbers should come as no surprise. In their frequent wars against African tribes, the Boers frequently used temporary cover to make up for a lack of numbers.[41] If cover was not available, and the odds against them were too great, the Boers often avoided a fight and melted away. That they continued to do so when fighting the British was simply good sense. Frederick Howland, an American correspondent writing for the British newspaper *Daily Mail*, noted, "The Boer fights determinedly only when in greatly superior force, when seeking to extricate himself from a desperate situation, or when snugly entrenched behind well-nigh perfect cover, which he knows so well how to find."[42] Of course, Howland was writing for a paper in which "outraged in Kent" letters to the editor still feature so prominently, and his style fit with the appeal of the paper. Despite the tinge of sarcasm and hints at unfairness, however, he does have a point. Boers often did not put up much of a fight when caught in the open. Why would they? The British often greatly outnumbered and outgunned them. Standing up to fight in the open would likely have meant committing collective suicide.

Fighting from fortifications fit well the Boer style of warfare. Moreover, it allowed small numbers of them to have a disproportionately large effect. General de Wet described the result of such an encounter in his book *Three Years' War*, where the English captured Veldkornet (Field Cornet) Speller and his fourteen men only after a bloody fight to force them out of their entrenchments. The English suffered "a good many dead and wounded" doing so.[43] Elsewhere, Captain Reichmann noted that seventy-three Boer policemen entrenched at Bergendal farm, on the edge of a plateau, held out against two British infantry regiments for more than four hours. The Boers' entrenchments were half-section slit trenches.[44] They must have been very difficult for the British to spot, particularly given the broken nature of the ground, thus providing the defenders both cover and some concealment. In addition, given the small size of the Boer trenches, with few men in a single space, any artillery hits would have had only a limited effect.

It was not only the Boers who utilized cover to this end. The British also constructed blockhouses to guard their lines of communication and to restrict the burghers' movements. These blockhouses simply needed a small garrison to make them relatively secure. For example, Kearsey noted that a typical garrison consisted of solely "one non-commissioned officer and six men were left to guard each blockhouse."[45] Without effective fortification, securing the lines of communication would have been impossible to do without vastly increasing the number of British and empire troops in the country. This situation was particularly true given the enormous length of the lines in South Africa, where hundreds of miles of rail lines effectively had to be protected. British Lt. Col. R. M. Holden argued that "by relieving as many men as possible from the important duty of guarding the railways, he [General Kitchener] increases the number of men available for mobile columns in the field."[46] It was ultimately a combination of the blockhouse system and the use of mobile columns that wore down the Boer forces. Without secure lines of communication, the British would have found it vastly more difficult to chase the Boers down, and without using fortification, a much greater number of men would have been required to secure British communications. Likewise, the British use of fortification meant that the Boers could engage the blockhouses only when they possessed either greatly superior numbers or artillery.

General de Wet described how he was put off attacking the small, fortified, British position at Badenhorst after his initial probes were thrown back and obviously would have taken heavy casualties if they continued. Despite inflicting many casualties among the English garrison, the sixteen-day siege was unsuccessful, and de Wet eventually withdrew.[47] On another occasion, de Wet describes a small British force holding out against him: "He [de Wet's dispatch rider] came back with the customary refusal, and reported that although the enemy's force was not very large, still the positions held were so strong that I could not hope to be able to capture them before the English behind me arrived."[48] In that instance, it is important to note that time pressure forced his decision. Further, his comment clearly stated that this garrison's behavior was the norm. If even small garrisons routinely refused to surrender, as he suggests, then at the very least they plainly felt confident enough in their positions to put up a fight, even against quite long odds. Thus, well-constructed fortifications not only allowed small groups of men to hold off larger ones but also facilitated the work of the mobile columns, which could use the blockhouse lines as an anvil to their hammer.

Reinforcing Key Tactical Points

The enhancement of fighting power facilitated the use of fortification at key tactical points largely because it allows small numbers of men more effectively to hold ground against larger numbers of the enemy. This fortification might take the form of a tactical point on a battlefield, much like a redoubt at a key location, or it could be a point that controls access through an important piece of terrain. For example, in the *War Record of the York and Lancaster Regiment*, Lieutenant Kearsey described trying to block the movement of a larger Boer force through a key piece of hilly terrain. His account is worth quoting at length:

> Towards the middle of October [1901] Louis Botha went south with his army, and General Walter Kitchener with a big force followed him up, while all the available troops blocked the points at which Botha could get north again. As many men as could be spared from Volksrust, Wakkerstrom and Ingogo held the neks [mountain passes] round about, and at the same time parties of our men held Barsfield, Molls Nek, De Jagers Nek, and Wakkerstrom Nek. . . . We had plenty of alarms, and on Wednesday, October 16th, I and thirty of our men were sent out to Wakkerstrom Nek with orders to stop Louis Botha and his commando getting through. We started that day, each man with one waterproof sheet and one blanket only. After a very hot march of thirteen miles we reached the nek just as it was getting dark, and then had to make dispositions to hold the place. The country on both sides of the nek is tremendous, full of positions commanding each other, and to which the enemy might have come and sniped in order to attract our attention,

while their main body went through the nek. As there were many empty farms in the neighbourhood where they could shelter during the night, it was thought probable they would attempt to get through the nek at daybreak. We had posts on the most exposed places on the high hills north-east and north-west of the nek, and just as we were standing to arms early on Thursday morning, we heard firing on the hill north-west of the nek, at a post held by the 8th Hussars. A party of twenty Boers had crept up the hill trying to get round the post, who, however, returned the enemy's fire and prevented their advance, though they wounded the sentry. Had the Boers succeeded in taking the hill, they would have commanded the nek; we should then have great difficulty in ousting them, as it was a very stiff climb from our side, and we should have been under their fire all the way up. The rest of the day was spent in sangar-making and fortifying our position as best we could. We built little round forts for each of the isolated outposts, and a bigger sangar for the main reserve party. . . . [Despite the efforts of the pursuing column, Botha's force escaped to the north.] Failures of this sort frequently occurred, and as the columns alone proved insufficient to prevent them, so the blockhouse system was begun in real earnest.[49]

His last point is an important one: the combination of the use fortification with other methods is what makes it so effective. Digging in for the sake of doing so serves no real purpose other than to tire out the troops. Kearsey also highlights the importance of using fortification as a base for the reserves, and that aspect is discussed in more detail later.

On the use of fortification on key ground, American attaché Captain L'Hommedieu Slocum also noted that the kopjes formed "excellent defensive positions,"[50] and they often allowed a few well-entrenched men to cover a large area of front given the relative lack of cover and the long range of infantry small arms. A Lee-Metford or Mauser rifle could kill out to 2,000-plus yards; thus, a few men on a kopje could dominate a large area of ground. As his compatriot

Captain Reichmann noted, this scenario is exactly what happened at Poplar Grove on 7 March 1900, when a small force of forty Boers on a rocky hilltop held up an entire British maneuver column.[51] Captain Slocum observed: "Were it not for the railroads their [the British] force would be almost immobile. The Boers knowing this, pick out their position on the railroad, fortify it, and wait for the attack."[52] To a certain extent, this pattern of operations was later mimicked, consciously or not, during the Russo-Japanese War and Balkan Wars. The sheer volume of matériel required by a modern industrial army effectively precluded large-scale operations away from rail lines until the widespread availability of motorized transport and decent roads.

Well-sited fortifications were also important to the success of the blockhouse lines. The Boers were able to exploit a weakness in the positioning of a blockhouse and continue their mobile operations. To counter this problem the British built extra blockhouses as they identified gaps in the lines, much as the works at Plevna were enhanced based on the experience stemming from each of the battles there (see chapter 2). On this issue Kearsey wrote that an additional "two more blockhouses built near Klip River Post were a help in guarding against these attacks [Boer attempts to cross the blockhouse line], and strengthened our open and exposed position."[53] The supplemental fortification of key locations secured the line; thus, the location of these positions was crucial to their success.

Even if fortified positions were well sited and constructed, it did not guarantee that they could completely stop an enemy. The Boer Gen. Jan Smuts, in his report to President Paul Kruger of Transvaal, commented, "Toward the end of November, van Deventer and Kersten, in conjunction, attacked the forts of Toutelbosch-kolk [sic], north of Calvinia, and although they could not capture the forts, they took 400 horses from the enemy."[54] Thus, although the forts survived the encounter and resisted the enemy's attempt to capture them, they did not prevent him from gaining some tactical advantage. Smuts's report then makes clear that although mobile operations were often successful even against superior forces, operations against fortified posts were much less so. It was this protection, albeit imperfect, that made them effective as a base of operations.

Providing a Secure Base

The enhancement of fighting power facilitated the use of fortification as a secure base. In addition, a fortified point allowed forces to store war matériel securely. This point was particularly important in the war given the long and vulnerable British supply lines. One of the main problems that the British faced was protecting the railways from Boer attack. Given the long distances involved and the lack of sufficient numbers of mobile troops, a ready solution to the problem was the use of the lines of blockhouses. They provided much greater security for the long lines of operations. Their use also freed up more men to serve in mobile counter-Boer columns, which had more freedom to hunt down recalcitrant Boers.

The effectiveness of the blockhouses along the rail lines can be gauged by examining the number of Boer attacks on them. From 6 June 1900 to 31 December 1900, Boer attacks caused 145 interruptions of the railway, and from 1 January 1901 to 4 July 1901, there were 110, resulting in a reduction from an average of 7 interruptions to 6 every ten days. Admittedly, this difference does not appear significant, but by July 1901, the rate was down to about three attacks in ten days, a very large reduction.[55] In addition, the Imperial Military Railways became so effective at making repairs that Boer sabotage often took longer to carry out than the time needed to fix the damaged rails. By the summer of 1901, the cost to the Boers of attacking and disrupting the railways became so great that it was hardly worth the effort. The combination of blockhouses, efficient repair crews, and mobile columns drastically reduced the effectiveness of attacks on rail lines. However, without the blockhouses it is very unlikely that the British could have effectively curtailed them.

Before the expansion of the blockhouse system, Boer attacks on the rail lines had been both common and destructive. Writing during the war, Lieutenant Colonel Holden described the scale of the problem:

> The Royal Engineers have repaired no fewer than 25 bridges with a span of between 100 and 500 feet, 20 bridges with a span of 60 feet, and 180 culverts with a span of 6 feet to 20

feet, all of which had been destroyed by Boers. They have laid as much as ten miles of new lines round the bridges which had been destroyed. But the Boers have not only destroyed the bridges and pulled up the line; they have blown up forty-five of our rather shaky locomotives. The blockhouses aided by armoured trains, have caused an almost complete cessation of these destructive methods which were so frequent in the early and middle periods of the war.[56]

Combined with the previous evidence, this observation indicates the effectiveness of fortification in securing the lines of operations. However, if these posts were not well sited or were insufficiently manned, they were vulnerable to enemy action. This risk is highlighted by the Boers' capture of the post at Reddersburg along with 546 men of the Royal Irish Regiment on 4 April 1900.[57] This example demonstrates that the blockhouses and fortified points really needed to be mutually supporting to be fully effective. To achieve this advantage, secure bases of operations were needed within the fortified lines themselves.

Larger fortifications, usually big stone blockhouses, were also used as bases of operation and supply within the lines of blockhouses themselves. Kearsey commented on this arrangement:

> Major Byass, with E company, had already taken up the Botha's Pass main blockhouse, and his company was the first one put into the blockhouses as they were built [this is the blockhouse line being built from Botha's Pass to Vrede]. F Company followed, and both companies had their headquarters at Klip River Post, our next strong station after Botha's Pass. Here a large reserve of tinned food and ammunition was stored, and sixty non-commissioned officers and men were left to guard both the store and the fort. This latter was built with topsods, cut by hand, and it commanded the ford over the Kilp river [sic].[58]

The main blockhouses were used to support the outlying smaller blockhouses, thus also somewhat simplifying the resupply process. The garrison of a main blockhouse was also large enough to allow commanders to send more readily their men out both on patrol and in support of other blockhouses.

This use of blockhouses enabled the blockhouse system to be kept resupplied without stopping trains every several hundred yards, and it allowed blockhouses to be placed on the best available tactical ground. The change in the supply chain was impressed upon the troops in Maj. Gen. W. F. Kelly's British Adjutant-General's Circular Memorandum No. 52 of 3 December 1901, in which he stated, "Posts and Blockhouses between stations are not to depend on the train service for their daily rations and water."[59] This shift forced the men to use local supply stores, which they needed to protect properly from the Boers. It also freed up the trains for longer distance supply duties, which were a far more efficient use of transport. The connected lines of blockhouses that emerged through the process of protecting the supply lines facilitated British domination of the geographical space in which they were operating.

On a broader note, the use of a seemingly secure fortified position could be problematic. De Wet criticized General Cronjé's decision to stand and fight rather than to break out and retreat from the Boer laager at Paardeberg because of his bravery, as well as his unwillingness to leave a well-protected position with all of its supplies.[60] Thus, Cronjé essentially gave up his force to the British after a short siege. His best chance had been to break out when the opportunity had presented itself; however, much as Osman Pasha did at Plevna, Cronjé ended up being captured along with his army. The protection provided by the fortifications proved no match for the enemy's use of maneuver and firepower. Being able to abandon a position was often as important as being willing to hold it.

Dominating an Area

Both sides used fortifications to dominate the country. Early in the war, the Boers had constructed fortifications along rivers that intersected the rail lines on which the British were so dependent, with their positions on the Modder and Tugela rivers being the most famous, to block the British lines of advance into Boer territory. French attaché Col. Jules Charles du Pontavice du Heussey commented that the dominating Boer position covering the Tugela River required the British to spend time to bring up their siege guns, thus delaying their advance to Ladysmith.[61] Ultimately, Colonel du Pontavice noted, General Buller had to turn the position, which involved a long march away from the logistical support of the rail line.[62]

As the war went on, the British, in turn, used fortifications to dominate the South African countryside. In particular, the use of the blockhouse system to protect the lines of supply had the double benefit of facilitating British domination of the country. As the British extended these fortifications across the country, particularly along the rivers and rail lines, the Boers' freedom to move about became increasingly difficult. This constraint both reduced the effectiveness of the Boers' guerrilla campaign and made it easier for the British to corral them.

The division of the country into more manageable parts allowed the British more effectively to track and hunt down the Boers. John Fuller, a British subaltern during the war and later a famous military theorist, explained the use of the blockhouse system in this way:

> The only way to reduce the area strategically was to partition it off into comparatively small sub-areas, and to clear the enemy out of each in turn. This was accomplished by dividing up the theatre of war by wire fence, and by building blockhouses along them, closely spaced so that each fence could be swept by the fire of neighbouring blockhouse garrisons. Once an area was rendered horse-proof, so to speak, the next operation was to sweep it clear of the enemy, and when this was done, to establish another horse-proof area and to clear that in turn.[63]

Essentially, as mentioned previously, the blockhouse lines provided the anvil for a British hammer. Though these lines were well fortified, they were permeable. Boers frequently were able to cross them, albeit with great difficulty.

Some criticized using fortification in this way. De Wet disputed the effectiveness of the blockhouse lines, going as far as to mock them: "It has always seemed to me a most unaccountable circumstance that England—the all-powerful—could not catch the Boers without the aid of these blockhouses. There were so many other ways in which the thing might have been done, and better done . . . this policy of the *blockhouse* might equally well have been called the policy of the *blockhead* [italics in original]."[64] De Wet argued that the British would have been better off using a greater number of mobile columns than they had. He also claimed mobile columns were a far better tool for rounding up recalcitrant Boers, especially when they operated under cover of darkness. This assertion might well have been the case, but the mobile columns described in his example failed to catch him![65] Furthermore, mobile columns required large numbers of trained horsemen, who were in very short supply in the British Army until late in the war. In addition, although perhaps it was not so for the Boers, operating at night in unfamiliar country was always problematic for the British. In de Wet's book, he provided several examples of his commandos breaking through blockhouse lines as evidence that the policy was flawed.[66]

However, he also provided some hints that the policy actually worked. At Rhenosterpoort, de Wet discussed coming into contact with English outposts "almost every day," and he explained he had to choose whether "to break through the English lines as a horse-commando, as it necessitated leaving all these waggons [*sic*] and oxen in the hand of the enemy. But there we were between the cordon and the Vaal River [thinly lined with English outposts]."[67] In the event, he did manage to cross the Vaal River with his waggons, escaping the mobile troops pursuing him, but he had clearly expected to lose them in the process. Furthermore, his men also seem to have had very strong misgivings about the blockhouse lines, which he had to take into account when attempting to cross them.[68] Thus, despite this success, he somewhat contradicts his own claim that they were ineffective. De Wet also mentioned the problem of keeping the enemy's eyes off his troop movements. Any time Boers encountered a line of blockhouses, the British received intelligence as to which side of the line the Boers were operating. Essentially, de Wet then had to avoid blockhouse and outpost lines where necessary to prevent the English knowing where he was.[69] Otherwise, he would have been easier to pursue and capture.

De Wet's argument was challenged not only by his own words but also by those of his compatriots. General Smuts, a senior Boer commander, described fleeing from British columns in a report to President Kruger:

> No less than seven columns of the enemy, each from 500 to 1000 strong were pitted against my small number of men in the northern part of the Free State. The march through the southern part of the Free State was even more difficult. From the western frontier I found a line of forts and garrisons running along the Modder River, the water works and ThabaN-chu, right onto the Basuto frontier. It was not without great difficulty and considerable loss that we arrived at the Roux-ville District at the end of August. Commandant van Deventer broke through the above mentioned line at ThabaNchu and I crossed the Modder River near Abrahamskraal.[70]

Smuts pointed out he then had to deal with crossing the Orange River, which was "defended by an unbroken chain of blockhouses, forts, outposts and columns." Smuts was able to get his men across a few days later but only after several failed attempts.[71]

Kearsey too argued against de Wet, pointing out that "although de Wet has called our blockhouse policy a 'blockhead policy,' the Boers have confessed that they did not like facing these entanglements, since it usually meant having to cut the wires while under fire from a blockhouse on either side. When they had once run the gauntlet of this fire, they hesitated before facing it again in order to re-cross our lines."[72] The lines might well have been passable, but clearly they were an effective tool for restricting Boer movement and for controlling the countryside.

Despite this benefit, it took time to impress on all British troops that the lines served a useful purpose. Army Order No. 3 of 15 August 1901 instructed the men that "the railway fences are about to be restored and must in no case be cut again by the troops. These fences form valuable obstacles to the enemy's movement in conjunction with the blockhouses on the lines."[73] One can only wonder why the purpose of the fences had not been properly communicated to the men when they originally constructed the lines.

Requiring tactical depth in the defense, given both the terrain and the need for protection, the Boers sometimes developed a prepre-pared fallback position, a strategy that fit well with standard Boer tactics. As Count Adalbert Sternberg, an Austrian adventurer who tried to fight with the British before joining the Boers, explained, "Bilse, an untiring cicerone, showed me the whole battlefield of Mag-ersfontein, where so short a time previously war had raged with all its horror. The Boer trenches were in two lines, about 1,650 yards apart, between the hills and the river."[74] Thus, even had the British broken through the first line, they would have had to redeploy their artillery in order to assault the second one. Any infantry still needing to cross the open ground between the lines would have been at the mercy of the Boers until the supporting artillery was deployed. This problem proved to be one of the toughest to crack before the introduction of the tank.

Improving Technical Construction

The technical construction of fortifications during the war dem-onstrated the increased importance of concealment. Preventing discovery was much more important than it had been during the Russo-Turkish War of 1877–1878 largely owing to the improvement of munitions and firearms, particularly the extended range and accuracy of the modern rifle and artillery fire. In addition, the widespread use of smokeless powder meant that physically spotting those troops who were firing was very difficult, especially given the very long ranges at which infantry fights often took place. To that end, both sides used aboveground fortifications only where the soil prohib-ited the construction of proper trenches or where more permanent structures, such as blockhouses, were required.

Both sides extensively used sangars largely because the ground on top of the hills often was rocky; however, their use was risky in an era where concealment was important. What could be seen often could be hit. For example, the British use of stone walls—in all likelihood sangars of some kind—at Koedoesberg on 11 February 1900 was problematic as the Boer artillery found them relatively easy to physically hit.[75] Admittedly, as the war ground on, this lack of concealment became less of a factor for the British as the dearth of Boer artillery meant that a well-constructed position was more important than a hidden one.

John Fuller described the problems of constructing a sangar:

> This with great labour we eventually built, as many of the stones had to be dug out of the ground. In each point of the star [four-pointed], a tent was pitched, and some five tents in the middle. The spaces between the points of the star were filled in with a low wire entanglement, with all our empty jam tins hung up on it. Once this work was finished we felt much safer. Not only could we fire down on the bridge, but we were in direct helio and lamp communication with Heilbron. We were also much closer to the three pickets on the hill, and this gave them confidence. The only disadvantage was that we were further from our water supply; but the tanks we had been provided with were quite sufficient to keep us going for several days should it happen that we were cut off from the river.[76]

Where the use of artillery was no real threat, improvisation was often very helpful. The British quite commonly used surplus supplies to supplement the protection of a position. Perhaps this resourcefulness is not surprising given Fuller's experience using stone; however, using such materials also was problematic as it was predicated on the assumption that the enemy either had no artillery or could not deploy it. After de Wet captured the British positions at Roodewal Station on 7 June 1900, he wrote, "We were all filled with wonder at the splendid entrenchments the English had constructed from bales of cotton, blankets, and post bags. These entrenchments had been so effectual that the enemy's loss was only twenty-seven killed and wounded—a remarkably small number when it is remembered that we took two hundred of them prisoners."[77] These fortifications had been quite effective until de Wet brought into action three cannons. Once they started firing, it was not too long before the garrison surrendered.

Conversely, and despite the extensive use of aboveground fortification during the war, the need for effective concealment was of fundamental importance. With the increased power of modern weaponry, any troops that were spotted could successfully be engaged even at very long ranges. Captain Slocum, observing the battle at Paaderberg, noted that most Boer artillery did not fire "as they had nothing but black powder [almost all of their smokeless artillery rounds had been already used] and were afraid to use it on account of the target it would make."[78] Modern optical instruments facilitated their discovery, and recent developments such as the first prism binoculars provided much more effective tools to aid vision.[79] The improved quality and power of optical instruments such as binoculars made it far easier to see clearly over long distances. Thus, the combination of better optics and artillery meant that troops in the battle area needed to be aware of enemy observation, even if they were not in the front lines. Previously, being observed had mattered little. Though remaining unseen was better, it was not essential. This component of battle was starting to change.

A properly sited and well-camouflaged position was usually invisible to enemy observers; however, human activity could reveal the location even at very long ranges. Count Sternberg commented on his own experience in his book *My Experiences of the Boer War*: "They [the Boers he was with] advised me not to stand on the breastwork—that the English might see me and shoot at us [the British were 7,000–8,000 yards away]. After I had inspected everything, we set out on our return journey. We had hardly ridden a hundred paces when a shell came whistling through the air behind us and burst."[80] His own careless actions, even at a very great range from the enemy, served to bring the position under accurate fire. Thus, not being seen at all was important given the range of modern artillery.

Combining concealment and protection was the ideal. However, the limited amount of artillery and the short duration of major combat meant that this lesson was not fully absorbed. The problems subsequent to this oversight were repeatedly demonstrated during the Russo-Japanese War (see chapter 4). The importance of not easily being seen applied as much, if not more, to troops in the open as it did to troops under cover. Maj. F. A. Molony of the Royal Engineers noted that he was "lucky" the crossing of the Orange River on 15 March 1900 was not opposed "as the night before I had taken the Khaki [sic] cover off my brilliant red and blue puggaree so as to be known."[81] Clearly, only a few months into the war, he already understood the necessity for this camouflage.

The effectiveness of even rudimentary concealment was not lost on Maurice's official history. Of the fighting at Paardeberg, it noted:

> So long as the men lay flat on the ground they were little molested, as a growth of thistles hid them from the enemy's view, but any attempt to move brought upon them a shower of bullets, to which they were unable to reply with any effect, as the Boers, perfectly protected by their trenches or concealed by the vegetation which lined the river bank, suffered little from the shrapnel of the supporting British guns, and could not be seen by the infantry.[82]

During the same series of actions, Captain Slocum reported that the British Fourteenth Brigade got lost in the dark during an attack and was stuck only five hundred yards from the Boer laager. The troops had to lie down all day and wait until dark because of the lack of cover and the heavy Boer fire. Despite taking sixty casualties and achieving nothing, Slocum noted the "immunity from serious loss was due to their almost invisibility in their khaki uniform while lying down on the brown veldt."[83] Slocum also reported on the Canadians, who launched a night attack and were able to use the cover of darkness to get within ninety yards of the Boer positions and lay down fire.[84] On the basis of his experiences, Slocum recommended reversible uniforms, with one side green and the other khaki. He also called for increasing the number of available field glasses and for better reconnaissance.[85]

The difficulty of spotting concealed troops firing smokeless powder weaponry fed into the phenomenon of the empty battlefield.

Lt. David Miller of the Gordon Highlanders, a British junior officer, tried to explain the effect:

> It would be hard for you to describe a battle—there is so little to describe. The infantry soldier sees nothing except the men on either side of him and the ground in front. He hears the crackle of the enemy's fire somewhere—he does not know where—he hears the whit! whit! of the bullets, and every now and then he knows vaguely some one near him is hit—he feels the smell of the powder (cordite) and the hot oily smell of his rifle. He fires at the range given, and at the given direction, and every now and then he hears "Advance!" and he gets up and goes on and wonders why he is not hit as he stands up. That is all. Then the bullets cease to come and the action is over. . . . That is the infantry soldier's battle—very nasty—very tiring—very greasy—very hungry—very thirsty—everything very beastly. No glitter—no excitement—no nothing. Just bullets and dirt.[86]

This last point is important because it must have been very difficult to keep men moving toward an enemy they could not see, particularly if they also could not ascertain what effect they were having on their hidden foe. Thus, a good show of artillery fire, even if ineffective, was helpful to get the men to move forward. Count Sternberg described the battlefield of Magersfontein: "On December 9 the British began shelling the hills [overlooking the Modder River] with a murderous artillery fire. Not a stone, not a bush was left unscathed; all were smashed to pieces, but not a single Boer was killed. They were lying down in front of and near the hills, exactly where the English had been told they were not."[87] Despite the British not being able to see the Boer positions clearly, it is easy to understand their need for the artillery fire: it provided some encouragement for the attacking infantry and, given the difficulties of spotting well-concealed troops, was a sensible course of action.

The threat posed by a few well-concealed troops meant forces now had an increased need to reconnoiter by fire. Captain Trimmel observed that where machine guns had the advantage of a secure defensive situation and were not visible, the whole area had to be kept under fire.[88] It also meant that in the right circumstances, a few troops could have a great effect on the enemy without serious risk to themselves. Slocum observed such a problem southwest of Pretoria, where the British deployed and shelled a ridge from where they had earlier received fire. The enemy was invisible and apart from a few shots does not seem to have actively defended the position, but the British were held up for three hours.[89] Of course, had the British not deployed their artillery and some stubborn Boers were on the hill, the consequences could have been serious. French attaché Lt. Col. Albert d'Amade summed up his take on General Buller's thoughts regarding the effects of this phenomenon when he opined, "The phases of the battle are changing, in effect, so quickly that it is necessary to allow junior officers to use their own initiative to engage enemy troops who are only visible for a few minutes, because failure to do so risks losing many favorable opportunities to inflict significant losses on the enemy."[90] He went on to argue that the encouragement of individual initiative must be combined with oversight, and all of these factors had to be built into the training program.[91] The tension between the need for centralized control and individual initiative is one that continues to cause problems today.

Not being able to see the effect of fire was also problematic for morale. Previously, the hideous effects of accurate rifle and artillery fire were obvious to all who witnessed them. When firing at unseen troops, however, how could anyone know what effect that fire was having? Reitz described this uncertainty at Spion Kop, where Boer "casualties lay hideously among us, but theirs [British] were screened from view behind the breastwork [almost certainly the famous earthen trench, with the low stone wall, full of British dead], so that the comfort of knowing that we were giving worse than we received was denied us."[92] This last point is important, as it signals a new concern in war. Troops could fire all day with no idea of what actual effect they were having on the enemy. Previously battles were fought at ranges short enough where individuals normally could see the result of their own fire during the fight.

No longer was this scrutiny guaranteed, and an individual might never know the full effects of his actions.

These developments meant that proper reconnaissance was ever more important. Accurately locating an enemy made it easier to effectively engage him with fire. However, as Count Sternberg points out, "reconnaissance was practically impossible . . . because the bare plain offered no sort of cover for the scout."[93] The lack of cover and the difficulty of seeing well-concealed positions made approaching the enemy fraught with danger, particularly because troops armed with modern firearms could engage targets in the open out to 2,000 yards or more with virtual impunity. The advantage of possessing the high ground was of critical importance because it allowed a terrific field of view and posed a barrier to enemy observation. This vantage point increased the importance of aerial observation, as it allowed an observer to see over blocking terrain and to have a greater range of vision.[94] At Paardeberg Captain Slocum commented that a "balloon discovered four ammunition carts in river bed [sic], which the 4.7-inch guns north of the river exploded."[95] His implication was that the carts would not have been seen by any other means, short of the British occupying the banks of the river. The introduction of aviation would generate profound future changes in the field of observation.

The actual construction of fortifications varied during the war, largely depending on the ground. Though sangars were widely used, both sides were adept at digging trenches. Indeed, the Boers were particularly noteworthy in this regard, to the extent that these fortifications were often called Boer trenches. Frederick Unger and Captain Slocum both provided detailed descriptions of the Boer trenches in the south bank of the Modder River at Paardeburg (see figure 3.1). Admittedly, Captain Slocum provided more technical information. There, the Boers had cut five-and-a-quarter-feet deep trenches into the crest of the riverbank. They included loopholed head cover and had branches on top to provide camouflage and, presumably, some protection from shell splinters and shrapnel. Behind them, in the bank of the river itself and out of line of sight, were camouflaged bomb-proofs where the men could sleep and take shelter. The steep

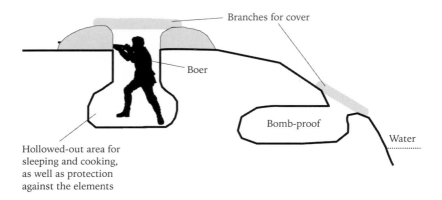

Branches for cover

Boer

Hollowed-out area for
sleeping and cooking,
as well as protection
against the elements

Bomb-proof

Water

FIGURE 3.1. Typical Boer-style trench and bomb-proof.

angles of the bank prevented an enemy who was firing at them on the same side of the river from hitting them without the use of very high-angle fire, and even then it would have been very difficult.[96] This construction was similar to the basic style of Turkish trench at Plevna, except for the camouflage, and it would prove to resemble even more those trenches dug during the Great War. Captain Trimmel, the Austrian attaché, also commented on the Boer trenches at Paardeburg, where he found that they "offered complete protection, from all sides, against English artillery fire, and the low profile significantly impeded their effective bombardment."[97] He also drew attention to the fact that they were often relatively small foxholes. Indeed, they are surprisingly similar to ones seen in the later stages of the First World War.

As noted, the other main type of fortification was the blockhouse, which needs describing in some detail because the British relied on them so heavily and constructed so many. Lieutenant Colonel Holden explained that there were two main types:

> The blockhouses in South Africa are of two kinds, corrugated iron or stout masonry. . . . The iron blockhouses are octagonal, hexagonal, or circular, and loop-holed, but the original idea has been so experimented upon that they are now found

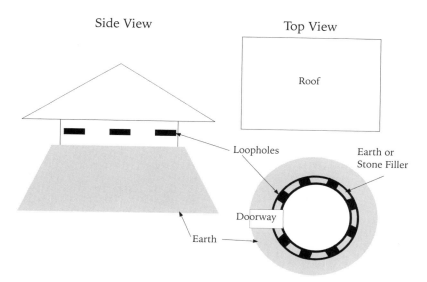

FIGURE 3.2. Typical design of a corrugated iron blockhouse.

in a great variety of shapes. The circular kind are generally preferred; they certainly take less material, which is a consideration when some four to five thousand are in course of construction. The general principle is, however, the same in all. Blockhouses are rapidly built, taking twelve men and twenty natives only about eight hours to erect.[98]

John Fuller gives an excellent description of the method of construction of a line of blockhouses. His observation warrants quoting at length:

First, a line on a map was selected and a blockhouse constructed at one end of the ground chosen. The distance of the second blockhouse from the first naturally depended on the country, but normally it was built at between one thousand and two thousand yards away from it . . . either on level ground or on a small kopje [hill] when such could be found. . . . Immediately round the blockhouse, that is between it and the wire fence, was dug a ditch four and a half feet deep and three feet wide; this was the sentry's beat during night time. . . . When digging

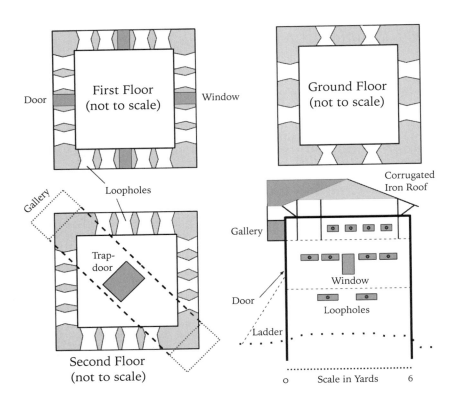

FIGURE 3.3. Typical design of a stone blockhouse.

was impossible the ditch was replaced by a stone *sangar* or loose stone parapet. Once the blockhouse had been rendered proof against enemy action, the next step taken was to prevent the enemy from crossing the intervals between the blockhouse and its immediate neighbours. This was done by linking up block-houses by a barbed-wire apron fence. . . . To alarm the garri-son of a blockhouse should the fence be tampered with during night-time, a single thin wire was run along, or rather through the fence; this, if cut, released a heavy stone, which falling on an empty biscuit tin would automatically sound the alarm.[99]

They took a great deal of effort to construct, and they required the expenditure of a large amount of resources too. The *War Record of the*

York and Lancaster Regiment mentions the cost difference between the early blockhouses, largely built of stone, and the simpler ones: "One of the first blockhouses was erected at Opperman's Kraal, thirteen miles north of Volksrust. It was built of stone, two stories high, and was altogether on a much more expensive scale than subsequent ones, which were principally made of corrugated iron with stone ballast between [the layers of corrugated iron]."[100] Holden points out the enormous cost difference between stone and iron block-houses, with the former costing from £200 to £600 and the latter £50 to £70. Of the roughly 5,000 blockhouses constructed during the war, the Royal Engineers listed 441 built from masonry.[101] The construction of masonry blockhouses often was restricted to key locations owing to their significant cost in both cash and matériel.

This cost had a significant effect elsewhere given the pressure it placed on other resources. Army Order No. 3 reads: "(a) Railway materials are not to be taken in future for constructing defences. These materials are scarce, and are required for repairing the railway. Where General Officers Commanding can arrange for the construction of corrugated iron blockhouses to replace defences made of materials required by the Imperial Military Railways they should do so."[102] Clearly, there was tension between the need to provide adequate fortification and the needs of the logistics system. However, once these tensions eased and British forces had standardized the style of blockhouse, their construction became that much easier. A small unit could construct several blockhouses a day with the help of an engineering officer and local black African labor.[103] Thus, within a few months thousands of blockhouses dotted the South African landscape.

The dreary nature of life in a blockhouse when combined with short periods of intense fear and excitement highlighted the problems of prolonged exposure to stress. John Fuller discussed this issue and its affect on the soldiers:

> It is true that there was little danger from the enemy, but the men being so isolated were frequently jumpy and were liable to fire at anything they saw moving. . . . By now [December

1900] most of the sentries had the jumps, and about midnight I started out alone for my tour of visits, and nearly got shot for my pains. . . . Besides the terrors of night work, alarums [*sic*] and excursions were fairly frequent. . . . On December 7th at 11.15pm. three shots were fired suddenly, followed by four others. Foljambe and I jumped out of bed, put on our shoes and greatcoats and seizing our carbines rushed out of our tent. A patrol was sent to where the firing was heard, and soon came back and reported that the sentry, Pte. Venn, had been sniped.[104]

Fuller gives his regiment's casualties from 1900 to 1902 as thirty-two officers and men.[105] Thus, the physical human cost does not seem to have been the main cause for the men's nervous state; rather, it appears to have been the threat of harm. This observation has parallels to what Col. Charles Brackenbury meant when he wrote about a soldier's supply of nervous energy and noted that prolonged exposure to stress contributes to a soldier's nervous exhaustion.[106] Life in the blockhouses typically involved the demoralizing effects of weeks of "constant sniping [that] caused us many sleepless nights."[107] No mention is made, in Fuller's example, of the number of physical casualties suffered, so they do not seem to be the main cause of the men's stress. Fuller again:

> The worst feature of blockhouse life was its demoraling influence on the soldier. Apart from sentry duty and minor fatigue work there was absolutely nothing to do except talk, smoke and gamble. Frequently no sign of civilization, or even of life, except for the two neighbouring blockhouses, could be seen for miles around, and this utter blankness of life undoubtedly carried with it a bad moral influence. Further, almost unceasing sentry-go [sentry duty], lack of natural exercise and monotony of food told on the nerves. Though they were in complete safety men would become jumpy and bad-tempered.[108]

The prolonged exposure to stress due to these various factors brought a whole new type of injury to prominence. The problems associated with shell shock would become well known during the First World War, where hundreds of thousands of men would suffer from it.[109]

Another of the affects of combat stress was the worry that men, once ensconced in cover, would be reluctant to move from it. On the face of it, this response is simple common sense given the relative lethality of modern arms. The commander's fear was that if troops took cover during an attack, they would be difficult to get going again, and any delay would risk even greater casualties. Reitz describes the downside of protection on the troops' martial spirit during a Boer attack on Red Fort in Ladysmith:

> The place was built on the brow of a low stony kopje immediately beyond the Harrismith railway line and, except where its earthworks formed an embankment, there was no cover. We had about four hundred yards to go, but the light was still uncertain, so we gained the safety of the ramp with the loss of only one man. This railway causeway proved our undoing, for had it not been there the chances are we should have gone straight on into the fort, but the sheltering bank was too tempting, and with one accord the men halted behind it to recover their breath. In the circumstances the delay was fatal, for we lost the original impulse that had carried us thus far and as the light was increasing and with it the fierce volleying, we became disinclined to leave cover and instead of resuming our advance, stayed where we were.[110]

It is worth noting that this attack was a costly failure. Of course, other attacks also stalled when men took cover during the advance, but whether the men's choice to lie low caused their failure at Red Fort is open to debate. Had the men continued to advances, they all might well have been butchered, making the whole point irrelevant. However, given that halted attacks often left the men dangerously exposed to enemy fire, it was reasonable to insist that they push the assault to their utmost. What dreadful consequences this order would lead to are all but evident from the events of 1914.

Conclusions

The Boer War saw a number of interesting developments in warfare. The issue of the need for protection was no longer really debated; rather, it became one of how to provide the required protection. Deep trenches, well camouflaged, were the most effective means, but they could not be constructed everywhere because of the nature of ground. Furthermore, as has been seen, they were not suitable for all situations. Another issue was the problem of clearly identifying enemy positions and dealing with them. The problem of combat stress had also started to raise its head; however, it would not become of major importance until the 1914–1918 war.

The use of fortification to prevent desertion in the Boer War is not really supported by the evidence, though its use in prisoner of war and concentration camps points to a new use. Admittedly, the creation of prisoner of war camps was not a novel idea. Prisoners had often been kept in old fortresses or on ships, and in the American Civil War, camps had been constructed for this very purpose. The large-scale use of concentration camps, however, was a change. Though it is outside the scope of this book to discuss this matter in full, it does serve to remind readers that particular fortifications were used for forced labor camps, extermination camps, and so forth.

The war again demonstrated that fortifications enhanced the troops' fighting power, with very small groups of Boers often holding up large British units for hours or days at a time. The Boers were particularly effective in exploiting fortification because of the lethality of modern weaponry, their skillful use of the ground, and their excellent use of camouflage. This combined well with the reinforcement of key tactical points. Simply occupying a key piece of terrain could make the enemy's ability to maneuver in the battle space extremely difficult. The idea that the enemy might hold a key piece of ground could delay an advance until the ground was properly cleared. Often this action involved deploying the artillery to shell the area and then sending troops up to scout it, a potentially long process.

The protection of a secure base was of vital importance during the war, particularly to the British. The long rail lines were incredibly vulnerable, and securing them effectively against Boer attack took a long time. The construction of the lines of blockhouses showed the use of fortification to dominate ground. Large numbers of blockhouses effectively boxed in vast areas of the southern African hinterland, though their utility was largely a product of the unique circumstances of the war.

The use by both sides of modern rifled firearms and artillery meant that enemy positions needed to be identified at long ranges or by effective close reconnaissance. Given the open nature of the ground in southern Africa, this type of detection proved very difficult. Troops lacked modern optical devices with which to observe the enemy in more detail from a safe distance, and crossing open ground to properly reconnoiter a potential enemy position was tantamount to suicide. Attacks were very tough to control once troops spread out, and the use of formed bodies of cavalry on the battlefield simply presented easy targets. The noted British military theorist Col. George Francis Robert Henderson spoke of these problems: "1. Infantry, attacking over open ground, must move in successive lines of skirmishers, extended at wide intervals. 2. Cavalry, armed, trained and equipped as the cavalry of the Continent, is as obsolete as the Crusaders. 3. Reconnaissance, even more important than heretofore, is far more difficult."[111] Essentially, this conclusion required completely rethinking the entire tactical system on which armies of the day were based.

The huge quantities of supplies that were necessary, particularly by the British forces, required an enormous and sustained logistical effort. By the end of 1899, the British were consuming 3 million rifle rounds per week, despite production at home being only 2.5 million weekly.[112] Clearly this could not last as the rate of production was insufficient to support demand indefinitely, and it was a relief when major combat operations ended in the summer of 1900. This last point also had a bearing on the First World War, as the use of artillery to reconnoiter positions greatly increased the use of artillery ammunition and, in turn, led to increased production. It seems reasonable to conclude that subsequent mechanical problems with the fuses,[113] which were precision pieces of machinery, might have stemmed from the massive expansion in their production. This experience provided a grim foretaste of what was to come in 1914–1915.

On the one hand, that much of the war was relatively static, particularly on the British side, did give rise to morale and other problems. On the other hand, it also allowed some of the luxuries of ordinary life to be available. The nature of steam-powered shipping and rail transportation kept the troops operating near rail lines, particularly those in static defensive positions, relatively well supplied. John Fuller noted the benefits of a railway, as he was able to ship "two dozen of whisky at six shillings the bottle; six bottles of brandy at seven shillings and sixpence, and three dozen of lime juice at two shillings and sixpence the bottle."[114] When he had time to drink all that booze, heaven knows, though it was likely some party.

Ultimately the main lessons of the war regarding the use of fortification reinforced the importance of digging in properly, of using concealed positions, and of the difficulty in taking them by assault. Men armed with modern weaponry demonstrated the power of these positions through the war. Discussing one in a series of attacks on strong positions, General Kitchener's take on the matter was that "if I had known yesterday, the 18th, what I know to-day, I would not have attacked the Boers in the river bed [at Paardeberg]; it is impossible against the rifle."[115] In addition, the Boers' use of defense in depth at Magersfontein, although it did not matter much to the tactical outcome, showed the way ahead. This last change became much more evident during the Russo-Japanese War, which is examined in chapter 4.

4

The Russo-Japanese War

The Russo-Japanese War of 1904–1905 was the first war to witness the widespread use of machine guns, wire entanglements, modern quick-firing artillery (the Russians were partially equipped with them), and large-scale defensive systems, all of which would not have been out of place a decade later during the First World War. The Russo-Japanese War also bore witness to the increasing scope of industrialized warfare in terms of the sheer size and scale of battles, which steadily grew during the war itself. For example, at the battle of Mukden approximately 250,000 Japanese soldiers fought 335,000 Russians on a front of sixty miles,[1] and the battle lasted more than two full weeks. Modern weapons had also brought about a reduction in the density of troop deployments partly because the troops needed to spread out to cover more ground, and they needed protection from greater firepower. Also fewer men were required in any one particular place owing to the improved firepower available to the defense.[2] In addition, the use of more modern weapons led to the increased use of field fortification because the battlefield was more dangerous, the troops needed protection, and the widely dispersed troops required a means to enhance their fighting power.

Building on its experience in the Russo-Turkish War of 1877–1878, the Russian Army continued with the program of reforms that had been instituted after the Crimean War; however, the army faced problems with who structured the reforms and how far they were implemented. After the Russian success in the Russo-Turkish War, Mikhail Dragomirov was appointed commandant of the prestigious Nicholas Academy of the General Staff between 1878 and 1889, which allowed him to mold the reforms with his ideology. Genrikh Antonovich Leer, who also possessed strong opinions, succeeded him in his post at the General Staff Academy. Both men chose to ignore the changes in the conduct of war that were rapidly occurring partly because of the conservative influence of the czars — Alexander III (1881–1894) and Nicholas II (1894–1917) — on Russian military thinking.[3] The 1881 infantry tactical regulations,[4] for example, were only very limited in their reforms as the reformers worried that control would be lost over the men if they were allowed to disperse. The regulations prescribed that all men be trained in digging and be equipped with entrenching tools, and Dragomirov wanted them to dig in, conceal their positions, and build obstacles. The regulations also emphasized the use of the night attack based on the Russian experience of fighting at Kars. However, they did not entirely do away with dense formations or the use of volley fire, and Dragomirov never fully adapted his pre-1877 ideas to the new technology and style of war.[5] The changes did not stop there, for the problems caused by the lack of high-angle fire capability to use against the Turks' trenches at Plevna spurred the introduction of a heavy mortar. By 1900 the majority of the armies of the Great Powers had introduced similar weaponry.[6]

Despite not being extensively studied today, the Russo-Japanese War was of great interest to the contemporary armed forces. Colonel Lombard, an attaché observing the war and representing the French Army, noted that sixteen military attachés were with him on campaign: six Englishmen, two Frenchmen, one Australian, two Germans, two Spaniards, one American, one Swiss, and one Austro-Hungarian.[7] As they had during the Russo-Turkish War of 1877–1878, the attachés gained excellent access to the ongoing fighting in the Far East. Though detailed reporting from the front lines during the war was often difficult, the German, British, and American armies compiled detailed official histories of the war based on their attachés' eyewitness reports and interviews with other observers and combatants.[8] The access given to the foreign military attachés, other officers, and journalists was demonstrated not only in their detailed reporting of the war but also through such incidents as the death in action of Lieutenant Burtin, a French officer serving with the Russians.[9]

Of course, reporting from the front lines was always a delicate balance between observing and interfering. Capt. Carl Reichman, an American military attaché with the Russian Army, noted in an unpublished report that "Major Cheminot [a French officer attached to the Russian Army] made himself obnoxious by asking too many questions and was banished to Samsonof's cavalry in the front and I received an invitation from General Stakeberg to join his headquarters."[10] Presumably, the general's invitation was a reward for the captain's appropriate behavior and facilitated the excellent access that his detailed reports demonstrated. That Reichman's comments about Cheminot were omitted from the official American report on the war indicates that it might well have been a sensitive topic. On the one hand, it also shows that secrecy allowed a greater degree of candor on the observer's part. On the other hand, it leads to the conclusion that not all possible questions could be asked and that the picture presented by the various attachés was subject to restrictions. The limitations imposed by both sides were considered reasonable in the circumstances, though some reporters obviously disagreed. The American journalist Frederick McCormick, a Reuters agent, purposely allowed the Japanese to capture him only to find their imposed restrictions even more stringent. So again he escaped, this time back to the Russian lines, and the Russians welcomed him back, despite his having sent an uncomplimentary telegram about Russian officers while he was with the Japanese.[11] (After those adventures, I am sure his evening meals with the Russian officers must have been rather entertaining.) Thus, the restrictions on both the movements and reporting of the observers in principle might have been fairly strict, but they were not always rigorously applied. And despite them, the observers had reasonably good access to the fighting and were able to provide very detailed reports of the events.

Most of the field fortifications that the military attachés examined and described were Russian rather than Japanese. The Japanese spent much of the war on the offensive, retaining the initiative and forcing the Russian Army to fight largely on the defensive. Thus, the construction of field fortifications played less of a role in the Japanese conduct of operations than they did in that of the Russians, who utilized them on a greater scale.[12]

Terrain and Soil in Manchuria

The terrain of southeastern Manchuria where much of the fighting took place consists of a series of mountain ranges, but none are particularly tall and rarely more than a thousand meters in altitude.[13] These mountains were largely barren and rocky, with extensive cultivation, particularly of a type of sorghum called *kaoliang*, in the valleys.[14] The soil was described as being sandy,[15] and French military attaché Gen. Marie-Félix Sylvestre said it was "particularly favourable for field fortifications."[16] Major A. Glasfurd of the Indian Army toured the battle sites in Manchuria in 1907 with the intent of providing a narrative and pictorial description of the terrain. He found the same general type in most of the places he visited. Because he inspected the area specifically to examine the ground, his comments on the subject have been relied on heavily for the related information contained in his report. Glasfurd's account concurs with Sylvestre's on the most important points about the ground, the layout of the terrain, the sandy nature of the soil, and the rockiness of some of the hilltops.[17] The ease with which the soil could be extracted facilitated the widespread use of field fortification, while more difficult digging conditions might well have restricted its use to those points where it was absolutely essential. One other point of interest regarding the ground was Glasfurd's comment on the color of the freshly dug soil: "The light reddish-yellow colour of the soil and the smooth grassy surface of all the higher ground combine to make the slightest scratch on the surface of these hills stand most sharply out, thus rendering it practically impossible to conceal trenches and excavations."[18] This last point emphasizes that temporary fortifications provided a clear point of aim for enemy artillery, thus providing a reason to fortify and camouflage a position properly. This task proved strangely difficult for the Russian forces to achieve early in the war.

Of the cultivated areas, the staple crops were beans and kaoliang. The latter is worth a brief description because of its use as cover during the campaign. Kaoliang is a cereal plant, which despite the relative stiffness of the stalk is not very strong, and stands an average of eight to ten feet tall when fully grown. It provided complete cover from view for all troops in a kaoliang field, which also proved difficult to navigate through.[19]

Owing to a shortage of timber and underbrush, which severely restricted the troops' ability to properly revet fortifications, troops frequently used sandbags and kaoliang instead. However, the firmness of the soil made maintaining the slopes possible without revetment, and trenches were often constructed without any revetment at all.[20] This lack of facing was a problem if the enemy possessed heavy artillery or high-explosive shell; then proper revetment was needed. Given the nature of the soil, most fortifications could be constructed belowground, which allowed the construction of bomb-proofs except in a few areas where the hilltops were too rocky. Though, as the reader will see, the rocky soil does not seem unduly to have hindered the Japanese in their construction of effective fortification.

The Campaign

The Russo-Japanese War began on 8 February 1904 with a Japanese attack on the Russian harbor at Port Arthur (see map 4.1). On the same day Japanese troops were landed at Chemulpo (modern-day Inchon), directly outside Seoul. Following these events Gen. Alexei Kuropatkin was made commander of the Russian land forces in Manchuria and arrived at Harbin on 28 March 1904.[21] However, he was powerless to prevent further Japanese landings taking place at Pyongyang on 29 March, as Japanese troops moved north toward Manchuria. Commander of the Japanese First Army in Korea Gen. Tamemoto Kuroki intended to cross the Yalu River into Manchuria close to Antung, repeating the Japanese maneuver from 1894 when they were at war with the Chinese, presumably because the ground was familiar to the Japanese commanders.[22]

The first important land engagement took place between the two armies when the Japanese Army crossed the Yalu on the night of

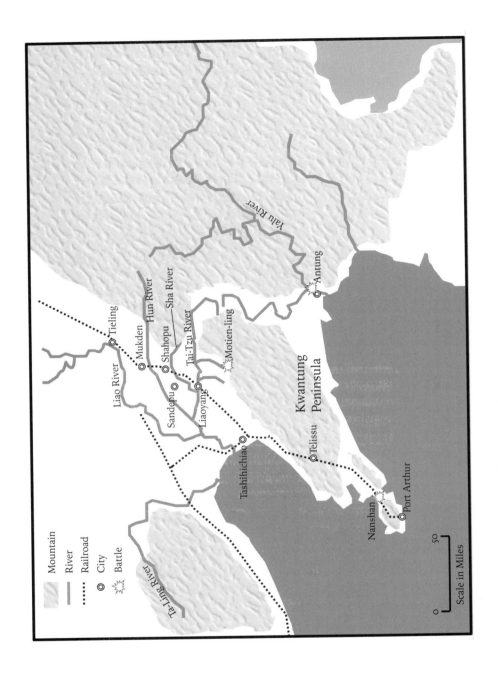

MAP 4.1. The Russo-Japanese War.

29–30 April. Presaging its own frequent future incompetence, the Russian Army failed to secure Tiger Hill, the geographic key to the position. The Japanese successfully crossed the river and forced the Russian Army into the first of many retreats.

During the early stages of the war, little use was made of field fortification, a fact noted in a report by Lt. Col. Walter Schuyler, an American military attaché with the Russian Army.[23] It is reasonable to suppose that the fairly rapid movement of the troops, as well as the fact that neither side at that time had faced sustained and determined resistance, made them unnecessary.

By 14 May, the Japanese had landed more forces in Manchuria and were threatening to cut off the Kwantung Peninsula. This development was important because Port Arthur, the main Russian naval base in the area, was situated at the head of that peninsula and would be completely isolated from the rest of the Russian Army if the Japanese sealed off Nanshan (Chinchou), which formed the neck. The position at Nanshan was small, but the defenses were formidable. It was also the first defensive point containing both machine guns and barbed wire that the Japanese forces would face.[24] The Japanese attacked on 25 May with three divisions and suffered 4,504 casualties while taking the position. The full scale of Russian casualties is unclear, but they lost at least 700 dead.[25]

At the beginning of June, Gen. Maresuke Nogi took command of Japanese troops shielding Port Arthur. He began building up his forces to take the fortress after the disastrous Russian attempt to relieve Port Arthur failed at the battle of Telissu (Wafangkou) on 14–15 June.[26] The Japanese pursuit was effectively prevented by the fall of very heavy rain,[27] which accompanied the onset of the monsoon season. A lull followed this battle, and the two sides did not renew heavy fighting until mid-July. Meanwhile, both armies brought up much needed supplies, but it proved a slow process given the effect the heavy rains had on the roads.[28]

In the meantime, on 29 June, the Japanese had occupied the important strategic pass of Motien-ling (ling is the Chinese term for "pass") on the line of advance to Liaoyang. Russian forces initially had abandoned this pass despite its geographically crucial position,[29] but then they were ordered to retake it. A night attack during the early hours of 17 July caught the Japanese by surprise; though the Russians had some initial success, they were eventually repelled. The British observer on the spot, Capt. B. Vincent of the Royal Artillery, was incredulous of the Russians' failure given the almost total surprise they had achieved, the circumstances of the battle, and the geography of the ground itself.[30] As the Russo-Japanese War progressed, the one-sided nature of the victories became less and less surprising with each Japanese success.

As the Japanese Army continued to advance toward Liaoyang, its forces again defeated Russian troops, this time at the battle of Tashihchiao on 24–25 July. General Kuropatkin blamed the problems his army faced on insufficient numbers of soldiers, poor training, the rain, and dysentery, conveniently omitting that the Japanese surely suffered from the last two problems too and that his command was the common denominator in most of the Russian setbacks.[31] The Russian defeat at Tashihchiao enabled the Japanese to proceed on their slow march to Liaoyang and to step up pressure on those Russian troops defending Port Arthur.

Following the battle of Tashihchiao, Russian forces in Manchuria were in full retreat to Liaoyang. The monsoon weather and correspondingly poor roads slowed the withdrawal, which lasted for much of August. However, Kuropatkin still intended to try to fight a decisive battle at Liaoyang, and he had prepared three extensive lines of defensive fortifications to protect the main routes of advance into the town. With his base of operations secured, he considered what were his two main options—to contain Kuroki and move against the other Japanese forces or to fall back on the main fortifications. The second option would allow him to free up enough troops to attack General Kuroki's part of the advancing Japanese force.[32] With his flanks under pressure from the Japanese, ultimately he chose a third option, which was again to retreat.[33] He made this decision despite the Russian Army in Manchuria possessing superior numbers: Kuropatkin gave his numbers as 150,000–180,000 troops,[34] while the Russians believed Kuroki's force had only 65,000–70,000 men.[35] (The Japanese force as a whole numbered approximately

125,000 men.) From 25 August through the Russian evacuation of Liaoyang on 4 September, heavy fighting occurred in and around the town, with the Russian Army withdrawing from the outer defenses to the inner defenses before completely evacuating the place. This Russian defeat made any attempt to relieve the garrison of Port Arthur much more difficult, owing to the sheer physical distance (around two hundred miles) that now existed between the besieged town and the main part of the Russian Army.

Port Arthur effectively had been cut off from the main Russian forces since their defeat at the battle of Nanshan on 25 May. From that point, the Russian garrison had been inexorably pushed back to the immediate defenses of the town. General Nogi, the Japanese in charge of the forces besieging Port Arthur, was tasked with taking the town as quickly as possible in order to relieve pressure on the Japanese Navy, which was blockading the Russian ships sheltering in the harbor. A victory would release his men to join up with the Japanese main force. Nogi's men chipped away at the outer defenses until they were ready to launch their first full-scale assault on the main Russian defensive positions. Preliminary attacks had started as early as 7 August, supporting attacks occurred six days later, and the main assault began on 19 August. The Japanese continued to launch large-scale assaults on and off for a further six days at the cost of 18,000 casualties. An additional 9,000 Japanese soldiers had already succumbed to disease during the monsoon.[36] After this first series of bloody attacks, the Japanese had little to show for their efforts and settled in for a long siege.

A few words are in order on the state of the defenses of Port Arthur. The fortress had many flaws in its layout, such as improperly covered approaches. The Russians had also gravely neglected its maintenance, leading to a degradation of its strength. In anticipation of the conflict, they made efforts to rectify this situation, with Russian engineers overseeing a vast amount of construction. Particular attention seems to have been paid to the construction of head cover and bombproof shelters for the men. However, lacking coordination, the Russians neglected some parts of the fortified area that should have been reinforced — with 203-Meter Hill being the most egregious example—and that oversight led to major problems later.[37] It is outside the scope of this book to go into great detail, thus interested readers should consult some of the excellent books that focus on the siege itself.[38]

Intermittent fighting continued over the next four and a half months, as the Japanese slowly tightened the siege and brought all of the Russian positions under very heavy bombardment. Only when Japanese troops captured the key tactical position of 203-Meter Hill on 5 December—at the cost of 14,000 Japanese and 5,000 Russian casualties—was it clear that the end of the siege was in sight. No longer were parts of the harbor hidden from enemy view, and the Russian fleet had no shelter from the incessant Japanese shelling. Consequently most of the fleet was put out of action by 9 December. On 2 January 1905, less than a month after the fall of 203-Meter Hill, the Russian garrison surrendered. The besieging Japanese force was free to join its compatriots facing Kuropatkin's army near Sandepu. The Japanese had captured Port Arthur at enormous cost, with casualties amounting to 91,549 killed, wounded, missing, or sick.[39]

During the siege of Port Arthur, the main Russian and Japanese forces continued to fight along the line of the Mukden–Port Arthur railway. Kuropatkin had again ordered his army to counterattack the Japanese forces in Manchuria in order to break through and try to relieve the beleaguered Russian garrison. This directive led to a major Russian attack and the battle of the Shaho, which began on 5 October and lasted until 17 October. The two armies fought each other to a standstill, with each side losing approximately 40,000 men.[40] The battle demonstrated little other than the ordinary Russian soldier could fight despite the incompetence of much of the Russian staff.[41] This Russian defeat removed any realistic chance of relieving the garrison of Port Arthur.

With the winter weather becoming increasingly cold and wet, military operations on the Manchurian part of the front continued only at a much-reduced tempo. The Russian Army in Manchuria was not able to build up sufficient forces to mount a significant threat to the Japanese until after the Russian surrender at Port

Arthur. Relieved of the burden of joint command after Viceroy Yevgeni Alexeiev was recalled to St. Petersburg,[42] General Kuropatkin was better able to plan for an offensive that was intended to begin at Sandepu on 25 January 1905 before the Japanese forces under General Nogi arrived. What should have been a well-planned and coordinated attack ended up a shambles, with surprise being lost and appalling weather hampering the movement of Russian troops. Three days of heavy fighting produced more than 9,000 Japanese and 20,000 Russian casualties, a demoralized Russian Army, and a failed Russian offensive.[43]

On the defensive after suffering regular defeats in Manchuria and with the stirrings of revolution at home, the Russian Army needed one final effort to stop the seemingly inevitable Japanese advance on the strategically important town of Mukden. Japan too needed a decisive victory, wanting to bring the war to a speedier conclusion. A great deal of pressure was exerted on Gen. Iwao Oyama to end the war with the coming battle; despite the almost constant success, the Japanese Army was under strain, and the Japanese economy was burdened by war debt.[44] Both sides pulled in their reserves during February, following the battle of Sandepu, and amassed more than half a million troops on the front lines. Kuropatkin had at his disposal 275,000 infantry, 16,000 cavalry, and 1,219 guns, against which the Japanese could muster 200,000 infantry, 7,300 cavalry, and 992 guns. Crucially the Japanese had nearly 1,000 machine guns to the Russian's 56.[45]

Both sides had determined to attack; however, the Japanese were better concentrated, as the Russian forces were thinly deployed along a front of nearly ninety miles. Thus, importantly, the Japanese started the attack on 22 February, preempting the Russians' plans by two days. The initial fighting was largely inconclusive, but the Russian forces were slowly worn down and outmaneuvered, with the Japanese bringing pressure to bear on their flanks. By 7 March, the weak Russian counterattacks had failed, and the Russians had again started to retreat. Within another three days, the main fighting was over, but the Japanese had failed to crush the Russians as Oyama had hoped. They had inflicted a severe and demoralizing defeat, causing 90,000 Russian casualties to 75,000 Japanese. Mukden proved to be the last large land battle of the war.

The war continued until 12 June 1905, when the Russian government accepted the offer of peace talks. Despite the almost constant bad news from the land campaign in Manchuria, this decision came only after the Russians' crushing naval defeat at the battle of Tsushima on 27–28 May and with severe economic and political disturbances at home. Japan's victory in the war worried the U.S. government in particular and demonstrated that Japan clearly had become a major regional power. In contrast, Russia had to overcome a revolution and reorganize and rebuild its armed forces.

The war witnessed the widespread use of the most up-to-date technology of the day. The armies of both sides and the scale of the battles were not too dissimilar in their extent and intensity from the armies and the fighting at the start of the First World War. Further, the Russo-Japanese War offered some very valuable lessons to those observing it. Perhaps the most important message was that one could be the strategic and tactical aggressor and overcome the destructive effects of modern weapons if one had sufficient moral power to overcome the defenders. This point was not lost on the observers despite many subsequent arguments to the contrary.

Fortifications: Preventing Desertion

Large-scale desertion was not an issue for the Japanese Army in Manchuria. This detail can be attributed to the discipline, courage, and patriotism of the Japanese soldiers,[46] as well as to the fact that they were consistently on the victorious side. While Professor Naoko Shimazu recently has challenged this view,[47] many eyewitnesses agree on the soldiers' bravery, whatever its reason, and this author defers largely to their impressions while taking some of the more extreme examples with a healthy dose of salt. During his assignment with the Japanese forces in Manchuria, Lt. Gen. Sir C. J. Burnett of the British Army detailed a list of crimes that soldiers of the Japanese Third Army had committed since 1 June 1904. The list included, but was not limited to, the normal types of crimes soldiers all over the world commit—disobeying orders, being unpunctual, being absent from duty, and so on—but, significantly, it does not contain one case of desertion.[48]

The Russian soldiers too were disciplined and courageous when under fire, yet the Russian Army in Manchuria suffered from desertion, particularly toward the end of the war. The Russian soldier was noted for being dependable,[49] so the problem of desertion in the Russian Army likely was largely caused by external factors, such as the unrest in Russia following the "Bloody Sunday" massacre in St. Petersburg on 22 January 1905, the general unpopularity of the war, and so on. Had desertions indeed been problematic, there would have been evidence of widespread desertions during and after the battle of Sandepu on 25–27 January 1905, when the army was already demoralized and the first news of trouble at home began arriving. It was not the case. In fact, the evidence from the foreign attachés shows only that the army had some minor problems with soldiers going absent.

Col. W. Waters, a British military attaché with the Russian Army, noted that in December 1904 orders were issued to stop the congregation of a number of Russian troops acting as porters and thieves at the railway station in Harbin. It struck Colonel Waters that because this issue had been a problem at Harbin for some time, the Russian soldiers' absence from their units had been hardly noticed and that discipline in those units must not have been properly maintained.[50] Given the circumstances of unrest at home, though not yet of full-blown revolution, or of defeat in the field, possibly the Russian officers did not want unduly to provoke their men by cracking down on discipline. It is important to note that when the order was given, although Harbin was situated well away from the front lines and was probably a relatively safe place for Russian troops to be out by themselves—given the local Chinese population's hostility to Russian occupation—the number of men seen there was not large.

This author has not found any detailed figures relating to desertion in the Russian Army in the foreign military attachés' reports. Evidence indicates that desertion did occur, although the scale is difficult to assess fully. Kuropatkin wrote in his account of the campaign that the reservists were unsteady and that there was a general lack of patriotism. He also noted that a "drifting to the rear of large numbers of soldiers,"[51] and that he specifically had to issue the order that "any men leaving the ranks in action under the pretext of accompanying or carrying away wounded men will be severely punished."[52] This order must have been given after some men disappeared from the field while "helping the wounded." Because much of his account is aimed at reducing the degree of his responsibility for the calamitous outcome of the war on land, his observations on desertion must be treated with some skepticism. However, in their respective books, Denis Warner and Peggy Warner and R. M. Connaughton also noted problems with desertion and self-inflicted wounds among Russian troops.[53] In addition, Colonel Waters's report bears out General Kuropatkin's complaints about the lack of courts-martial to punish cowardice and disgraceful conduct.[54] Even if we accept some exaggeration in General Kuropatkin's account, given that he had to issue two specific orders on the matter, the essence of his writing was almost certainly accurate: the Russian Army in Manchuria had a problem with desertion.

One way to estimate the numbers of desertions is to examine the numbers of men listed as missing. When comparing the numbers for each army, some interesting differences emerge in the proportion of troops listed as missing. Col. John Hoff, assistant surgeon general of the U.S. Army, was attached to the Russian troops in Manchuria, where he commented that one should not presume that the missing had deserted to the enemy. Although the evidence he accumulated indicated they indeed might have done so, he also readily admitted that this theory was impossible to prove. His findings showed that the number of Russian soldiers missing was roughly equivalent to the numbers of men killed at each battle prior to the battle of Mukden. At that battle the number reported missing was almost four times greater than the number of men listed as having been killed. The numbers of officers reported missing were much lower, but they too showed a significant increase at the battle of Mukden.[55] During the war the Russians reported 39,729 officers and men as missing, of whom almost 30,000 disappeared at the battle of Mukden. Some of the missing were possibly killed and abandoned, but the sheer numbers involved do not support the idea that these men were all killed or wounded and left on the field. In contrast, when the Japanese published their casualty lists for the war, only some 3,000 officers and men were listed as missing.[56] Admittedly, this report was published after the war when the Japanese had possession of the ground that had been fought over, so they could make as full a tally of all of their casualties as possible. Even so, the evidence indicates that desertion was a large-scale issue for the Russian forces at the battle of Mukden.

The nature of the battle itself contributed to the ease of desertion. Many factors might have caused a Russian soldier to want to desert: bad weather, poor conditions, constant defeats, poor leadership, unrest at home, and so on. Yet the soldiers had not deserted in large numbers until the actual battle itself. Prior to the battle and for much of the winter, the soldiers had been housed in field fortifications in relatively close proximity to the Japanese. Thus, the opportunities for desertion were too limited and dangerous. As was shown in chapter 3, leaving well-protected trenches in the face of the enemy was potentially deadly, and the troops had this lesson drummed into them through bloody experience. Once the battle of Mukden was under way and the Russian troops had started their retreat, they would have had much greater opportunities to desert. Not only were troops already outside the protection of their fortifications, but also they were spread out over a massive area: the Russian front line was close to ninety miles long. These details, when combined with the confusion of retreat, would have made desertion a much simpler proposition. Further, the large numbers involved made the deserters relatively safe from the attentions of bandits and the like, as well as from military justice. Once the situation had started to stabilize and the gap between the two armies had closed, the opportunity to desert would almost certainly have gone; moreover, the men would have needed to return to their fortifications when in proximity of the enemy.

Given that desertion really only became a problem for the Russian forces toward the end of the war, it is perhaps no wonder that the issue of desertion was not discussed more widely in the literature.

Had the war continued longer than it did, the increased incidence of desertion among the Russian troops might have been more formally addressed through the construction of fortifications designed to combat the problem rather than simply giving orders that dealt with the more visible issues.

Providing Physical Protection

The Russo-Japanese War bore witness to a much wider usage of field fortification for physical protection than ever before largely because of the new nature of the weapons deployed and the sheer scale of the fighting. The advanced weaponry made it more essential to protect the men when they were in the proximity of the enemy. Because of the technological advances, this dynamic had altered. The enemy's proximity had changed in relation to distance; it reached beyond the 2,000–3,000 meters of effective range seen in previous large-scale wars and extended the depth of the battlefield to at least 6,000–7,000 meters. This difference forced greater numbers of troops to be spread out over a wider area. The increased use of modern technology and its corresponding lethality also required them to dig in.

The advances in weapon technologies, particularly the power of artillery, meant that field fortifications had not lost their usefulness. Despite the increased power of artillery and rifle fire, they still provided protection for those men sheltering in them, if they were sufficiently well constructed. Observing the battle of Telissu on 14–15 June 1904, Lt. Col. A. L. Haldane noted that General Oshima's troops were prevented from leaving the protection of their shelter trenches because of the Russian troops' determined fire raining down on them.[57] So although the men were unable to move into the open while under fire, they were relatively safe as long as they stayed in the protective embrace of their trenches. American Capt. Carl Reichmann, who had served as an attaché during the Boer War of 1899–1902 and later taught at West Point, noted in his report on the Russian Army that "wherever practicable the standing trench was employed as being the best protection against shrapnel fire. The kneeling trench was not employed unless lack of time or the character of the ground made the standing trench impracticable. The lying-down trench I never saw."[58] Thus, a well-constructed trench provided protection against shrapnel, whereas troops in the open were very vulnerable.

This latter point is emphasized in the comments of Lt. Gen. Sir Ian Hamilton, who observed a Russian attack on the Motien-ling on 17 July 1904. He described how a Japanese artillery battery caught a large group of Russians advancing in very close order in the open at about 3,000 yards, causing more than a thousand casualties.[59] This encounter took approximately thirty minutes of firing and clearly demonstrated the power of modern artillery fire. Hamilton also noted that the effect of artillery fire on the morale of those troops caught in the open "was most noticeable."[60] Being in the open, exposed to enemy fire, had a negative effect on troops; it follows that placing them in fortifications of some sort improved their morale and, therefore, their ability to fight.

The experience of Capt. John F. Morrison, an American military attaché with the Japanese Army who went on to teach at the U.S. Army Staff College, reinforced this observation. He contrasted the effect of being protected against artillery with being exposed to it, and he is worth quoting at length:

> On the evening of August 30 a concentrated rapid fire of nearly 200 guns was poured into the Russian infantry position on the Shoushanpou for one hour, and this followed nearly an all-day's slower bombardment. The following desperate assault by the Japanese infantry was repulsed. I was told, the Russian infantry, under the cover of their works during this artillery fire, suffered practically no loss and were ready for the infantry attack when it came. . . .
>
> Shrapnel fire made many places absolutely impassable, as, for instance, the little valley at the east end of Scrub Hill [southeast of Shoushanpu hill, Battle of Liaoyang]. It was reported by the Japanese to be very effective in holding back the pursuit at Telissu, where two Russian batteries sacrificed themselves to save their army from heavy loss. The same was true

at many other places. The Japanese found it effective in pursuit in more than one instance.[61]

This description is significant because the Japanese possessed high-explosive shells, and it indicates that the field artillery was not particularly effective against troops in well-prepared fortifications.[62] Morrison's example hints at the problems posed to armed forces of the period: they needed larger and more powerful weapons and plenty of high-explosive shell to neutralize well-fortified opponents, as shrapnel was virtually useless against well-protected troops. This problem proved to be particularly troublesome for the Russians because, as American attaché Capt. Peyton March noted, unlike the Japanese "the Russians have no shell [high explosive] with their field artillery."[63] Thus, the Russians lacked any real ability to defeat Japanese troops who had taken advantage of cover, particularly if that cover had splinter-proof protection.

In describing the protection that field fortifications offered even against heavy fire, March quoted Major General Okasaki of the Fifteenth Brigade, Second Division, in describing his unit's part in the battle of Liaoyang of 1–3 September 1904. Okasaki's comments also address the command dilemma when contemplating leaving the protection of field fortifications:

At this moment [just after 8 a.m.] the Russians opened fire, a little short but it wounded Ito, my adjutant, and then all of the Russian artillery began a rain of fire, making it impossible to stay on the hill [this coincided with having to take cover too]. All the soldiers were on the bottom of the intrenchments, and Major Watanabe and I came down to a pit where Colonel Baba, of the Thirtieth Regiment, was, and we stayed there an hour without moving. There were few casualties, because we all laid down. Then the Russian artillery distributed their fire, but some guns continued to fire at Manjuyama [the hill that General Okasaki's troops had captured], and it was not possible for the soldiers to get food, fire, or water. They had to stay in the intrenchments and eat uncooked rice. During this fire I believed the Russians would attack, either then or at night. Their fire was very rapid, sometimes 10 shots a second from the more than 40 guns around the hill. At 11 o'clock the Russians occupied the hill (910-foot). I sent an order to the battalion of the Fourth Regiment to retire. The Russian intrenchments there were in a semicircle facing Manjuyama, and I knew it was the preparation for an attack. The Japanese artillery could not change position to approach the Russian artillery [Russian guns were generally more technologically advanced, and frequently the Japanese found themselves outranged]. I went to the Sixteenth Regiment and took with me the Second Battalion of the Thirtieth Regiment, which was the reserve of the brigade. When I arrived there I saw that the Russians had stopped on Shutun. I received a message from the commanding officer of the battalion of the Fourth Regiment, asking permission not to retire. I replied "not possible," adding that I was sending two companies to assist during the retreat. The two companies lost 100 men and the three companies for the Fourth 170 men during the withdrawal. . . . The soldiers on Manjuyama were very tired, even sleeping under fire, the snoring of men being heard between the shells. . . . The Russian artillery fire against Manjuyama stopped after 6 p. m.[64]

From this account the battalion commander of the Fourth Regiment clearly wanted to stay in the relative safety of the field fortifications despite the obvious risk of Russian attack. Logically this choice was preferable to losing so many men while abandoning a position, however temporary that move might have been. Further, this bombardment occurred in a tactical situation that lasted a full ten hours prior to an infantry assault.

The effectiveness of well-constructed field fortifications was also noted in a report from Col. J. Tulloch, a British attaché who observed the battle of Liaoyang: "No redoubt was captured by assault on front or flanks — some were entered by the gorge, but most were abandoned before the Japanese got into them. In the redoubt of which a plan is attached [see figure 4.1] there are upwards of one hundred

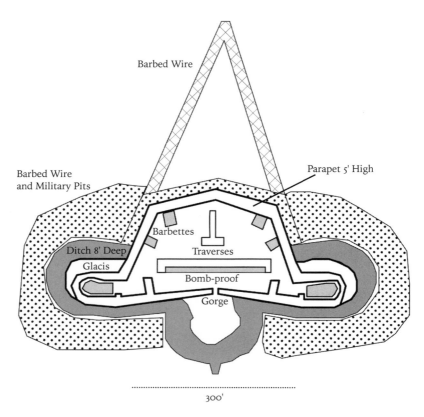

FIGURE 4.1. Russian redoubt at Liaoyang. Based on *Reports from British Officers Attached to the Japanese Forces in the Field*, vol. 2, held in WO33/1520, National Archives, Kew Gardens, London.

shell marks on the parapets and bombproofs from projectiles of, it is believed, field mortars, and possibly a few high-explosives, but no appreciable damage was done to it."[65]

These particular positions were also extensively protected with military pits and wire entanglements; thus they protected the men from both the worst effects of the enemy's fire and physical assault. Capt. B. Vincent observed that the Russians had improved their field fortifications since the battle of the Yalu—presumably because they had to, after the heavy casualties they had sustained—and that they now provided much better protection against rifle and shrapnel fire.[66] In the same report, he also noted the willingness of Major General Okasaki to order his men, even though they were very tired, "to dig deep pits as protection against the artillery bombardment which it is certain they would receive in the morning. The hill is very rocky and therefore difficult to entrench."[67] Even in tough ground, the men had to make the best of the situation. It must also have been essential, even if unpopular (as this author can testify), to order them to do so during the night when they needed rest.

Through the protection offered by field fortifications, clearly the men were better able physically and mentally to withstand heavy enemy fire. Indeed, they possibly could not have functioned without them, because the casualties would have rendered them ineffective very quickly. As Colonel Lombard noted, the Japanese artillery put up epaulements any time they stopped, unless speed was of the essence, because they did not have gun shields for crew protection.[68] These points tie in with the effect field fortifications had on the ability of men to resist. When men felt safer, they were better able to fight to their full potential, and they were more likely physically to last longer in action without harm.

Enhancing Fighting Power

The journalist Frederick Palmer spoke to the effect of fortification on fighting power, with a degree of artistic license, while he was on the road to Liaoyang and outside Fengwangcheng:

> The heights beyond the town were seamed with trenches and cut with roads for the artillery. Not one has been required in action. It was not thought that they ever would be. Their value was "moral." They made fifty thousand men as good as a hundred thousand men for defence, and they held safe on Kuropatkin's flank an army which could be thrown into his rear the moment that he should advance with his whole force to the relief of Port Arthur.[69]

Though this quote is rather dramatic, its basic premise was sound: field fortifications enhanced fighting power.

Lt. Col. E. Agar, a British military attaché in Manchuria, backed up this idea when he noted that the Russian infantry positions near Tiehling provided excellent protection for the soldiers, allowing them to remain steady while they shot at the Japanese. Indeed, he postulated that it helped them to shoot as well as other Europeans did,[70] with the implication being that the fortifications—not the men's insufficient training and leadership—gave them the confidence to take the time to shoot straight. Captain Reichman, too, wrote of the solidity of Russian troops under fire when trenches protected them:

> As evening approached the fire gained in intensity and consisted of shrapnel and high explosive shells. The aspect of the battle was magnificent and terrible beyond description. The enemy showed the bayonet to make the Russian troops show and expose themselves to the artillery fire, but the attitude of the Russian infantry in the well constructed trenches was firm. The attack on the hill, held by the 3rd East Siberian Rifles was repulsed and the enemy's infantry did not advance beyond the *kaoliang*.[71]

These observations are in line with Colonel Agar's: field fortifications helped troops to stand and fight, especially against greater numbers of the enemy.

This idea was important given the considerable distances over which the armies deployed and operated. Small forces needed to be able to hold up, or at least delay, an enemy until reinforcements arrived or a change in plans was made. During the war, the Japanese made many attempts to outflank the Russian Army's positions, and their threat to the Russian flanks had facilitated the Russians' withdrawal at the battles of Liaoyang and Mukden. Had the Russian troops dug in better, they might have withstood the Japanese pressure. Further, the lesson was that if pressure successfully could be applied to a flank, then the enemy might be induced to withdraw, negating the need for a head-on assault. However, if no flank was available, as at Nanshan (until the tide went out) or Port Arthur, a bloody frontal assault was the only real option.

Reinforcing Key Tactical Points

Field fortifications were used to reinforce key tactical points, particularly so during the battle of Liaoyang, where the featureless terrain demanded the use of fortifications to help secure the infantry line. Colonel Tulloch described Russian redoubts used for this purpose:

> The redoubts were all of a semi-permanent nature. Their command varied up to as much as 12 feet. The ditches 6 feet in depth and 15 feet wide and flanked by orillons. They were constructed for garrisons of 500 infantry or less, and for machine guns, and were never more than 1,400 yards apart. The total length of the work was about ten miles.[72]

Wire entanglements further protected the works, and their construction also protected and dominated the Russian front line. Given the garrison's size, they also could have been used as small bases of operations within the lines themselves. These last two points tie in well with the other reasons for utilizing fortifications.

Captain Morrison described similar Russian positions thus:

> At Haicheng, in addition to the infantry trenches, they had forts constructed as salients in the line, with deep ditches and heavy parapets. These were for the infantry. . . . The inner line around Liaoyang consisted of eleven redoubts prepared for infantry and machine guns. These were all very similar in plan and construction. Between these redoubts were the usual trenches and minor works. Covered ways were constructed leading into the redoubts and trenches both at Nanshan and Liaoyang.[73]

So well constructed were the Russian redoubts that Morrison noted that at the battle of Liaoyang the Japanese only captured one while it was still manned.[74] In addition, American military attaché Maj. Joseph Kuhn pointed out that despite the increasing power and accuracy of artillery, redoubts did not lose all of their importance as key tactical positions in the support of a defensive line.[75] Again, if fortifications were well constructed, they were very difficult to neutralize without the use of heavy artillery and could be used to anchor a defensive position.

At the battle of Mukden, British attaché Capt. D. Robertson also witnessed this type of use: "Sites for redoubts had been selected with great judgement, generally on slight undulations, which very often formed the parapet itself. The slopes were always very gentle, and the works were generally invisible at a few hundred yards, even when no attempts were made to conceal them."[76] The use of slight undulations in otherwise flat and open ground provided an excellent field of fire to the defender. In addition, using the ground this way when constructing redoubts helped both to conceal the redoubt and to speed up its construction. Thus, such a position could easily be relied on to anchor the defense in otherwise featureless terrain. This point was particularly pertinent during the Great War given the geography of Flanders, where very slight rises in the ground played a prominent role in tactical and operational battles. Defending these otherwise featureless positions became even easier when combined with the skillful placement of machine guns. Oberleutnant Hoess, an Austrian attaché with the Japanese, noted the guns' impact when he described the attack of Twenty-Third and Forty-Eighth Regiments, Sixth Division, on the afternoon of 31 August 1904, and they took very heavy casualties from only five or six machine guns.[77]

Providing a Secure Base

Now that moving supplies and men was so crucial, it was not surprising that Colonel Tulloch commented that all of the Russian defensive positions had been set up to protect, or at least cover, the rail line that served as their main line of operations in Manchuria.[78] Indeed, the Russians frequently had retreated in the face of a threat to their lines of communication. But the Russian Army subsisted via a single railway line thousands of miles long, and the army certainly would have been defeated far more quickly had it lost access to this railway line. Major Kuhn observed that "many of the Russian positions had been prepared with great care and with an abundance of time. The main Russian fortified positions along the railway were at Nanshan, Telissu, Kaiping, Tashihchiao, Haicheng, Anshantien,

Liaoyang, the Sha River, the Hun River, and Tiehling."[79] It is important to note that the railway was heavily fortified: protecting the lines of advance and retreat had become increasingly important because the army was consuming ever-increasing volumes of material in a modern industrial war. At Liaoyang the Russians went so far as to construct earthen parapets along the actual rail line itself, and they certainly helped during their withdrawal at the end of that battle.[80]

This protection provided to the lines of communication was particularly important given the massive use of ammunition by modern armies. Captain March noted the very heavy ammunition usage at the battle of Liaoyang, where Okasaki's brigade alone fired almost 425,000 rounds in three days of fighting.[81] Lieutenant Colonel Schuyler reported a Russian battery of eight guns fired 4,800 rounds in a small combat at Tashihchiao on 24 July.[82] The massive quantities concerned also reinforced the need for an army to remain relatively static in order to be fed and supplied.

Troops also used field fortifications for protected rallying points, if and when soldiers needed to withdraw in the face of the enemy. Schuyler discussed this point in his report:

> At that time [during the initial phase of the war] it was an ever-present idea in the minds and in the speech of the officers that the genius of the Russian Army was for attack and for forward movements, there being a very widespread impression shared in even by those highest in command, that the enemy would not be able to withstand the Russian bayonet. This no doubt had something to do with the lack of care in the location of field works, as they were only to be depended on for rallying points and to enable an inferior force to withstand the attack of numbers.[83]

The last part of the quote is worth noting, as it tied in with the other reasons for troops to dig in and demonstrates that these themes were not usually independent of each other.

While field fortifications were used to provide a rallying point, they also offered a jumping-off point for attacks. Capt. D. Robertson described this idea in the style of the day, putting it in a socially and racially descriptive context: "Indeed it may be said that the works of both sides exemplify, in a singular manner, the military characteristics of the two nations: those of the Russians built solely for defence, their many lines encouraging the inclination to retire; those of the Japanese mere footholds, whence to spring forward when the moment came."[84] These views fit in well with the social Darwinist ideas of the time regarding racial characteristics. They also reflect the mind-set of at least some of the war's observers, who chose to see the war's developments in these terms, thus contributing, perhaps, to some of the later misapprehensions about the lessons of the war.

Dominating an Area

Certainly field fortification was used in the Russo-Japanese War to dominate an area. The positions at Nanshan and those protecting Motien-ling, Telissu, Liaoyang, and Mukden all clearly did so.

The best example is probably found at Nanshan, where the position was formidable: here the land narrows to an isthmus, and the fortifications completely cut off any access by land to the rest of the peninsula as a whole. Further, the rest of the peninsula afforded no suitable place for an amphibious landing. This situation served to increase the importance of the Russian fortifications.[85]

The position itself was a very strong one. Its front was narrow, the hill upon which the fortifications were dug afforded a view over most of the surrounding country, and the terrain was relatively smooth, thus facilitating defensive fire. The sea secured both flanks of the 3,000-strong Russian force manning it under the able command of Col. Nikolai Tretyakov. In addition, the Russians had constructed extensive field fortifications, to which they had added a considerable network of barbed wire. However, they had placed their artillery batteries on the skyline, and the Russian entrenchments lacked concealment. The reports of Lt. G. R. Fortescue and Lieutenant Colonel Haldane implied that this position should have been virtually impregnable, but as the successful Japanese assault on 25–26 May 1904 showed, it was not.[86]

The pivotal moments of the Japanese attack also demonstrated some of the main tactical points to come out of the war: the destruction of a key Russian machine-gun position, the intervention of the Japanese gunboats with their heavy guns, and the cutting of the barbed-wire entanglements.[87] Silencing the enemy's machine-gun fire and cutting his barbed wire, as well as relying on heavy artillery to facilitate the process, were virtually identical to the issues that both sides faced later during the Great War. The Japanese had the additional advantage in that they were able to move some troops around the flank of the Russian positions, after they had sent a force to wade through the water at low tide. Thus, they threatened to cut off the Russian troops from their line of retreat, something not possible for the armies fighting on the western front.

Elsewhere, Captain March described the dominating positions at Bunsuling that the Russian Army had abandoned:

> At 7 a.m. on the 30th [June 1904] we moved out, passing through the Russian works at 10.30 a.m. These were in successive lines, well chosen, well made, with good roads cut to all points of the lines. The first line was on a saddle perpendicular to the road. It contained gun pits for 8 guns on the right of the road and for 24 on the left. These were supported by infantry intrenchments which followed the natural line of the hills and gave a slightly converging fire upon the valley, up which the Japanese must advance. The flanks of the position rested upon high hills, and these hills themselves were crowned with infantry intrenchments. The position could not be commanded by any point within effective range and covered the general line of retreat. The intrenchments and gun pits had been constructed at leisure and were typical, presenting no new features, except that it may be said that they were vastly superior to the Russian earthworks at the Yalu crossing, which were extremely poorly made both as to type and to position.[88]

Clearly these positions were constructed to dominate the routes of approach to them. Captain March went further: "Bunsuling is the natural line of defense for Motienling against an advance from the south. The abandonment of these strong positions by the Russians without any fighting was a surprise to the Japanese and was undoubtedly a serious strategic blunder. The determined attempts of the Russians to retake the Motien pass on the 4th and 17th of July show that they realized their blunder thoroughly."[89] These fortifications were constructed to dominate an important strategic pass, which the Russians then failed to hold. Unfortunately this episode was typical of the Russian performance throughout the campaign.

Improving Technical Construction

During the war the technical construction of fortifications changed (see figure 4.2 for a more common style early in the conflict).[90] At its start, they had tended to be less sophisticated, and they were certainly not dug as deeply as they were toward the end of the conflict. Though normally not an issue, at times the ground was sufficiently hard or stony to reduce the troops' ability to dig deep fortifications. For example, the ground on top of the hills was often stony, and during the winter the ground was sometimes very firmly frozen.

In a report relating to a small action at Saimachi on 7 June 1904, the British military attaché Capt. J. B. Jardine described poorly constructed Russian trenches without head cover and no properly cleared field of fire, although the Russians had plenty of time to fix both. In this case, the Russians stuck around long enough for the Japanese artillery to start shelling them, and for their infantry to advance, before they quit the position. Jardine contrasted this fortification with a Japanese position of a similar size: it was well laid out, protected with abatis, had an excellent field of fire, was carefully concealed, and possessed top cover where necessary. His sarcastic comments about the quality of Russian generalship indicate that this disparity was not unusual:

> It is difficult to understand why the Russians attacked with such a force in such a way—it is charitable to suppose that not only were they in ignorance of the force opposed to them, but had no idea whatever about the Japanese prepared position—a frontal attack on a very strong prepared position held by troops far exceeding them in number both in guns and men,

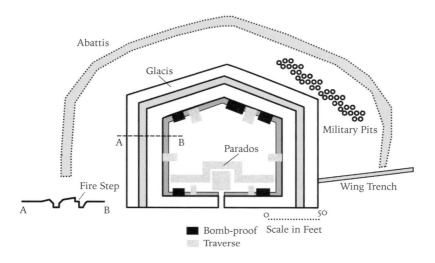

FIGURE 4.2. Russian redoubt near Likuanpu. This illustration and the plans in figures 4.3 and 4.4 show changes in the general pattern of Russian redoubts. Based on plans found in volume 3 of the War Department, Office of the Chief of Staff, *Reports of Military Observers Attached to the Armies in Manchuria during the Russo-Japanese War*, 5 parts (Washington: Government Printing Office, 1906–1907).

with apparently no scheme or plan of any kind. . . . Russian methods seem no better in attack than they are in defence.[91]

Eventually, the fortifications used during the war had more in common with the wars of the twentieth century than they did with those of an earlier age. Following the battle of Nanshan, Lt. Col. W. Apsley Smith visited the site and gave his impressions, which bear out this idea:

Guns in semi-permanent works *en-barbette*, with splinter proofs and ammunition recesses, platforms, stone and sandbag revetments. All work, even advanced works, closed all round by shelter trenches. Shelter trenches, 5 feet deep, two or three tiers in places, revetted sandbag loopholes, traversed, zigzag communications, but in many cases too wide for their depth, insufficiently flanked and traversed, and affording slight cover to distant oblique artillery fire. Very few, however, appeared to have been much damaged, though the pit-marks caused by the Japanese artillery testified to the accuracy of their fire. The size of the craters were also some proof of the effectiveness of their high-explosive common shell. Front and flanks of position, a network of barbed wire entanglements, with a number of mines (naval pattern). No facilities which we could detect for a counter-attack. Two searchlights. A number of machine-guns which were shifted as required.[92]

Describing the change in techniques, Major Kuhn cannot have foreseen what was to happen ten years later, but he noted that the field fortifications he examined in the inner line at Liaoyang "conformed to the generally adopted standards for field fortification. They were properly traversed, both bombproof and splinter-proof protection were provided, and the defending fire from the positions was interlocking and covered by military pits and wire entanglements."[93] Kuhn also pointed out that the redoubts discussed were situated on level ground and that none of them provided for the emplacement of artillery within them. This omission is significant in that artillery now possessed the range and destructive power to be kept out of the front line and thus better allowed for its own protection. Further, the infantry in the redoubts, equipped with breech-loading magazine rifles and machine guns, were better able to defend themselves without the need for close-range artillery support. The reduction in tactical depth of the redoubt's profile (see figures 4.3 and 4.4) limited the size of the target presented to the enemy artillery, thus increasing the difficulty of targeting and hitting the redoubt. The downside of the design, for the defender, was that it restricted the volume of flanking fire from the redoubt; however, when the defender used machine guns, that problem was not an issue, provided the defender possessed sufficient numbers of them. Thus, the increased firepower that a machine gun afforded also allowed for the construction of smaller, more compact, and better-concealed defensive positions.[94] It also enabled the defender more easily to use positions that supported each other and covered gaps

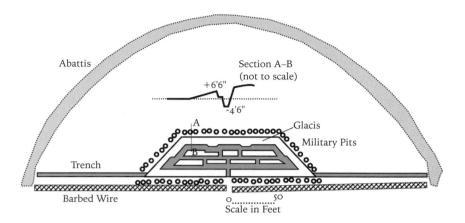

Abattis

Section A–B
(not to scale)

+6'6"

-4'6"

A

Glacis

Military Pits

B

Trench

Barbed Wire

0..............50
Scale in Feet

FIGURE 4.3. Russian redoubt near Shanlantzu. Based on plans found in volume 3 of the War Department, Office of the Chief of Staff, *Reports of Military Observers*.

in the line with fire rather than having to construct an unbroken line of trenches (see figures 4.5 and 4.6).[95]

Lieutenant Colonel Schuyler reported on the changing physical shape of the field fortifications:

Two of these regiments [part of the Russian attack on the Putilov position on the Sha River line 16 October 1904], advancing from the north, partially covered by knolls and villages, constructed hasty intrenchments as they progressed, and especially at the point where they halted to await the orders for the final assault. These works consisted simply of trenches constructed with the field-intrenching tools carried by the men and were entirely for kneeling or lying infantry. . . . It was quite early apparent that the shallow field trenches, hastily made under fire, would afford but little protection from shrapnel, and, in fact, the semi-permanent works at first constructed at Liaoyang and to the south of that place were much too open. At first there was a tendency to speak with derision of the narrow trenches found in the Japanese positions, but it was gradually recognized that this was the proper type; and after the battle

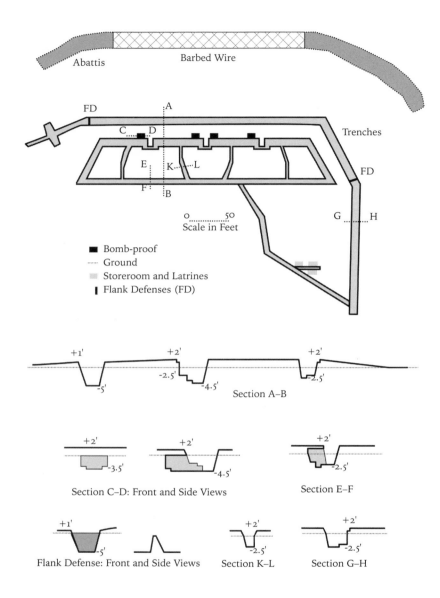

Abattis

Barbed Wire

FD

A

C D

Trenches

E K L

FD

F B

0 50
Scale in Feet

G H

■ Bomb-proof
⋯⋯ Ground
Storeroom and Latrines
▌ Flank Defenses (FD)

+1'   +2'   +2'

-2.5'

-5'   -4.5'   -2.5'

Section A–B

+2'   +2'   +2'

-3.5'   -4.5'   -2.5'

Section C–D: Front and Side Views   Section E–F

+1'   +2'   +2'

-5'   -2.5'   -2.5'

Flank Defense: Front and Side Views   Section K–L   Section G–H

FIGURE 4.4. Japanese field redoubt near Kangpienhsien. Based on plans found in volume 3 of the War Department, Office of the Chief of Staff, *Reports of Military Observers*.

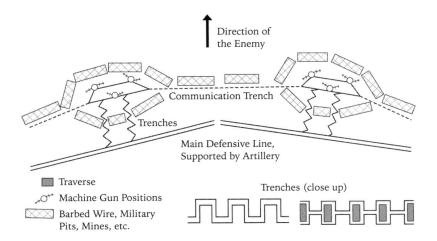

FIGURE 4.5. The Russian defensive system by 1905. This illustration and figure 4.6 are based on the plans of French attaché Lt. C. Bertin and show the sophisticated machine-gun positions of the Russians, as well as the width-depth ratio of the Russian redoubts. Bertin described it as the "Barrier of the Palladin Knight." 7 N 1700, Service Historique de la Défense, Château de Vincennes, Paris.

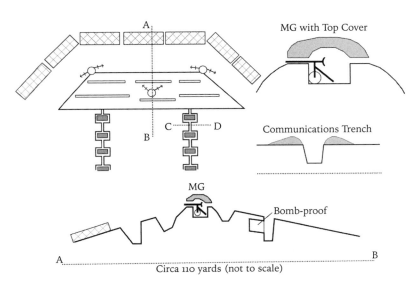

FIGURE 4.6. (*Detail of figure 4.5*) Another view of the Russian defensive system by 1905. Based on Lt. C. Bertin, 7 N 1700, Service Historique de la Défense, Château de Vincennes, Paris.

of Liaoyang all Russian trenches were made deep and narrow and furnished as speedily as possible with splinter-proofs so situated as to be quickly accessible as a protection from ordinary shrapnel. These blindages, so called, were covered with timber of about the size of railway ties and then with from 10 inches to a foot and a half of earth.[96]

Troops had used this style of deep, narrow trench during the fighting in and around Plevna during the Russo-Turkish War of 1877–1878. Thus, it is surprising that the Russians had to relearn its effectiveness from the Japanese.

Prior to the battle of Liaoyang, Captain Morrison commented that the Russians used breastworks of a "depth of trench 3 feet; height of bank, 1 foot 6 inches; making 4 feet 6 inches protection." However, they were frequently much shallower with a taller parapet (see figures 1.1, 1.2, and 1.4).[97] Seeing that this type of fortification would have presented a reasonably good target to Japanese fire and would have not provided a great degree of protection from Japanese shell fire might account for Captain March's comments on the issue.[98]

Choosing appropriate positions was an important part of the art of fortification. In a report Lieutenant Colonel Schuyler described some of the Russian positions he saw:

> The selection of positions was not always wise nor skilful, and it was apparent that the engineers, as well as many of the commanding generals, were novices. In illustration of this point I mention simply the tendency to put works on the sky line and to make the intrenchments the most conspicuous objects in the landscape. After the battle of the Yalu and especially after Telissu, there was much improvement in this respect, and as time went on much of the work done by the army and less by contract [much of the initial work, away from the front lines, was contracted to large numbers of Chinese laborers].[99]

A report of Capt. Carl Reichmann's somewhat contradicts Schuyler's observation. Reichmann noted that

in the First Siberian Corps and in the East Detachment [outside Liaoyang] the senior sapper laid out the work; the troops furnished the labor, the sapper officers superintended it, and for each company working in the trenches the sapper battalion detailed four men, who directed the work and saw that the dimensions, etc., of the work were correct. The trenches were constructed on the military crest and generally disguised. At Anshantien the trenches of the outpost brigade west of the railroad were constructed just inside kaoliang fields, and in some instances kaoliang had been planted on the superior slopes. In the main position the trenches were not disguised and the streaks of excavated yellow earth marking the trenches were visible a long way. When the commanding general caused the trenches to be manned the troops immediately gathered grass and grain from the fields and covered the excavated earth. At Liaoyang little, if any, attempts had been made to disguise the trenches.[100]

The differences between these two reports could be attributed to something as simple as the engineers being unavailable to help the troops whom Schuyler observed rather than the engineers being inherently inexperienced. However, British attachés also observed similar issues with the Russians. At the battle of the Shaho, Lt. Col. C. V. Hume observed simple Russian entrenchments on a hilltop that were no better than shell scrapes.[101] Admittedly, on the tops of most hills the ground was not always favorable to constructing fieldworks. Indeed, the rocky earth on the hilltops frequently limited the depth of trenches and forced troops to build them up, thereby presenting an improved target to enemy gunners.[102] That being true, constructing the works farther down the hillside or, as the Japanese did, digging them properly despite the rocky soil would have made more sense. Captain Jardine witnessed the Japanese working on their fortifications: "Owing to the difficult nature of the soil, the Japanese entrenchments were slight at first, but of course improvements were made as the hours passed. Generally speaking, the entrenchments, on being improved, took the form of breastworks with a very shallow trench, revetted with stones, of which there were plenty lying around about, and sods. The top was sodded to prevent splinters."[103]

The superior construction of Japanese works was again not lost on the observers. It is odd that the Russians themselves failed consistently to carry out these kinds of simple tasks, which would have better protected their men. This problem is highlighted by the proper works that forced Chinese labor constructed, thus indicating that the Russians did not necessarily lack technique.[104] One can surmise that their shoddy fortifications were owing to the poor quality of many of their officers and to the inexperience of their troops.

Later in the war this lack of proper preparation had started to change. Captain Morrison described various Russian defensive positions at Shoushanpu:

> In their rear, usually on the reverse slope, shelter was provided for men not in the trenches. These were generally covered so as to be splinterproof. . . . A zigzag covered way led back to the supports and reserves, at this point about 400 yards, and 1 mile respectively. The covered way was constructed by digging a trench about 5 feet wide and deep enough so that the earth excavated and thrown up on both sides would afford about 7 feet of cover. The supports and reserves were in villages, which afforded protection from shrapnel fire. Nothing new was offered in construction. Our manuals contain practically all I saw in that.[105]

So, despite the improvements that the Russian forces made, the Japanese were still digging deeper. The latter almost certainly did so because the Russians possessed modern quick-firing guns, and the Japanese had to provide deep fortifications in order to properly protect their troops. Captain Vincent noted a similar improvement during the fighting on the Shaho, where the Russians at last had made an effort to provide head cover for their troops.[106] By the end of January 1905, the Russians had worked to solve this problem. General Sylvestre reported that both Generals Siniewitch and Alexander Kaulbars had issued standing instructions for their troops to construct "deep trenches" as soon as a location was occupied. The orders also required enfilading trenches for redoubts, as well as the obstacles in front of a position to block or slow an enemy.[107] Thus, the Russians were catching up with the Japanese and finally doing what they should have been doing since the start of the war, particularly given their experience in 1877–1878 (in which General Kuropatkin had played a part).

Captain Vincent followed up the point about deep trenches, noting that the Japanese were digging deeper and improving the concealment of their fortifications. Again, at the battle of the Shaho he observed, "At 2:30 p.m. a Japanese battalion suddenly emerged from a trench north-east of Chien-tao to get water from the village. Even from my position on a high hill a few hundred yards behind, the network of trenches, covered ways, and underground shelters was extremely hard to detect in the bare brown soil. The whole Japanese army seemed to be underground."[108] The profile of the field-works were lowered based on the experience gained during the war. As Major Kuhn discussed in his report, the profile of fortifications reflected the differing needs of the two sides:

> In general the Japanese fortifications were characterised by lower parapets, with flatter superior slopes, and wider trenches than the Russian works, a portion of the excavated material being thrown to the reverse side of the trench. The form of parapet adopted by the Japanese lends itself better to concealment, but the width of trench renders it more exposed to shrapnel fire. The greater width of trench has for its object, of course, the securing of lateral communication.[109]

Clearly the Russians were trying to restrict the effects of Japanese shrapnel and shell fire, while the Japanese wanted a trench that reduced the ability of Russian small arms fire to hit it and that increased the Russian artillery's problems in locating it. The Japanese emphasis on the attack also required wider trenches that were easier to vacate and that facilitated the lateral communication necessary for enhanced coordination of forces. Given that the Japanese were primarily on the offensive and the Russians on the defensive, the two sides had adapted the type of fortifications that best suited their respective purposes.[110]

In an exception to the general trend of the war—that of improving the protection of fortifications—not all positions were being provided with head cover, despite the medical observers' observations about the locations of wounds. In a report on the Japanese medical services, Maj. Charles Lynch, an American medical officer who served with the Japanese forces in Manchuria, noted that not only had the location of soldiers' wounds changed but also the number of head and neck wounds had greatly increased largely because entrenchments reduced the men's exposure of other parts of their bodies.[111]

Despite this evidence Captain Morrison again noted, "As far as I could observe or find out by questioning, the hasty cover, either kneeling or standing, was safe cover from shrapnel while the men remained close behind it. Loopholing or giving head cover was not universally used as I had expected it would be where the works were deliberately prepared."[112] Major Kuhn also noted that overhead cover was generally not used in the firing line except where the lines were held for a long period of time, in which case overhead splinter-proofs were constructed.[113] Thus, despite the increasing lethality of artillery and infantry fire on the battlefield, unless each side deliberately could prepare fortifications in advance, neither one made much of an effort to provide head protection for the troops. The terrain offered little brush that conveniently could be used to revet fieldworks; thus, unless it was properly camouflaged, head cover was often dangerously visible.

The issue of concealment on the battlefield was now arguably more important than that of head cover. If positions could be seen, then they could be hit. Lieutenant Colonel Hume noted the contrast between the Japanese and Russian entrenchments at the battle of the Yalu on 30 April 1904:

[The Japanese positions] were very thoroughly prepared and entrenched, the entrenchments being made in the soft, sandy soil. Every advantage was taken of nullahs and any slightly rising ground, and everything possible done to conceal and disguise the trenches and pits with branches, tree, &c. . . . The

Kazanluk Redoubt in modern-day Bulgaria. Note model for scale. *Author's collection*

Boer trench, Pieter's Hill. *U.K. National Army Museum*

Boer shelter trench. *U.K. National Army Museum*

Boer trench, Magersfontein. *U.K. National Army Museum*

Dead British on Spion Kop. *U.K. National Army Museum*

Military attachés examining a trench on 203-Meter Hill. *Österreichishes Staatsarchiv*

Japanese approach trenches viewed from 203-Meter Hill and looking toward 74-Meter Hill. *Österreichishes Staatsarchiv*

Russian bomb-proof at Port Arthur. *Österreichishes Staatsarchiv*

Port Arthur forts before the siege. *U.S. National Archives*

Japanese dead in a Russian trench on 203-Meter Hill outside Port Arthur, Manchuria, during the Russo-Japanese War. *Österreichishes Staatsarchiv*

A view of 203-Meter Hill after the fighting. Military attachés can be seen examining this scene of the intense fighting. *Österreichishes Staatsarchiv*

Almost certainly Japanese dead, next to a destroyed wire entanglement at Port Arthur. *Österreichishes Staatsarchiv*

Improvised Japanese gun position, unidentified location. Note the gunner is below the level of the ground. *U.S. National Archives*

Russian trench at Liaoyang. It's worth noting the lack of head cover and any effort at concealment. *U.S. National Archives*

Russian wire entanglements and military pits at Liaoyang. *U.S. National Archives*

Bulgarian entrenchments at Adrianople. *U.S. National Archives*

Greek 12cm gun outside Bizani during the Balkan Wars of 1912–1913. *Service Historique de la Défense*

Greek artillery near Janina. *Service Historique de la Défense*

Greek field piece near Giannitsa, Greece. *Service Historique de la Défense*

Greek Nordenfelt gun at Janina. *Service Historique de la Défense*

Bulgarian shell scrapes. *U.S. National Archives*

Bulgarian artillery at Adrianople. *U.S. National Archives*

Hastily dug Turkish trenches at Lule-Burgas. *U.S. National Archives*

Turkish dead next to a poorly constructed earthwork at Kirkkilisse. *U.S. National Archives*

Turkish dead in a trench at Lule-Burgas. *U.S. National Archives*

[Russian] infantry trench consisted of a trench about three feet square in section with a high parapet revetted by branches. It was more in the nature of a breastwork and, as there was no attempt at concealment, was very visible.[114]

Consequently, Japanese artillery fire at that battle proved very effective. In a report written on the same day as Colonel Hume's, General Hamilton observed that the Russians had made little attempt to conceal their positions, while the Japanese had gone to great lengths to conceal theirs, including rearranging trees to cover some artillery pieces so that the woods appeared to be in the same place and placing some very conspicuous trenches for the Russians to see. As a result the Japanese were able to fire these guns without the Russians locating them throughout the action.[115] Thus, concealment in this context increased the physical protection that the Japanese-built fortifications provided. One of the lessons that the French attachés drew was that "invisibility was the only safeguard of artillery," and once it had been located, artillery was easy to destroy with modern weapons.[116] Occasionally, however, the Russians did surprise the Japanese, as at Haykontai in January 1905. Here the Japanese had crept up to within 200–300 meters of the Russian lines before launching their attack. Their assault was repulsed with heavy casualties by six Russian machine guns, which had remained concealed, thus protecting them from the more effective Japanese artillery.[117]

In addition, the Russians and Japanese increasingly used the kaoliang fields for cover both in attack and defense, particularly once they had grown to their full height. In a report on the battle of Liaoyang, Captain March quoted General Okasaki when describing his unit's action of 1–3 September 1904: "When darkness came, the artillery fire ceased, and the brigade in the *kaoliang* began to advance. It was the first time that we had fought in the *kaoliang,* which I think assists an attack, with care."[118] March continued with this idea when observing the battle of the Sha River, writing that the field of fire had been cleared of kaoliang and was thus exposed to fire from the flank.[119]

Not only was kaoliang used as cover, so too was night. Lt. Col. Edward McClernand, an American military attaché with the Japanese Army, noted that the available firepower provided an incentive to attack at night, and Japanese casualties were lower than expected. His implication was that night attacks reduced casualties.[120] March also noted the same tactic: if the infantry could not suppress the defender by artillery fire so that it could attack, then the infantry attacked at night.[121] Despite the confusion caused by marching at night on bad roads, troops were even forced to do their approach marches at night given the dangers of traveling during the day when the enemy was nearby.[122] Another benefit was the opportunity to remove defensive obstacles while relatively well protected by the cover of darkness, an operation that would have been virtually impossible to accomplish during the day.[123]

As it was not always possible to deal with obstacles at night, the men improvised a solution and used an updated version of a *pavis*. Usually it involved some type of armored shield that the engineer needing protection could shelter behind and move forward while going about his work.[124]

Concealment combined with the scale of the battle meant that knowing what was going on grew increasingly difficult; consequently, it had become virtually impossible for a commander fully to control his troops. General Sylvestre commented that the great extent of the modern battle space and the problems of the empty battlefield made it "impossible to follow the phases of combat."[125] A commander could not even easily observe his own troops once they were in action, let alone those of the enemy. This problem was to become all too familiar on the battlefields of the Great War.

The increased use of concealment mirrored the improvements in the use of field fortifications elsewhere. Captain Morrison noticed that where the Russian positions had once been poorly camouflaged and visible, later they were much better constructed and concealed.[126] Major Kuhn wrote of the Japanese artillery that

in selecting gun positions great attention was shown in the matter of concealment. Much of the firing was indirect, being controlled from an observatory or a near-by eminence or from a tree top. At Liaoyang, during the attack on the Shoushanpu position, the Japanese artillery took up its position in the fields of kao-liang, which had at this time reached its maximum growth, the fire being directed by observers located in tree tops, house tops, or on stepladders carried by the batteries and of sufficient height to enable the observers to look over the top of the kaoliang.[127]

Most likely the Japanese resorted to these techniques because their field artillery was inferior in quality to the Russian field artillery, with its more modern quick-firing guns and heavier weight of shot.[128] The Russians too had improved their ability to conceal them by that stage in the war.[129] Thus, the Japanese could not get their guns into action as easily as they had earlier in the war, unless they were concealed, lest they lose them to Russian counter-battery fire.

The Russo-Japanese War witnessed an increase in the use of obstacles, which became increasingly valuable with the rise of fire-power. Obstacles that delayed the attacker but did not obstruct the defender's field of fire were the ideal. So important had they become that the absence of obstacles and the poor construction of field fortifications were two main reasons for the Russian failure at the battle of Telissu. According to Lieutenant Colonel Haldane, because the Russians' fieldworks lacked sufficient strength, concealment, and any obstacles to impede the attacker's progress, the Russian defenders failed to make the most of their positions.[130] Thus, the increased weight and volume of defensive fire were no longer enough to hold a position. The attacker had to be held up and kept under fire, the defender had to remain concealed as much as possible, and the defenses had to be quite strong in order to withstand the enemy's artillery. With the attackers' artillery firing until the attacking troops were almost upon the defenders, delaying the attacking infantry as close to the front of the defensive positions as possible was very important. If done, the attacking infantry was likely to receive casualties from its own artillery fire, assuming it kept firing until the attackers were on the defensive position. If the artillery stopped firing while they were still held up on the obstacles, the defenders could emerge and pour fire onto the exposed attackers at short range. This issue continued to provide a problem for attackers during the First World War and was not fully solved until sufficient mobile firepower became available.

Most of the types of obstacles used in this conflict were not particularly new. Captain Morrison described, at length, the extensive Russian use of obstacles and the problems of dealing with them:

> Their removal cost many lives and added to the difficulty in carrying the positions. The Japanese custom was to detail engineer troops to precede the infantry line to cut the wires and remove obstacles. On a portion of the line August 31 three detachments of 22 engineers each were sent forward to open a way for the infantry assault. Of these 66 men 45 were killed or wounded. . . . High wire entanglements and deep pits were the most extensively used obstacles. The former was the usual form of high wire entanglement, the stakes being 3 or 4 feet high. Comparatively little barbed wire was used. It was chiefly heavy No. 8 wire such as is used on their telegraph lines. The deep pits were in three rows in quincunx order. They were about 6 feet in diameter and the same in depth, conical in shape, generally with sharpened stake at the bottom. These pits were sometimes added to by stringing low wire entanglements over them. . . . The mines were the stone fougasse, fired by electricity. Their moral effect or the dread of them was out of all proportion to any damage they ever did.[131]

The Russians expended an enormous amount of labor in constructing military pits, which would not have looked out of place at the siege and battle of Alesia in 52 BC, but they were largely ineffective as was much of the wire used during the campaign. The available wire was frequently smooth iron telegraph wire rather than barbed wire, and the men often did not stake it out securely. Such wire obstacles forced the Japanese to use troops to clear a path through them ahead of the main assault; however, they did not seem unduly to have hindered them. As mentioned previously, the absence of timber and brush did not permit much use of abatis, though both the

Russians and Japanese devised a type of wooden tripod that proved quite effective. The Russians sometimes cut the kaoliang eighteen to twenty inches from the ground to form a simple but effective obstacle.[132] The obstacles used during this war did not offer anything particularly new to warfare expect perhaps the extensive use of wire entanglements, although they were perhaps not as consistently effective as they might have been.

Conclusions

The Russo-Japanese War again demonstrated the importance of field fortifications. General Sylvestre, commenting on their general use and importance, said that "their utilisation incontestably is down to the effects of fire."[133] Though his comment is a little simplistic, it does sum up the situation. Both sides recognized fortifications' importance right from the start of the conflict, though the Japanese certainly treated their construction with more concern and skill than did the Russians. The Russians eventually did improve their fieldworks, but the Japanese had already moved forward and were digging deeper and better-concealed fortifications when compared to the Russian forces' by the end of the war.

Despite the improvements in technology, field fortifications still provided protection to the troops manning them as long as they were properly constructed. Their construction had become an important issue with the arrival of the modern high-explosive shell. Captain March discussed the effects of shell fire after witnessing an action on 26 August 1904:

> These guns opened at 10 a. m. with shrapnel, and after firing for half an hour changed to high explosive shell. In less than ten minutes after the Japanese began using this projectile the Russian infantry began to break and leave their trenches, and the Japanese infantry, charging up the hill, occupied the position. An examination of these trenches after the fight showed them full of Russian bodies with heads, arms, and legs torn off, lying in heaps, so that it was impossible to tell to what body the members belonged. The effect of this shell is enormous,

and we were destined to see exactly the same effect produced by it later—i.e., entrenched infantry break under it.[134]

Later in the same report, while on the road to Liaoyang, March also noted the densely packed Russian troops who would have been very vulnerable to accurate Japanese artillery fire despite their use of cover. He further noted, after observing an action that took place on 28 August 1904, that the Russian infantry fired volleys.[135] This action indicated that the Russian troops were not fully capable of independent action and that their officers needed to closely supervise them so that the troops would function as required. It also showed that the troops needed to be in field fortifications in order to be relied on to fight at all. This last point demonstrates the force-multiplying effects of fortifications. Perhaps understandably, the Russian troops would not have been likely to stand had they been forced to do so without proper cover.

Field fortifications reinforced the key tactical points on the battlefield. As the war progressed, the battlefields began to consist of long lines of trenches interspersed with redoubts to reinforce the key tactical points or to provide them where no geographic ones were available. What really helped in defending the key tactical points were machine guns. Major Kuhn described the Japanese forces' tactical use of machine guns:

> Tactically the guns are used primarily for defense and reserve their fire for short and mid ranges, up to 600 or 800 meters. On the defensive line of the Third Army after the battle of Mukden many machine-gun emplacements were noted. These consisted mainly of blinded casemates, 8 feet wide, 10 feet deep, and 3 feet 6 inches high, with from 18 to 24 inches of overhead cover. Importance is laid on concealing the guns, and it was claimed than none had been knocked out by the Russian artillery.[136]

This Japanese claim is credible given their care in using concealment and the Russian artillery's lack of high-explosive shell along with the corresponding reliance on shrapnel. With the thick layer of top cover described, shrapnel would largely have been ineffective against such a well-fortified position even if it had been spotted. This problem would become familiar and formidable to the troops fighting the Great War. It is no accident that both sides fully appreciated the effective results from, and value of, machine guns used in key tactical points.[137]

The Russian Army heavily fortified points along the railway line into and through Manchuria. This issue had become increasingly important because the industrialization of warfare and the long duration of battles placed a considerable strain on the logistic capacity of the fighting armies. It also placed a burden on the artillery, as the guns had to be moved continuously if they were to play their full role.[138] Logistics would become particularly problematic, for forces needed larger and larger guns to blast the enemy out of his increasingly sophisticated fortifications, but these guns were too difficult to move far from a rail line until the introduction of good all-weather roads and reliable motorized transport.

The Russians constructed lines of fortifications outside towns such as Liaoyang. They were designed to provide a base of operations from which to advance or retreat as the situation developed. They were very long, with the outer lines at Liaoyang being about fifty miles in length and those at Mukden measuring almost twice as long. They also served the purpose of dominating the area in front of them, much as the positions at Nanshan completely dominated access to the Kwantung Peninsula. However, unless these long lines were securely anchored on a fortress or a geographical obstacle, they were still vulnerable to a turning movement, which was amply demonstrated during the war.

Some relatively new features of the war included the regular use of the cover of night and the greater weight of artillery required to shift well-dug-in troops out of their positions. Captain March described the increased use of the cover of night and the consequent rise in the importance of cold steel:

In the Battle of the Sha River the use of night attacks by both sides, to which I have referred in previous reports, was again very noticeable. . . . Neither the Russian nor the Japanese army made surprise a feature of night attacks. Generally, before the attack, the position they desire to take is overwhelmed with artillery fire for an hour or so before darkness sets in and even after dark. Then the infantry makes its advance. . . . One of the most striking lessons of the Japanese war is the return to the use of the bayonet and sword upon the battlefield. This is greatly increased by the constant use of night attacks by both sides.[139]

This statement appears significant because of its implications for future warfare; yet March had either not seen or chose to ignore the medical evidence that contradicted his statement.[140] If he was being honest and did not have his own agenda, the night battles he observed possibly took place at much shorter ranges. Thus, the fight was not decided until the troops came into close proximity, creating the impression that it was won at the point of the bayonet—even if its use had only been threatened.

The American attachés observing the war were under no illusion about one of the main lessons. Captain Morrison described the use of field fortifications: "Great reliance was placed on field intrenchments, and their use was very general. Once in the presence of an enemy the intrenching tool seemed next in importance to the rifle and ammunition. The rule on both sides seemed to be to always cover their positions with entrenchments as soon as taken up, even when held only for a short time."[141] Lieutenant Colonel McClernand stated that the U.S. Army had fallen behind others in adding entrenching tools in the routine equipment distributed to soldiers and that the Russo-Japanese War clearly demonstrated the need to do so.[142] Though this next opinion was not universal, Major Kuhn wrote that the war did not demonstrate any dramatic developments in the use of field fortifications and seems to think the war imparted nothing new.[143] It is worth noting that the U.S. Army ordered entrenching tools to equip American troops in 1913.[144]

The increased use of field fortifications, particularly deep trenches, led to the need for heavier guns and indirect fire. A heavier shell could blast apart fieldworks, and indirect fire both better protected the artillery from counter-battery fire and allowed for steeper plunging fire, which was more likely to hit a trench than a gun firing along a flat trajectory. To that end, the Russians made widespread use of indirect-fire artillery at the battle of Liaoyang in August 1904 and continued its use thereafter. Lieutenant Colonel Schuyler made an interesting observation about some unforeseen problems with the weight of the Russian guns: "The new field gun, being heavy, was ill adapted to travel on Manchurian roads in the wet season, and in addition to the exhaustion of the animals, guns and ammunition wagons were several times lost through abandonment in the mud. A notable instance of this was the loss of a battery by the rear guard of the First Corps on the withdrawal from Anshantien to Liaoyang in the latter part of August."[145] This example is significant because although forces required heavier and heavier guns to break up enemy defensive positions, there was not a sufficiently developed road or rail network capable of handling larger artillery. In that situation, any advance would stagnate until the heavy guns were put into position. Thus, in the future inadequate transport networks would cause major attacks to stagnate quickly, assuming they could even get started—a problem that became all too familiar during the First World War. Thus, heavy guns would make an army become increasingly static simply in order to deploy and supply them properly. At the same time, they were necessary to resume mobile operations and blast defenders out of trenches. Once an army had again become mobile, its attack would break down if it encountered further defensive positions—until sufficient heavy guns were brought forward to restart the cycle. This defensive-offensive relationship provided the Gordian knot of the Great War.

5

The Balkan Wars

The Balkan Wars of 1912–1913, which provide the last of our case studies, were chosen because they occurred immediately before the First World War and had many parallels with that conflict. They bore witness to heavy fighting between conscript armies that were organized along the lines of the contemporary European models (except for Montenegro, which lacked a general staff), were equipped with a variety of modern weapons, and were ideologically nationalistic.[1] The armies were also fairly large in relation to the size of the states involved: Montenegro's active army had 35,600 men; Serbia, 190,000–230,000 men; Greece, 120,000 men; Bulgaria, 350,000 men; and Ottoman Turkey, 400,000 men, with large manpower reserves.[2] The Balkan Wars were also the last conflicts before the great upheavals of the twentieth century to include large numbers of foreign military observers. Thus, they provide a convenient end point to this book and highlight many of the changes that first came to worldwide attention shortly afterward.

Following their defeat in the Russo-Turkish War of 1877–1878, the Ottomans were keen to reform their military. The sultan himself, Abdul Hamid II, formed a commission of inspection to identify the causes of the military failures, and he established a German military mission beginning in 1882. Lt. Col. Colmar Freiherr von der Goltz served this mission until 1896, during which time he exerted a powerful influence on the direction and shape of the reforms of the Ottoman military. The reform measures improved the structure of the army and overhauled its system of conscription. Tactics were changed to reflect von der Goltz's understanding of modern war and his belief that an entrenched enemy could be attacked only with the proper coordination of infantry and artillery. They were further revised after the Russo-Japanese War of 1904–1905, where Col. Pertev Bey had been an observer and had stayed in close contact with von der Goltz (who still retained influence in Turkey) during the conflict. The officer corps also was rebuilt, and large numbers of elderly and incompetent officers were forcibly retired though not without strong resistance. By the early twentieth century, the Ottoman Army had grown in size and confidence.[3]

The army had its problems too. Frequently, the reserves (the Redifs) were very poorly trained and lacked the necessary ammunition and money to practice required skills.[4] The burden of service fell mainly on the peasantry from Anatolia, with exemptions for Arabs, Kurds, and others.[5] There were shortages of modern rifles, so older models had to be used,[6] with units suffering all the consequent problems of using nonstandard equipment. Heavy artillery was in short supply as most of the newly purchased modern weapons went to equip permanent fortifications.[7] The army also had woefully insufficient numbers of pack animals and other transport to haul weapons and supplies, placing a severe strain on the army's ability to conduct mobile operations. Finally, a new wave of reorganization of the army's entire structure and deployment was instituted in 1911, which was scheduled to take ten years to fully complete.[8] Thus, despite reforms much work still needed to be done. When war broke out, the Ottoman Army was in a state of flux, which goes some way to explain its poor performance.

Similar to the Russo-Turkish War of 1877–1878 and—to a lesser extent—the Russo-Japanese War of 1904–1905, the Balkan Wars have not been widely studied. This oversight is because the Great War started right after the Balkan Wars, eclipsing them in brutality, scale, and intensity. The Balkan Wars were, however, of interest to the contemporary armed forces. Indeed, as during the Russo-Japanese War, attachés from a large number of countries traveled to witness the conflict, with almost all of the European nations represented.[9]

The observers in the theater of war experienced several problems. During the First Balkan War, the Turks and Bulgarians banned both attachés and correspondents from their frontline armed forces, and they also forbade any discussion of military operations.[10] That being said, the ban was ineffective and had only a limited impact on the reporting of the first conflict. It neither stopped the attachés from reaching the front nor prevented them from traveling with the various headquarters.[11] However, banning the attachés from the front lines during the Second Balkan War—following the Greeks' decision to prohibit military attachés' visits to the front owing to their suspicion of the activities of a Hungarian officer, Colonel Tanczos—as well as the second war's short duration made it more difficult to report on that conflict.[12] Attachés had little time to circumvent the ban and make their own way to the front. Understandably, most of the best eyewitness accounts came from those men who observed the First Balkan War. Further, as the reader will see, their reports contradict historian Richard Hall's assertion in his book *The Balkan Wars, 1912–1913: Prelude to the First World War* that the military attachés "ignored many of the tactical lessons" and that they failed fully to note the impact of "various aspects of field fortifications."[13]

Terrain and Soil in the Balkans

The geographic area over which the Balkan Wars were fought (see map 5.1) had a distinct influence on the course of the campaigns. The terrain in the southern Balkans is very difficult, consisting of several mountain ranges that run obliquely north to south. In addition, the southern slopes are generally steeper and more difficult than the northern slopes, meaning that access to the north through the ranges from the south is much more arduous than vice versa. Heading south, the mountain ranges tend to lead toward the ocean. On the coast there were no easy lateral communications other than by sea.[14]

In his article "Balkan Geography and Balkan Railways," Lord Noel Buxton similarly described its geography. He also noted that the valleys frequently were fertile and rocky and that communications were poor, reporting one road he took as being the "only road in European Turkey that appears secure and employed for commerce."[15] He

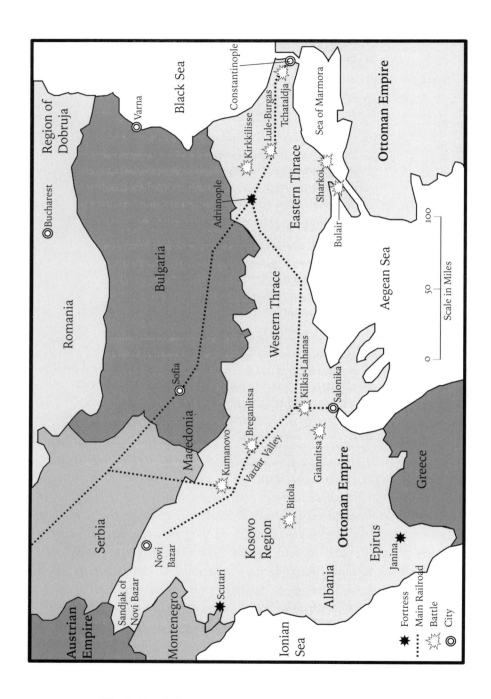

MAP 5.1. The Balkan Wars, 1912–1913.

went on to comment on the Turks' "dislike of cover" and that they had "cut down all of the forests in the vicinity of towns."[16] Presumably this measure was to prevent the local peoples from ambushing the Turkish troops and indicates that the Turks did not have full military control of many areas. The rocky ground did not appear to have hindered the movement of infantry,[17] showing that the rocks alone did not form major obstacles. Given these and other factors, Ottoman power in the lower Balkan Peninsula rested largely in the southeastern part of Rumelia (eastern Thrace), close to Constantinople.[18] This area was heavily cultivated, and according to the American military attaché Lt. Sherman Miles, the soil was "easily turned with the spade."[19] The area also had the best rail network and port access close to the Ottoman capital, both of which were vital for moving reinforcements from Asia Minor during a crisis. Finally, as this last area was relatively open and much less mountainous, it was where most of the heaviest fighting took place.

The Campaigns

The Balkan Wars were rather confused with several different countries all fighting with their own agendas at the same time, and as such only the major events will be discussed. Serbia, Montenegro, Bulgaria, and Greece collaborated to form the Balkan League, whose aim was to assert its national claims against the weakening Ottoman Empire. Following several years of crisis and tensions, the first of the Balkan Wars erupted on 8 October 1912 when the Montenegrin Army tried to besiege the Ottoman troops in the fortifications at Scutari (Shkodër). Given the small size of the Montenegrin Army, it could only accomplish this goal with the aid of Serbian troops, who joined them on 18 November 1912. The Montenegrins' premature attack gave the Ottomans notice that they would have to fight in the Balkans and allowed them time to make peace in their war with Italy before the major fighting started.[20]

The geography of the southern Balkans greatly influenced the flow of the wars, and as such the campaigns will be dealt with according to the geographical area in which they took place. The Bulgarian and Serbian General Staffs decided that their main military effort would take place in Thrace and Macedonia, respectively. This decision was dictated not only by geography but also by the relative size of their respective armed forces. Bulgaria, possessing a larger army, was to take on the bulk of the Ottoman troops in eastern Thrace, which also had the physical space for their deployment. Bulgaria was also aware that it would need to conquer Macedonia from Thrace, as the mountains and transport network did not allow a more direct approach from Bulgarian territory.[21]

Though Greece was not expected to play a major role on land, the cooperation of its navy was essential to the plan and was tasked with preventing the Ottoman fleet from landing troops on the coast of southern Thrace. This action would limit the Ottoman Army to ferrying troops across the Sea of Marmora and delivering them to the meager transport network available there.[22] The league recognized that this would offset the larger numbers of men available to the Ottoman Army once the reserves started to turn up in force.

The plans of the Ottomans and the Bulgarians were similar. Both sides wanted to take the offensive in Thrace. The Bulgarian plan sought to destroy the Turkish Army but did not envisage an attack on the fortifications at Adrianople (Edirne), because it was deemed to be at odds with the central aim.[23] In contrast, the Ottoman plan was, essentially, defensive and called for a more passive posture in all areas.[24] The Ottoman minister of war Nizam Pasha countermanded this plan and ordered a general offensive against the Bulgarians.[25] The goal was to draw the Bulgarian forces into a battle of annihilation.[26]

The Ottoman Army's forward movement led to disaster at the battle of Kirkkilise (Kirklareli), 22–24 October 1912. The battle took place along a thirty-six-mile-long front between Kirkkilise and the fortress city of Adrianople. Kirkkilise was also an Ottoman fortress, though the fortifications had not been maintained and amounted to little more than a "few neglected earthworks."[27] Furthermore, the two main forts in the town had only four artillery pieces between them.[28] After the first contact, many Ottoman troops retreated, their morale broken by the pouring rain, the poor conditions, and the combat with better-armed, trained, and motivated Bulgarians.[29]

Following its victory at Kirkkilise, the Bulgarian Army was slow to pursue the retreating Ottomans because of the poor roads and the heavy rain. This delay allowed the Ottomans time to set up a twenty-mile-long defensive position from the Erkene River running past the village of Lule-Burgas (Lüleburgaz) northeast, to a line of rugged hills anchoring the Ottoman right flank. The position itself was quite strong, being a virtually unbroken ridgeline between two geographical features; it also possessed a good field of fire for the defenders. The Ottomans had dug in, but their entrenchments frequently were shallow and poorly constructed. The battle opened on 29 October with a Bulgarian attack on the whole Ottoman line. Four days of rain, regular attacks by the Bulgarians, and heavy fighting eventually took their toll on the Ottoman forces, which fought better than they had at the battle of Kirkkilise, almost certainly because they were entrenched. But with their ammunition supply dwindling and their right flank threatened, the Turks eventually panicked and ran.[30] The largest battle fought in Europe between 1871 and 1914, it cost the Bulgarians 20,000 men and the Ottomans 22,000.[31]

Delays followed owing to supply problems, and the Bulgarian Army again was unable to pursue the retreating Ottoman Army effectively. This respite allowed the Ottoman forces to withdraw to the lines at Tchataldja (Çatalca), which were hastily being improved for the defense of Constantinople.[32] Despite the positions there being incomplete, they formed a strong line, and the new works were well suited for the defense.[33] The Bulgarians launched several large attacks, but they neither broke through the Turkish lines nor had the means to turn the flanks of the position that were anchored on the coasts.

With the help of Serbian troops, the Bulgarians had also started to besiege the fortress at Adrianople, which guarded the main rail line to Constantinople. The Bulgarian General Staff did not launch an attack on the fortress given the likely cost, especially following the failure at Tchataldja. At this point a stalemate ensued in Thrace.

The western Balkans also witnessed heavy fighting but not on the scale of what had occurred in eastern Thrace. Montenegro had attacked the Turks at Scutari, with little success, and had occupied parts of the region between Montenegro and Serbia (the Sandjak of Novi Bazar).[34] However, the Montenegrin people felt they had little to show for their efforts, in part because their minor success paled in comparison with that of the Greeks, the Serbs, and the Bulgarians.

The Serbian Army also had moved troops into the Sandjak of Novi Bazar and advanced south toward the Vardar River valley from Serbia. Ottoman troops in the valley advanced north to attack the Serbian troops, under the same orders as their compatriots in eastern Thrace. The battle of Kumanovo on 23–24 October led to disaster for the Ottomans. In what proved to be the decisive battle in the Macedonian campaign, the Ottoman Army panicked and then fled, and a Turkish soldier attempted to assassinate the Ottoman commander, causing further confusion.[35] Following another brief fight, the Serbian Army occupied the town of Monastir (Bitola) on 19 November. Thus, within a few weeks, the Serbian Army had occupied most of Macedonia, Kosovo, and parts of northern Albania.

The Greek Army's main goals were the port of Salonika (Thessaloniki) on the Aegean coast and the fortress town of Janina (Ioánnina) in Epirus. The flow of the campaign was similar to those of the Serbian and Bulgarian forces, with the Ottomans soon retreating after putting up only a very brief initial fight. They did stand and fight on 1 November at Giannitsa (Yannitsa), where they were joined by troops retreating from the Serbian advance on Monastir; yet despite the reinforcement, the Ottomans were still defeated. The Greek forces continued their march to Salonika, which the Ottoman garrison surrendered to them on 8 November (the Greeks having offered better terms than did the approaching Bulgarian troops, an event that sums up much of the politics of the war). The advancing Bulgarian Seventh Division asked to join the Greek Army in the occupation of Salonika. The Greeks initially refused this request but later relented, and a joint occupation was begun. Cracks were starting to open up in the cooperation between the opponents of the Ottoman Empire.[36]

In Epirus, the Ottoman forces under the command of Esad Pasha put up a much stronger fight, contesting the Greek advance every step of the way and over some of the roughest terrain in the region.

The Greeks were able to advance only very slowly. Though the Greek troops eventually reached Janina, at first they were unable to surround it.[37] The Ottomans, meanwhile, had reinforced the garrison there and supplemented the permanent works with field fortifications constructed in the stony ground.[38] The Greeks did not have sufficient men or artillery to take the fortress and thus became stalled outside the town.

The First Balkan War came to a halt with victory for the members of the Balkan League and an imperfect armistice on 3 December. Both sides had been exhausted by their efforts and chose to start negotiations, except the Greeks continued their active operations in an effort to capture Janina before any deal might be reached. The Greeks kept the Ottoman garrisons at Scutari and Adrianople in a state of informal siege and cut them off from outside help. Having carried out most of the heavy fighting and having taken on the bulk of the Ottoman troops in the theater of war, the Bulgarians demanded a greater share of the spoils. This stance led to tension with their erstwhile allies, and relations with Romania also deteriorated due to the increased strength of the Bulgarian position.

This armistice came to an end following a coup by the Young Turks—not their first one—on 23 January 1913 that overthrew the Ottoman government. The aims of this coalition of progressive reformers included continuing the war to retake some of the lost provinces and to avoid ceding some islands in the Aegean to Greece.[39]

In an attempt to relieve pressure on Adrianople, the Ottomans launched an attack from the lines of Bulair (north of modern-day Demirtepe on the Gallipoli Peninsula) on 8 February. The Bulgarian advance to Tchataldja had cut off the Ottoman forces on the Gallipoli Peninsula, where they sheltered behind fortifications that the British and French had originally built during the Crimean War. During the lull in the fighting, the Ottomans reinforced their troops there, using their control over the Sea of Marmara to transport men and supplies. They launched their offensive with 50,000 men—a 5:1 advantage in manpower—however, the Bulgarians had more artillery,[40] which was to prove decisive. In some of the bloodiest fighting of the wars, the Ottomans launched repeated attacks against the Bulgarian positions. In the face of fierce artillery and machine-gun fire, they gained some initial success but at a very heavy cost, and eventually they were pushed back to their starting positions. The attacks cost the Ottoman forces 6,000 dead and up to 18,000 wounded; Bulgarian losses were less than a thousand men.[41] This difference clearly indicated the cost of attacking an entrenched, highly motivated enemy on a narrow front who was well equipped with machine guns and artillery. The Ottomans' task was made even more difficult given that there were no flanks to turn. This experience was repeatedly borne out during the 1914–1918 war.

Supplementing the attacks at Bulair, the Ottomans launched an amphibious assault at Sharkoi (Şarköy) to the northeast of Gallipoli. Initially they were successful, but they were forced to withdraw in the face of Bulgarian resistance and the failure of the attacks at Bulair.

The collapse of the armistice and the Ottoman attacks at Bulair and Sharkoi increased both the military and political pressure on the Bulgarian Army to take Adrianople. It resumed the shelling of the fortifications and town, though the artillery was not sufficiently powerful to do much damage. The Bulgarians lacked sufficient heavy artillery and had to request help from the Serbs. Serbian heavy artillery arrived on 13 February, and pressure on Bulgarian commander Gen. Mikhail Savov to assault the fortress increased.[42] He resisted. His men were struggling with the cold and wet winter, and he was worried about the probable heavy casualties. He was also aware by the middle of March that the garrison had only three weeks' supply of food left and that it would be a simpler matter to await its surrender.[43]

However, eventually he was forced to give in to the political pressure, and he ordered an assault for the evening of 25 March. The attacks were greatly successful, and the fortress surrendered the next day. Presaging artillery's role during the First World War, the key to the successful assault was the brief but ferocious fire that the heavy artillery brought down at the critical point of attack. The Bulgarians had stocked up ammunition for this precise purpose and secretly had moved the Serb guns into position ahead of time.[44] Col.

Jean Frédéric Lucien Piarron de Mondésir, who studied the fortifications shortly after they fell, stated that the 12cm and 15cm howitzers rendered great service to the success of the attack.[45] However, despite this triumph, relations between Bulgaria and Serbia worsened owing to increased tensions over the fate of Macedonia. Furthermore, this assault cost the Bulgarians almost 11,000 casualties, a portentous result.[46]

In the western Balkans, the Greeks still continued their sieges (to use the term loosely) at Janina and Scutari. They also pressured the Ottomans and reinforced the troops outside Janina by drawing on those troops who took Salonika. From December 1912 to February 1913, they wore down Janina's defenses, launching several attacks before finally taking the town by assault on 5 March.[47]

In northern Albania, despite the occasional Montenegrin shell, the armistice had allowed the Ottoman defenders of Scutari to rest, improve their positions, and await developments. Once the armistice broke down, Montenegrin king Nikola I ordered the immediate capture of Scutari. Launched on 6 February, the assault failed with heavy Montenegrin casualties of 4,000 men. The main reasons for their defeat were they lacked both heavy artillery and sufficient troops for an effective attack. Therefore, the Montenegrins turned for help to the Serbians, who dispatched 30,000 men and seventy-two guns.[48]

The Montenegrins' failure to capture Scutari was unexpected,[49] and it presented a problem to them because the Great Powers were busy localizing the conflict and deciding the future shape of the Balkans.[50] Without possession of Scutari, the Montenegrins would not be likely allocated it as a part of any postwar settlement. Thus, their taking of the town assumed ever-greater importance as time went on and the Great Powers moved closer to an agreement. Eventually the Great Powers reached a consensus on the town's fate before Scutari fell, which left the Montenegrins with a difficult decision: either give up the siege to pacify the will of the Great Powers or defy them by continuing the siege and presenting a fait accompli to the world. They chose the latter. After being effectively cut off from help for several months, the Ottoman garrison at Scutari surrendered on 22 April owing to the severe lack of food.[51] However, with the Austro-Hungarians prepared to take military action and an assortment of ships representing the Great Powers off their coast, the Montenegrins were forced to give up the town on 5 May.[52] This last action signaled the end of the fighting in the First Balkan War.

The Treaty of London, of 30 May 1913, ratified many of the gains of the Balkan League and created an independent Albania. Crucially, it satisfied neither the Balkan League nor the Ottomans, and all parties wished to revise the details. Thus, within a few short weeks, fighting again broke out. For the second round of combat, Bulgaria rather than Turkey was the object of attack. The Bulgarians, Greeks, and Serbs squabbled over Macedonia; the Romanians attacked Bulgaria to press their claims to Dobruja; and the Ottomans wanted to take back Adrianople.[53]

Bulgaria wanted to gain control of Macedonia and believed that its army's victories against the Ottomans would allow it easily to brush aside both Greek and Serbian forces. Fearing their attack, the Bulgarians under General Savov launched a strike against the Serbs on 29 June 1913. Confusion in Sofia—King Ferdinand favored renewing the fighting and the government opposed it—did not help the decision to attack. Savov was fired, reinstated, and fired again, all within the opening few days of the war. This disruption led to immense upheaval in the Bulgarian Army, and it is not surprising that the force's attacks were repulsed. In the south, the Greeks easily overwhelmed the small Bulgarian garrison in Salonika. The Greek Army then took the offensive in Macedonia and, after heavy fighting at the battle of Kilkis-Lahanas, forced the Bulgarian troops to retreat.[54]

The Bulgarians were still withdrawing from Macedonia when the Romanians decided to press their claims to Dobruja, declaring war on 10 July. The Ottomans then joined the fray on 12 July and advanced. Understandably, the Bulgarians were in a very difficult position. Having withdrawn almost all of their troops to fight the Serb and Greek forces, the Bulgarians were unable to defend themselves against the new aggressors. Romania quickly occupied the territory it claimed, and the Ottomans did the same, recovering Adrianople without firing a shot on 23 July.[55]

Despite the Ottoman and Romanian interventions, the Bulgarians were able to stabilize the situation with the Serbs and Greeks but only after some heavy fighting. Both sides were exhausted by this stage and eager to seek an armistice, which was agreed upon on 31 July and brought the fighting in the Second Balkan War to a close. The treaties of Bucharest and Constantinople set new boundaries and stripped Bulgaria of most of the original land it had conquered, though it retained a part of western Thrace that included an outlet on the Aegean. Serbia, Romania, and Greece all gained territory, but the settlements were temporary. The Great War erupted less than a year later.

Fortifications: Preventing Desertion

The use of field fortification prevented desertion in the Balkan Wars of 1912–1913, as it had done in previous conflicts. No direct evidence indicates that it was used for that express purpose, but it had that effect nonetheless. Desertion was only an issue of note for the Turkish forces during the first conflict and only seems to have been a major problem in that war's opening stages. After the initial battles, when the war had settled down into a series of sieges, desertion became less of an issue, though the political machinations in Turkey continued to cause problems.

This pattern stemmed from the regular defeats that the Ottoman Army suffered at the start of the war and from the confusion and lack of cohesion precipitated by the Young Turks' coup of 1913 and the military's ongoing reforms. In addition, large numbers of non-Muslims in the Ottoman Army, including ethnic Bulgarians and Greeks, perhaps understandably, deserted at the first opportunity. This opening presented itself with the first Ottoman defeat and subsequent chaotic retreat at the battle of Kirkkilise, where the American military attaché Lieutenant Miles commented that Ottoman deserters provided a useful source of information for the advancing Bulgarians.[56] Following their defeat at the battle of Kumanovo, British vice consul C. A. Greig in Monastir likewise noted that "many

[Ottoman troops] have deserted and are in hiding."[57] As with Russian troops in the latter stages of the Russo-Japanese War, demoralized and disaffected Ottoman troops took advantage of the chaos of retreat to desert.

As previously shown, troops found it safer to desert when away from the dangers of the battlefield itself; however, there is a difference when examining the issue of desertion from fortified places. During the Balkan Wars, men deserted the fortifications at Adrianople and Janina. Consul L. L. R. Samson, the British military attaché at Adrianople, commented on the non-Muslims and Bulgarians in the Ottoman ranks, "many of whom have deserted at every possible opportunity."[58] He went further in another letter, stating, "There have been a large number of desertions during the armistice, but these too have been mainly confined to non-Moslems."[59]

At face value these examples might indicate that field fortification was not effective in preventing desertion, but the important point is that the desertions took place during the armistice, which was a relatively safe time to leave fortifications and especially to desert. Further, non-Muslims and Bulgarians had much less to fear from their enemies across the barbed wire, and it was probably easier for the deserter who was not obviously an ethnic Albanian or Turk. In addition, Hall mentions in *The Balkan Wars* that desertion from Janina was easy because it was not completely surrounded.[60] The local population in northern Epirus contained more Muslims than did other areas in Macedonia and western Thrace, making it safer for Ottoman soldiers to desert there.

That Scutari is not mentioned with the other fortresses regarding desertion is important. Its defending troops initially were not completely cut off, but they were some of the few Ottoman troops who had successfully held their ground in the early stages of the war. In addition, a larger number of Muslims was among the garrison, and the Montenegrin besiegers of Scutari never fully lifted their military pressure on the fortress. So the defenders of Scutari had less reason to desert than did their compatriots elsewhere, they were farther from safety, and they had enjoyed success. Thus, they were less likely to consider desertion in the first place.

Providing Physical Protection

The Balkan Wars really drove home the importance of providing protection for troops because any lack of proper physical cover on the battlefield often proved deadly. Major Yanikieff, chief of staff of the First Brigade of the Fourth Division of the Bulgarian Army, compared the use of cover with a lack of it: "The fire of the enemy's batteries was harmless, because the battalions were already entrenched and because the shrapnel burst too high. . . . Only the space behind their [the Ottoman] left flank formed an exception [to the few casualties in the trenches]. That was literally covered by their dead."[61] Clearly this example indicates the importance of cover; however, simply throwing up some earthworks was no longer sufficient. Indeed, they had to be properly constructed in order to be fully effective, because the power of modern guns had increased, and larger numbers of them were available to the warring sides. Full account had to be taken of the enemy artillery, which had superseded the rifle as the dominant factor on the battlefield.

Given the range and power of artillery, all sides quickly found that their troops in the area of the battle needed to be properly entrenched. This lesson, though, was lost on the raw recruits of the Ottoman Army who frequently failed to dig in adequately. In a report on the Serbian Army, the fate of poorly entrenched Ottoman artillery was clearly noted: "At Monastir the whole of the [Serbian] heavy artillery went into action at ranges varying from 5300 to 6000 yards and as at Kumanova the target was the Turkish batteries and the heavy artillery did fearful execution against a gun position containing 14 guns situated at a road junction just north of Monastir."[62] Lieutenant Miles commented that "against the shallow trenches of the Turks at Lule-Burgas the Bulgarian shrapnel was very efficient, and was an important factor in the victory."[63]

French military attaché Lieutenant Colonel Fournier reported that Turkish trenches at the battle of Kumanovo were shallow breastworks of only half a meter deep with a one-meter-tall profile. Properly constructed works with head cover meant that troops were almost invulnerable to shrapnel, but without such fortification the Turkish infantry suffered greatly.[64] The Bulgarians suffered too. American attaché Maj. J. R. M. Taylor noticed the same problem during the fighting at Tchataldja, where "the Bulgarians left some 1000 dead mostly killed by shrapnel against which their hastily constructed trenches did not afford protection."[65] The Bulgarians had not had time to entrench properly, and they were punished for it. This circumstance was certainly not down to routine bad practice, as the French officers Capt. G. Bellenger and Colonel Piarron de Mondésir pointed out that "the Bulgarians always entrenched even their reserves when they came under fire, but their trenches were often constructed for shelter only, and had no field of fire."[66] Presumably, surviving the enemy's artillery fire was now of greater importance than gaining a good field of fire partially because the defender's artillery had become more critical in defeating an attacker. Indeed, artillery had become a key enabler for both the defense and the attack. Thus, the fire of the defending infantry was less consequential for defending a position, provided the infantry had good artillery support.

This is not to say that entrenching a position was pointless. On the contrary, it was more important than ever, and properly constructed works were very effective. Rudimentary field fortifications also provided some benefit; even if they did not protect against the full effect of the enemy artillery, they could still be useful against small arms fire. With the increasing use of machine guns, the combatants normally took this important point seriously. As their allies did, the Serbians too routinely dug in when their infantry advanced: "The stages of several infantry attacks could be followed by the regular lines of intrenchments built during the advance. Intrenching tools were almost invariably used when attacking, and in view of the open nature of the country this was absolutely necessary."[67]

The Bulgarians also dug in while advancing, as Major Yanikieff's experience at the battle of Lule-Burgas demonstrates: "Under the deadly cross artillery and machine gun fire our infantry halted temporarily, and began to entrench."[68] Despite this halt, they went on successfully to assault the Ottoman positions. Clearly, these hasty intrenchments proved of some value. Of course, properly dug fortifications were better. British military attaché Lt. Col. G. Tyrrell observed the protection provided by gun pits at Tchataldja: "During the three days I had a good opportunity of observing the effect of Bulgarian artillery fire against two field batteries in gun-pits on left of Mahmudiyeh redoubt. These two batteries were about 50 yards behind the crest. About 2,000 shell fell in and around them. Two men were killed (one in each battery), and five wounded. Other result nil, though the shields were struck by many bullets."[69]

It is important to note that the Turkish artillery at Tchataldja was under the supervision of a major named Lehmann, and the Ottoman Eighth Division was under the command of Lieutenant Colonel Lossow, both of whom were German officers attached to the Turkish forces.[70] Their need for German advisers is perhaps best explained by the fact that during the First Balkan War, this level of Turkish competence was frequently the exception: "The Servian [*sic*] Artillery always took up covered positions and fired by indirect laying. Even in these positions the guns were frequently entrenched and in consequence their losses in personnel and horses were insignificant. The Turks, however, either placed their guns on forward slopes or just behind the crests of hills and their losses were enormous."[71] Thus, the Ottomans' failure in providing protection was not simply about their inadequately constructed fieldworks but also about their lack of concealment. Given the increased range of artillery, concealment had become an important part of the art of fortification and almost as important as the use of the spade in its construction. Bellenger commented, "All the belligerents agree that a battery seen on the move is lost."[72] Accurate and long-range fire could quickly be brought down upon it once spotted. According to Major Taylor, the skillful use of cover was a reason for the effectiveness of the Turkish artillery at Tchataldja as "the initial positions for Field Artillery, howitzers and heavy batteries are invariably 'covered', well behind the crest so that in most cases not even the flanks would be visible."[73] He continued to explain in a later report:

> It is difficult if not impossible to accurately judge the effect produced on a line of defiladed batteries. This is proved by the battle of Tchataldja. The Bulgars began by an interminable

bombardment of the Turkish batteries. They, well sheltered behind parapets or in positions behind the crests valiantly endured a storm of iron and fire without suffering anything but very small losses. The Bulgarians thought they had sufficiently paralysed the Turkish artillery and threw their infantry forward with the results we know [a very bloody failure].[74]

The Turks' success also relied on their gunners' fire discipline, which helped to persuade the Bulgarians to attack. Yet neither this discipline nor their use of covered positions was universally applied. As the Bulgarian officer Lieutenant Colonel Alexandroff, who commanded a group of the Bulgarian Fourth Field Artillery, commented in an interview with Lieutenant Miles,

> Nothing can be said for direct fire. Everything is in favor of indirect fire, except in the event of the enemy's approaching so near as to be in the dead space formed by the mask of the guns. . . . At Karagatch the Turks had flank batteries so well hidden that they fired all through the first day without being located by us, and kept up a cross fire on our fighting lines which eventually brought them to a standstill. They also took up direct fire positions with many of their batteries from the first day, and eventually left 36 guns in position there, most of them disabled.[75]

This report is again clear evidence that concealment is an important component of protection. Direct artillery fire was too dangerous even to consider in anything other than an emergency. Yet, with the exception of the deployments at the lines of Tchataldja, the Turks routinely used direct fire, which gravely exposed their artillery to the enemy. They consequently lost 300 of the 530 guns they used in the first conflict.[76] Thus, even when they were concealed, troops still needed to be well dug in, so in case they were observed they could have a decent chance of survival.

Enhancing Fighting Power

That fortification heightens a force's fighting power was again demonstrated during the Balkan Wars, particularly in the case of the reservists. Consul Samson, a British official in Adrianople, did not doubt the benefits of fortification in relation to the fighting power of troops when he commented on the Ottoman reservists there:

> The *moral* [italics in original] [sic] of the Turkish troops has not recovered from the shaking which it received at the commencement of the campaign when the forces covering the town were driven into it. The Turkish rank and file with whom I have spoken on the subject freely admit the superiority of the enemy, and seem to have lost confidence in their own officers. Many of the latter also allow that the redif divisions are of doubtful value, and that it is courting disaster to oppose them to the Bulgarian regular troops. These divisions have, of course, by now gained a certain experience in fighting, but it is not yet safe to employ them in the open, for their officers are not equal to the task of handling them. There is, however, every reason to believe that behind earthworks they could be depended upon to give further proof of the stubborn defensive qualities which have characterized the Turkish soldier in past campaigns.[77]

Following the disasters of the early part of the campaign in eastern Thrace, the Ottomans were forced to use Redifs to help man the last defensive line guarding Constantinople. The Bulgarians expected to face poor-quality, demoralized troops "largely supplied with Martini rifles."[78] The considerable efforts put into strengthening the lines at Tchataldja with field fortifications improved the Ottomans' confidence enough to resist and repulse three days of Bulgarian attacks on 17–19 November 1912.[79]

The Ottomans did manage to hold off the Bulgarians at Tchataldja, though they were loath to admit that Redifs were in the front line. As Taylor reported,

> It will be noticed that two Redif Divisions have been sent across the causeway [on the extreme left of the Turkish lines]. One Redif Division alone is kept in the front line and placed where it is least liable to attack and where retirement is most

easy. The staff officer with the party insisted that there were no Redifs in the front line, implying they were not fit for such a position, and it was only from Muhieddin Bey that it was discovered that a division of the class was holding the right flank. Apologies were constantly made when Redifs were passed, who did not stand to attention or salute, that they were poor ignorant children and not regular Turkish troops. . . . The trenches which run along the whole line of the main position are well sited, generally about 400 yards forward of the crest line and enormous labor has been expended in digging them. There are wire entanglements in place in front of them. Numerous communication trenches afford complete cover for the approach of supports etc.; these latter are dug down about five or six feet and are about three feet broad.[80]

It is important to note the extent to which the Ottomans went to make the lines fully secure. Admittedly these lines were covering the capital, but the Turks needed to ensure that many of the available troops actually stood their ground, given that previously they had struggled to do so and given the numbers of Redifs in the front line. French military attaché Lieutenant Antoniat explained that the Turkish infantry sheltered behind field fortifications and, while holding the lines at Tchataldja, had "found something of the combatants of Plevna." In addition, the fortifications were much more important to their fighting power than the "threat of the invasion of Stamboul [sic] by Christendom."[81] The idea that fortification enhanced fighting power was further reinforced later in the war when "the Turkish infantry which had taken part in the retreat from Kumanovo and Monastir to Janina fought bravely at Janina and performed deeds of valor hardly to have been expected from soldiers who had suffered so many defeats."[82] As noted previously, after much neglect, the original permanent fortress of Janina—similar to that in Adrianople—was so in name only.[83]

Field fortification also facilitated better infantry fire as the firer used its solid surface to help physically support his rifle. This physical support allowed more accurate shooting. Yanikieff commented after the battle of Lule-Burgas that "our infantry stood higher in this respect. With its fine offensive spirit, it did not neglect the aid of the spade. It took advantage of night and every suspension of fire to create covering for more accurate and undisturbed fire."[84] This point is important, because with the stresses of combat, the vibrations of explosions, and so forth, troops under attack were less likely to have been able to hold a rifle steady. Further, given the physical support of the fortification itself, less well-trained reservists at least could be relied on to keep the muzzles of their rifles relatively level.

Where the enhanced fighting power provided by field fortifications really stood out in the Balkan Wars is when they were combined with the widespread use of machine guns and barbed-wire entanglements. This combination allowed small groups of well-protected men to put up resistance far in excess of their number. The comments of Major Velitcheff, a Bulgarian battalion commander in the Macedonian Division, speak to this point:

> The Servians [sic] used their maxims well — in many cases holding a position from 20 minutes to a half hour longer by the sacrifice of one maxim. In this way they were able to inflict serious losses on us when we took the position, and also secured the retreat in good order of perhaps a whole regiment to the next position. By deciding to sacrifice one or two maxims, for instance, all other maxims and all troops occupying the advanced trenches attacked have time to get back to the next line of trenches before the enemy can take the first trenches, guarded by the maxims. And the enemy loses severely in the attack.[85]

He continued:

> At Lukavitza I saw a Montenegrin lying dead across a heap of two or three thousand cartridges, which he had fired until our men got within 30 meters of the trench, and killed him. On the ridge between Bezikovo and Kamenitza I saw a Servian [sic], alone, stick to a maxim in a trench until we got within 20 meters of him. Then he got up and ran. . . . The moment

we appeared on the sky line we were received by the fire of the troops who had left the trench a few minutes before under cover of the maxim, and who were then installed in their second line of trenches.[86]

Velitcheff's observation is significant because the effect of machine-gun fire was commented on during the Russo-Japanese War but not in this context. Fewer machine guns had been available to the troops during that war, which, combined with their great effect, made it less likely that they would have been risked in this fashion except in extremis. Thus, when combined with fortifications, machine guns were an excellent means of enhancing fighting power. This effect was compounded by their effect on enemy morale, as commented upon by Miles: "It is the weapon for which the soldiers have the greatest respect. The men do not seem to worry much whether they were opposed by one or two of the enemy's batteries, and they seldom knew. But they always took a keen interest in the number of maxims they had to face, and seemed to regard it as a question of personal interest whether there were 5 or 6, or only 2 or 3."[87] This comment presaged what would occur on a massive scale only a few months after the report was submitted in April 1914. It also indicated why artillery had become so important: fortified defensive positions equipped with machine guns could effectively be dealt with only by artillery, which, if the defender was well dug in, needed to be both heavy and plentiful.

Reinforcing Key Tactical Points

In the Balkan Wars, troops again used field fortification to reinforce key tactical points on the battlefield. Often the landscape lacked good cover, which meant it had to be provided, and as such the importance of creating key tactical points ties in with the need for protection. With the increasing power of machine guns, well-placed fortifications with clear fields of fire were more useful than ever. The enhanced fighting power produced through the combination of the two meant that a well-chosen position on a battlefield could dominate the action at little material cost to the side possessing it. These factors combined further to enhance the fighting power of the troops.

During the Balkan Wars the observing attachés did not comment on the fortification of key tactical points as often as they had in previous conflicts. Almost certainly, its use was now taken for granted. Now they frequently mentioned redoubts without referring to their purpose. Indeed, what caused more comment was the absence of fortification in reinforcing key tactical points. Studying the field fortifications at Adrianople, Miles noted that "the line contained no strong supporting points, so necessary on that narrow ridge. Consequently, once it was broken, a series of flank attacks was practically certain to roll up the entire position."[88] It should be noted that the Turks had neglected the fortifications at Adrianople, not fully used many of the permanent forts, and dug most of their fortifications after the conflict had started.[89]

In contrast, the Bulgarian positions outside Adrianople were well constructed. As Miles comments,

> At Adrianople, as on the open field of battle, the Bulgarians showed great energy in entrenching. Their infantry redoubts and gun emplacements were made with the greatest care and labor. The redoubts, of which there were 34 in the East Sector alone, were generally in the form of ellipses, usually about 140 yards long and 50 yards broad. They consisted of deep standing trenches. . . . The trenches were run very irregularly, so as to bring fire to bear in all directions. They were excellently traversed. Communication trenches zig-zagged across the redoubts. Paradoses were built on the sides away from the enemy. Between, and sometimes in front of the redoubts, were the infantry trenches, also well constructed. All communications trenches were covered.[90]

It is important to note that he mentioned the positions the Bulgarians prepared elsewhere too, with the implication being this type of usage and construction was routine. The other notable point is the plan of the redoubts was remarkably similar to the newer forms witnessed in the Russo-Japanese War.

The use of fortification to reinforce a key tactical point was also applicable to the attack as well as to defense. Properly digging in facilitated an attacker's defense against an enemy counterattack. The original, captured fortifications might not be in the best position to defeat an attack from the opposite direction and would need to be strengthened if the new owner of the ground was to remain there. The Bulgarians made particularly good practice of this strategy at Lule-Burgas, as Yanikieff reports: "If the enemy had advanced, he would have found in the center of his former position E. of Karagac, an interesting and improved redoubt, with many traverses, communicating trenches and covered ways, and a well fortified position on the opposite crest. During the advance our infantry worked with the rifle and spade, and in many cases under the enemy's strongest fire."[91] With the addition of the portable firepower of machine guns, this redoubt could easily be turned into a veritable fortress.

Of course, should the combination of machine-gun fire and fortification not prove sufficient, obstacles could be added to assist the defense. Lieutenant Colonel Fournier noted, "The most important field fortifications are always protected by barbed wire entanglements [underlined in original]."[92] These defenses were quick to erect, portable, and very effective, and they formed an immense problem for the attacker when they were combined with machine guns and artillery.

Providing a Secure Base

Troops commonly used bases protected by field fortification during the Balkan Wars. The fortresses at Janina and Adrianople were such in name only, and they provided real value to the defenders only after they dug supplementary works. The same can be said of the lines of Bulair and Tchataldja, yet these places all provided secure bases for the Turkish forces in Europe. Thus, the Turks largely relied on the hasty construction of field fortifications in support of old, decrepit permanent fortifications. Even where the equipment necessary to the defense was available, they did not always use it. For example, they did not install the barbed wire at Adrianople before the war started, despite having already purchased it.[93]

In contrast, the Bulgarian and Serbian officers had their soldiers routinely dig in wherever they were. This preparation allowed them to use their positions both for protection and as a jumping-off point for the next move, secure in the knowledge that they would have a rallying point for their troops should it be needed. Further, given the long ranges over which modern artillery could fire, the routine use of field fortifications provided protection to the rear area services upon which the frontline infantry depended. Further, they were less susceptible to the harassing fire of enemy artillery.

The Serbs constructed three lines of field fortifications that covered and anchored on Kumanovo and Küstendil.[94] They both acted as a base of operations for their advance into Macedonia and dominated the area in front of them. Of the Serbs' routine entrenching, Fournier noted that "the Serbian soldiers very actively worked in the construction of field fortifications, protecting them with a network of barbed wire entanglements."[95] Field fortifications were relatively quick to dig, and barbed wire could be speedily set out, thus providing a convenient and fast method of securing a position. Given too the dangerous nature of the modern battlefield, troops usually were willing, if not always happy—as this author can attest from his brief service in the Territorials—to dig themselves in when ordered.

The fortresses already mentioned were also used at the strategic level. The Turkish Army in Thrace initially deployed with its left flank secured by Adrianople, which "forms a pivot of manoeuvre [being fortified] for the Turkish field armies, and may be used either as a base for offensive operations against Bulgaria, or as a support for the left flank of the Adrianople-Kirk Kilisse defensive line."[96] It is also important to note that when the siege took place, Adrianople was not a modern "manoeuvre fortress. It was at best but a position of temporary character."[97] The Austrians also shared this view at the time.[98] The Ottoman Army in Epirus retreated upon its base at Janina in face of a strong Greek advance, just as its compatriots in Thrace had withdrawn to the fortified lines at Tchataldja and Bulair—both using them as a secure base.

Dominating an Area

Extensive use was made of field fortifications for dominating an area, with the lines at Bulair and Tchataldja being the most prominent examples. These lines also served to provide a secure base as well as to protect the lines of communication. Following the experience of the First Balkan War, troops made even greater use of lines of fortifications in anticipation of the second conflict, preparing a number of them during the short period of peace between the two wars. Given the nature of the terrain in the Balkans, it was often a simple matter to anchor these lines on geographic features in order better to secure them and increase their utility. Increasing the scale of this example provides a prescient glimpse of the western front.

The lines at both Bulair and Tchataldja long predated the wars, but they had been largely neglected. Forces began working to reinforce both positions once the first war started. Despite the lack of regular upkeep, both positions were made quite formidable with the addition of extensive field fortification. Major Taylor commented that "the works of Bulair date from the time of the Crimean war, but they have been improved and connected by trenches and unless subjected to fire from the Gulf of Sarros will probably prove as difficult to take as the Bulgarians found the lines of Tchataldja."[99] Their flanks were anchored on the coast, and any attempt on them would have involved a full frontal assault. Thus, they completely dominated land access to the Gallipoli Peninsula. Furthermore, they also operated as a protected base for the Ottoman troops sheltering behind their protection.

Likewise, the lines of Tchataldja, which originally had been constructed during the Russo-Turkish War, had not been completed and required the extensive construction of field fortification to secure them. Similar to the lines at Bulair, they also had their flanks secured by the coast,[100] and they dominated the approach to Constantinople. Again, this arrangement meant they could not easily be turned. As with Plevna and the fortifications at Nanshan, the only real option for attackers at Tchataldja was a direct frontal assault with the risk of very heavy casualties. The Bulgarian expectations regarding the resistance they would meet at the lines of Tchataldja are interesting to note and are contained in an unpublished French report from before the war:

> These currently comprise only one main organised defensive line, but the two flanks have the sea to cover them, they present a front of 40 kilometres of admirable fields of fire, they are easy positions to defend, and they are difficult to force. In front of this new Torres-Vedras that bars the entry to the Byzantine isle, and which will defy Bulgarian attacks for a long time, but it will not be enough for the 40 days needed for the arrival of [Ottoman] reinforcements from Asia. Soon the ammunition will run out and Bulgarian élan will succeed.[101]

They did expect stiff resistance, but they believed that the morale of their men would be enough to overcome the Ottoman defenders, as the lessons of the Russo-Turkish War and the Russo-Japanese War had demonstrated so clearly. Though their preconceptions were misplaced regarding the lines at Tchataldja, they were proven to be correct at both Kirkkilise and Lule-Burgas. Thus, the Bulgarians could more easily put down their lack of success at Tchataldja to their own failings, rather than acknowledge the extensive fortification work and moral effect it had on the Ottoman defenders.

The Ottomans were capable of constructing fortifications where they were needed, even when there were no preexisting ones to work with. Vice Consul Greig in Monastir wrote,

> It is anticipated that an attempt will be made to hold the Kirli Derbend (north of Sorovitch) [present-day Amyntaio in Greek Macedonia]. If that position is forced from the south, or turned by a Greek force approaching, as is suspected, on the east from Vodhena and Ostrovo, a stand will probably be made at Banitsa, where Javid Pasha is reported to be entrenching so as to command the railway and the junction of the Sorovitch-Monastir and Vodhenir-Ostrovo-Monastir roads.[102]

Covering the rail lines, as was done in the Russo-Japanese War, was particularly important in the Balkans given the poor state of many of the roads, the limited options regarding transport, and the very difficult terrain in much of the region. This issue also highlights the importance of the fortress at Adrianople, which sat astride the main rail line to Constantinople.

Prior to the Second Balkan War, the Serbs were busy fortifying a base of operations and their positions dominating the railway lines along any potential line of advance against Bulgaria. To do so, they constructed "field works covering the line Trnovca–Kratovo–Uljari in Macedonia, and Pirot–Krupac in Serbia."[103] Likewise, the Greeks fortified the hills north of the Kresna defile. As Commandant Devignes, French military attaché in Athens, reported, "To the north of the Kresna defile was the large rough plain of Simitli, also closed to the north by a line of heights formed in half-circle, which form an excellent defensive position, like the first line at Simitli."[104] The Bulgarians, in anticipation of a second Balkan war, also were in the process of constructing works to guard potential invasion routes into their country: "The general method employed should be to create, at all points, strong detached fortifications, which, situated in the middle of the space to be defended, would make the passage impossible, or to constitute a line of forts which rests its flanks on two solid places (they copy our example, in the defense of the Hauts de Meuse)[the hilly area to the east and southeast of Verdun, in France]."[105]

Thus, increasingly all sides were using field fortifications for this purpose. They were starting to think about the best means for doing so when the Second Balkan War started.

Improving Technical Construction

What emerged from the Balkan Wars was that field fortifications, if they were to work effectively, needed to be dug deeply into the ground. It was rarely sufficient to dig breastworks or shell scrapes, particularly when in range of the enemy artillery. Further, they needed to be dispersed, with support trenches and reserves deployed farther away from the main fighting line in order to protect the men better. They also needed to be concealed, even when they were not in the immediate firing line. Top cover and splinter-proof cover were also needed, though the attachés rarely commented on them unless they were lacking, indicating that its provision had become a routine part of digging in too.

One of the most important observations about the First Balkan War is that the Balkan allies invariably were better dug in than the Ottomans were. Lieutenant Miles observed the Turkish field fortifications at Kazankoj during the battle of Lule-Burgas and commented, "The main line of trenches ran along the sky line, and no attempt was made to use the lower slopes. Often the trenches of supports of reserves were to be found within 100 yards of the firing line. The trenches were shallow and very inferior to those of the Bulgarians."[106] Having observed a later action he continued the theme: "Turkish kneeling trenches lined the crest of the ridge. They were a little better than those at Kazankoj. . . . Two Roman burial mounds form a prominent land mark. They rise to a height of about 30 feet. Extending in both directions were long lines of Turkish Infantry trenches, mostly of the converted type of kneeling trenches . . . badly made and shallow. Trenches for the supports were often within 30 yards of them."[107]

One could surmise from Miles's comment that the only well-constructed works in the Ottoman positions were Roman burial mounds, and his tone in the report is one of surprise when he does not see trenches, particularly deep ones. This report needs to be contrasted with his observations of the Bulgarians:

> Near the battery's position were several scattered Turkish skirmisher shelters facing a little west of north. On the eastern face of the spur there were two lines of Bulgarian skirmisher shelters; each line of a half company. These lines ran along successive small spurs of the main spur, separated by a distance of about 200 yards. They faced south of east. The little rock shelters were cleverly made by piling up rocks on top of each other or utilizing big ones for protection.[108]

Despite the rocky ground of the position, clearly these fortifications were superior to the Turkish works he had seen. He continued: "On top of the western spur of the ridge there was a line of deep and well made Bulgarian infantry trenches of the kneeling type. They were cut into the soft limestone rock."[109]

Other witnesses reinforced the veracity of these observations. Major Yanikieff viewed the battle of Lule-Burgas as a participant, commenting on the two sides' use of fieldworks: "The Turkish trenches were defective. They were mostly designed for individual skirmishers or groups with large intervals. There were also trenches for larger groups, and in places there were several tiers. But all of them were shallow, and gave no good cover from shrapnel fire. . . . The Turks, masters of entrenchments in the past, practically neglected the use of the spade during this war."[110] The inadequate Ottoman fortification practices contrast poorly with what French military attaché Lieutenant Colonel de Matharel observed: the Bulgarian infantry made extensive use of head cover to protect against the effects of shrapnel.[111]

The main exception was the fortification of the Ottoman artillery at Tchataldja, where Major Taylor reported,

> No epaulments [sic] were seen: the gun-pits being invariably sunk about 2 feet below the surface of the ground, the difficulty of dead ground and clearing the crest being overcome by the raised platforms in the right rear of each gun-pit. . . . In most gun-pits there was a splinterproof constructed in the parapet to the left of the guns, sunk a foot or so below the level of the floor and capable of sheltering all the detachment and also of forming an ammunition reserve.[112]

Clearly these fortifications were well constructed and concealed, though it must be remembered a German officer supervised these troops in their work. It is important to note that the Ottoman artillery first gained the upper hand over the Bulgarians at Tchataldja. Colonel Pomianowski, Austro-Hungarian military attaché in Constantinople, commented, "All the military attaches had the impression that the Turkish artillery fire was more accurate than the Bulgarian."[113] Again, this ability to fire more accurately was probably because of the Germans' influence. That is not to say that the proper construction of field fortification was the deciding factor in the series of battles there, but it certainly played an important role in the turnaround of events.

Concealment had become more important than ever before. Lieutenant Antoniat reported on the location of Bulgarian artillery positions at Lule-Burgas that they "established defiladed positions behind the crest, which were impossible to see."[114] Pomianowski also noted the Bulgarian artillery used concealment during the initial fighting at Tchataldja, where he observed that they "were very well dug in and were only detectable from the flash as they fired."[115] Regarding the concealment of infantry, he noted that "the khaki uniform of the Bulgarian seems to be too dark. Both with binoculars and the naked eye men can be seen at 4,000 to 5,000 m as though they were wearing black uniforms."[116] Thus, even the color of uniforms was becoming of greater importance in concealing men, and colors needed to be sufficiently drab to avoid easy detection. At the ranges he was discussing, the fear was that artillery would catch observed infantry in the open, which would mean almost certain slaughter.

Because of the power and range of artillery, it was important to conceal troops not only while they were in action but also when they were in the proximity of the enemy, and that distance now meant up to four or five miles. Lieutenant Colonel Tyrrell noted that "[the Bulgarians] appear to have dug trenches during the night, as each day fresh lines were visible nearer to the Turkish position, but all attempts of Bulgarian infantry to advance across the open during the day were easily defeated by the fire, both of artillery and infantry."[117] If night did not provide sufficient concealment, then screens could be used to block the line of sight to the men working.[118]

Fire discipline also became more important, as the infantry learned not to open fire unless it was necessary, given the corresponding loss of concealment and its likely consequences. Bulgarian officers commented that soldiers, once willing to open fire at anything in sight, became hesitant to open fire at longer ranges "due to the conscious desire of the infantry of both sides not to disclose their positions to the enemy's artillery, or to attract its attention."[119] This change in behavior does not seem to have affected the Montenegrins, as Capt. Gustav Hubka, an Austrian military attaché, commented,

"Fire discipline in the field is an almost unknown quantity."[120] This indiscipline might help to explain their relative lack of success when compared with their allies.

It is worth reiterating that the fortresses of Scutari, Adrianople, and Janina were a mix of permanent and temporary fieldworks. In the words of an unnamed Turkish officer, "the fortifications about Janina with the exception of the original ones built of concrete had all been improvised during the war. They are open trenches parapets [*sic*] built on a stony ground and piles of sandbags. Barrels filled with earth were also used. . . . The shelter trenches were made for men standing and well adapted to the terrain. [There were only a few of these properly constructed.]"[121]

Of the trenches at Adrianople, Miles observed, "They were never provided with head cover or sand bag revetments. Very few of them were loop holed. Consequently the men had to expose themselves when they rose to fire on the wire. This was particularly the case in the trenches which were above the entanglements. Considered as trenches of a besieged permanent fortress, they were remarkably poor."[122] He went on to point out that the artillery positions there were poorly concealed, if at all.[123] In defense of the Ottoman troops at Adrianople, Miles could have been commenting on the temporary trenches that lay farther out. An unnamed Russian officer described the outer trenches in a similar fashion while those of the main line of defense blended "very cleverly with the landscape and were well concealed from observation."[124]

At Scutari, an Austrian report noted that the Turkish trenches were about 1.7 meters (5 feet 7 inches) deep plus head cover; thus, they were deep enough that a man could stand without having to expose himself to enemy fire.[125] In addition, effective strongpoints added protection to the defensive lines (see figure 5.1). Scutari was also better protected by barbed-wire obstacles than Adrianople was.[126]

Obstacles were limited largely to the use of barbed-wire entanglements most likely because of their utility and the ease and speed with which they could be set up. Barbed wire, as had been shown during the Russo-Japanese War, was also difficult to destroy. The Serbians and Montenegrins discovered this fact at Scutari, where the

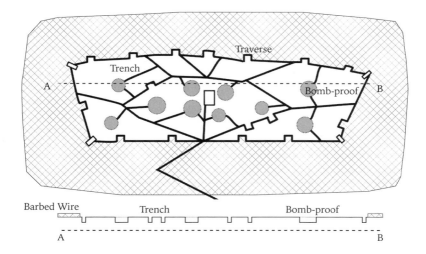

FIGURE 5.1. Turkish strongpoint at Scutari. The rectangles at the corners of the defensive position appear to be for machine guns, but this detail is not explicit in the original. Based on AOK-Evidenzbüro 3464; Die Befestigungen von Scutari und die militärische situation vor Scutari Anfangs Marz 1913.

effect of "artillery fire against the obstacles [barbed wire] was only small, overall they were left intact."[127] Miles reported the issues at Adrianople, where troops had made extensive use of barbed wire:

> The wire entanglement extended completely around the main line of defence, except in the north section of the East sector, where there were two small gaps. . . . It was the only obstacle used by the Turks. . . . The wire was run in every direction over the stakes and in such profusion as to form a jungle. It was laid on loosely, so that it sagged in the middle. This enabled it to resist shell fire and bombs very well. . . . As a rule the explosion of a shell did not sever it. . . . The only practical way of cutting it was by means of special cutters whose long handles gave them a powerful leverage. . . . The only unfavorable criticisms, which can be made on the entanglements are — (a) It was not high enough to prevent men crossing by throwing their overcoats and equipment on it and stepping on them. In cer-

tain places it was even low enough to admit of being walked across at the cost of torn clothing and flesh. Entanglements of the wire at Scutari, for instance, were from 1 to 1½ feet higher, and it was impossible to cross them except by cutting a breach or by raising them up on rifle butts and crawling under.[128]

This insufficient height for the stakes supporting the wire led to the erroneous reports that the attacking Bulgarian soldiers had thrown "their overcoats on the wire and succeeded in passing them by this strange expedient."[129] Miles contradicted these accounts: "Observing foreigners who visited the lines a few days afterwards remarked that no bits of torn clothing or equipment were to be seen stuck on the barbed wire. There is no doubt some men did get through, individually, by using their fixed bayonets and entrenching tools as axes, and hacking down the wire."[130] Clearly getting through the wire was difficult, whatever method was used, and for this reason Miles also noted that "the main object of the trenches was to enable fire to be brought on the wire and prevent its being crossed."[131] Serbian Gen. P. Bojovic noted that to make the job of the attacking infantry even more hazardous, the defenders at Scutari "attached blast grenades to the barbed-wire entanglements."[132] Presumably they served to deter the enemy infantry from attempting to cut the wire. It also foreshadowed the lengths to which defenders would go in order to protect their wire during the Great War.

Conclusions

The Balkan Wars clearly showed the importance of field fortifications. They also witnessed the ever-increasing need for better concealment and belowground protection. Even simple fortifications were of less use, as they did not provide sufficient protection against artillery fire, though they were still necessary to protect against rifle fire. The Balkan Wars also demonstrated that artillery had become the dominant arm in combat, as the infantry was unable effectively to attack or defend without its continuous support.[133] It had proved to be the key enabler for both attacking and defending positions, and without its support, success was difficult to achieve.

Field fortification also provided protection for the troops manning them; however, even more so than during the Russo-Japanese War, it was essential that they were well built. Achieving any noticeable effect on the troops manning well-constructed fortifications without the use of heavy artillery and high-explosive shell was very difficult, particularly if head cover and splinter-proofs had been built. As the Ottoman defenders at Adrianople found out, inadequate cover was of little benefit against an enemy with artillery as "the trenches and batteries, lacking head cover, loop holes and embrasures, were indefensible under the powerful artillery fire brought to bear on them."[134] Their compatriots at Janina were in the same situation: "The Greek shells inflicted great damage, the shrapnel on the other hand did almost no harm. The shells destroyed the Krupp guns and the artillery men were put out of action by horrible wounds."[135] This experience had important implications for the future. Wherever troops were positioned, if they were in range of the enemy artillery, proper cover had to be provided for them, including splinter-proofs and head cover at the very least. Even the battlefield communication routes had to be entrenched.

The protection provided by field fortification also enhanced the fighting power of the troops manning them, especially when combined with the machine gun and barbed wire. Though artillery had become the dominant weapon, the infantry most feared the machine gun. Miles observed, "The efficiency of the machine gun, particularly as a weapon for the defence of wire entanglements, impressed itself upon all Bulgarian officers. They spoke of it, always in connection with the wire, as the weapon they most feared, and the one which caused them the most losses."[136] This description presages one of the main tactical issues of the First World War. The combination of field fortification, machine guns, and barbed wire enabled relatively small numbers of defenders to defend key tactical locations against much greater numbers of attackers.

The sieges of the Ottoman fortresses and the fortified lines demonstrated that fortifications protected and provided a secure base. As Sir Gerard Lowther pointed out in a letter of 1 February 1913, the Ottomans in Adrianople had at that time already held out for 120 days, and they were accomplishing what their forebears had done at Plevna in 1877. They were tying up large material and human resources of the Bulgarian Army. He even commented that some Ottoman officials, unofficially, were hoping that these sieges financially would exhaust their enemies so that they would consider peace.[137] The stalemate induced through the extensive use of fortification helped lead to a more attritional form of struggle.

With the relative sizes of the armed forces and the spread-out nature of the area over which they all were competing, it was logical that field fortification was constructed to dominate an area. Given that they protected the troops and that relatively few men could be relied on to defend a position, this use of field fortification was the defender's cost-effective way of restricting the enemy to lines of attack chosen in advance.

The technical changes in the construction of field fortifications reflected the growing power of artillery; properly digging into the ground, as well as providing splinter and head protection, became more important. Without all of this effort, a position was exceedingly vulnerable to the effects of enemy artillery fire. If a position was properly fortified, however, the only reliable way that attackers could shift the defenders out of it without enormous casualties was through the use of heavy artillery and high-explosive shell. Observers regularly commented on this fact both during and after the war. Colonel Papadopoff, the chief of staff of the Bulgarian First Army, believed heavy guns were essential to support an infantry attack, and he advocated that his troops "should have howitzers of 12 and 15 cms. (4./" [4 ½"] and 6") attached to divisions."[138] Colonel Zagorski, another Bulgarian officer, also supported the idea that heavier guns are needed when facing well-dug-in troops and is quoted as saying, "A 3' howitzer is only a toy."[139] In addition, the use of high-explosive shell with delayed-action fuses proved effective,[140] as the delay allowed the shell to penetrate cover before it exploded.

The veracity of these views is borne out when examining the amount of Bulgarian artillery ammunition used, particularly the numbers of shell and shrapnel fired, as well as the amount of heavy artillery ammunition expended.[141] (See table 5.1.)

TABLE 5.1. Bulgarian artillery ammunition usage in the Balkan Wars, 1912 and 1913, by rounds fired.[142]

| Size of piece | 1912 | | 1913 | |
	Shrapnel	High explosive	Shrapnel	High explosive
75mm QF	52,600	145,166	5,000	27,708
70mm QF	9,700	20,225	2,230	7,267
12cm cannon	91	729	881	2,467
15cm howitzer	370	323	298	761

Note: QF stands for quick firing.

These figures indicate the vast increase in the amount of heavy artillery ammunition used during the second war, despite its more limited duration.[143] They also show an exponential increase in the use of high-explosive shell despite the lack of sieges. Lieutenant Colonel Alexandroff points out the usual role for each: "Shells [high explosive] were used for destroying trenches, earthworks, buildings, artillery and artillery positions. . . . Under certain circumstances we also used shell against moving troops, as when they were on sloping, rocky ground. . . . Shrapnel was commonly used against troops in all circumstances, and (with shell) against transport and artillery."[144] Thus, one reason for the greater use of high explosive was that gunners were starting to fire them more often and in a wider range of circumstances. They were also needed to break open field fortifications in order to support the infantry.

The large amount of artillery ammunition expended was important in that it pointed to a new issue that proved to be a problem for all sides at the beginning of the Great War—that is, providing an adequate supply of artillery rounds. The problem of supply was further complicated by the sheer quantity of small arms ammunition fired too. The Serbian Army used 13 million rifle rounds in the First Balkan War and 21 million in the second (in a month's fighting).[145] The Montenegrin Army used two-thirds of its stock of 20 million rifle and machine-gun cartridges in the war against Turkey.[146] Given the immense difficulty of keeping the troops fully supplied during the Balkan Wars, the large modern armies of industrialized states were likely to run short of ammunition unless the front was relatively static and convenient and efficient transportation routes were available. Until there was a sufficient number of good roads and reliable motorized transport, large-scale mobile operations eventually were likely going to be beset by logistical problems caused by the sheer scale of demand for ammunition; correspondingly, operations with a high tempo would soon get bogged down and grind to a halt.

The difficulty of destroying barbed-wire entanglements was again reinforced during the Balkan Wars. Lieutenant Colonel Fournier commented on the effects of artillery fire against fortifications and wire: "The experience of the Serbo-Bulgarian war confirmed the observations from Scutari of the difficulty for artillery, whatever its calibre, to produce a material effect or to destroy field fortifications and barbed wire entanglements."[147] This experience mirrored the problems faced during the Russo-Japanese War, and the troops adapted. According to British vice consul Harris, "The Bulgarians have hand-grenades, wire-cutters, and shields to protect them from rifle fire; in fact, all the paraphernalia the Japanese used in the storming of Port Arthur."[148] The enormous problems of dealing with barbed wire, however, later plagued troops during the First World War.

The Balkan Wars witnessed very heavy casualties for all the main combatant nations. The following figures include those caused by disease, but they do indicate the ferocity of the fighting. Bulgarian losses were 66,000 dead and 110,000 wounded, evenly split between the two wars. Greek casualties were almost 8,000 dead and 43,000 wounded; Montenegrins, 3,000 dead and 7,500 wounded; and Serbians, 36,550 dead and 50,000 wounded. The Ottomans lost an estimated 125,000 dead and 215,000 wounded or taken prisoner.[149] Acting consul general James Morgan, in Salonika, commented on the consequences of the scale of casualties, despite the brief length of the two wars. He noted that the Greeks were forced to broaden the conscription of troops to meet the army's needs; consequently, "fresh troops arrive daily from Greece, the recruits of 1913 having been called up, also those who for various reasons were exempted from service in 1902, 1903, 1904."[150] Thus, in a relatively short period of time, the Greek Army experienced a shortage of soldiers, as would the major combatants of the Great War; however, this shortfall did not seem to dampen the Greek combatants' martial spirit. Earlier Morgan had commented on a successful Greek attack at Kukush in Macedonia: "According to eye-witnesses the Greek troops showed astonishing courage and enthusiasm. The Bulgarian artillery fire is unanimously described as being of remarkable accuracy, but neither this nor the rifle fire of the enemy, strongly entrenched, seems to have been able to check the Greek advance."[151]

This point is the most important one of all: an attack against troops who were well entrenched and armed with modern weapons frequently was successful, much as the Japanese had been in 1904–1905, largely owing to the strength of the attackers' martial spirit. A number of major actions during the Balkan Wars bore this observation out: Kirkkilise, Lule-Burgas, Kumanovo, Janina, Adrianople, Giannitsa, and others. What they all had in common is the strategic and tactical aggressor in each case emerged victorious. The evidence of the Balkan Wars further reinforced a key lesson of the Russo-Japanese War: attacks under modern conditions could succeed, despite much evidence and argument that seemed to indicate the contrary. Indeed, it could be argued the failed attacks that provided evidence to contradict this lesson—those at Bulair and Tchataldja—were unsuccessful because they lacked adequate artillery support and a convenient flank to threaten. Such flawed execution and the unusual circumstances of fixed flanks hardly make them good evidence to the contrary. The reader is left with a set of lessons from the Balkan Wars that reinforce the preconceptions gained from examining the previous conflicts. These preconceptions about the feasibility of the attack were completely reasonable in the context of the time. However, during the first years of the Great War, they were ruthlessly exposed as being brutally out of touch with reality.

6

The State of Military Thinking in 1914

What, then, was the general state of military thinking and doctrine going into the First World War? Despite the obvious costs of recent conflicts, offensive warfare was still seen as possible or even likely, and, by and large, military doctrine emphasized the offensive as the key to winning wars. Some had significant differences of opinion with this view, most notably Ivan Bloch, a Polish banker who had written *The Future of War in Its Technical, Economic, and Political Relations: Is War Now Impossible?*[1] Bloch's views held that the offensive in a modern war was impossible, owing to a mix of economic and technical factors, as clearly demonstrated by recent experience. Much of the criticism of pre-1914 thinking has focused, often rather narrowly, on Bloch's writings, pointing out that his arguments about war and his views on the subject were correct and that he had largely been ignored. It was certainly not the case, and as usual things were much more complex than that rather simplistic view. This subject will be examined after the doctrine of the main powers has been discussed.

Following on from the defeat in 1904–1905, the Imperial Russian War Ministry introduced a new field regulation in 1912. Much simpler than the previous version, it upheld the principle that the offensive was the best means of deciding a conflict. While the stress on the offensive remained, the regulations did change their emphasis, with firepower now expected to play a much greater role in both the attack and the defense. In addition, following the experiences of the Russo-Japanese War, the regulation required that the defense be more active and that the defender construct field fortification, consisting of strongpoints, "obstacles, and interlocking cross-fires."[2] (See figures 4.5 and 4.6.) The regulation, however, still had a particular emphasis on the assault with the bayonet, though it made no provision to integrate artillery fire into the assault's final stage to facilitate its use despite the good coordination that the infantry and the artillery had obtained at the battle of Liaoyang.[3] Indeed, during the field maneuvers of 1912, the Russians worked their guns as they would have done in the early nineteenth century, starting to fire at 1,700 yards (well within modern machine-gun range) and galloping them in the open to a final position only 400 yards from the enemy.[4] In modern conditions this tactic was suicidal, but the Russian Army was still greatly affected by the traditional ideas of the offensive spirit, which is not surprising given the lesson taught to them by the Japanese. They had made some concessions to the increased importance of well-defended field fortification: the artillery was reorganized, and a 4.8-inch howitzer (at corps level) and an 11-inch siege mortar were introduced.[5] Furthermore, following their widespread use of indirect fire during the battle of Liaoyang, the Russian Army had persisted with this technique. However, its introduction and use was not properly coordinated with other arms, it was distrusted as a technology, and it was thus rendered much less effective than it otherwise might have been.[6]

This problem affected many other armies too. In France, similar ideas also held sway. In his book *The Lessons of History*, the historian Michael Howard quotes Col. Ferdinand Foch of France: "To charge, but to charge in numbers, therein lies safety. . . . With more guns we can reduce his to silence, and the same is true of rifles and bayonets, if we know how to make use of them all."[7] Thus, modern defenses would be overcome through sheer weight of numbers, combined with incredible bravery on the part of the troops. The need for very high morale to successfully achieve this was directly linked to the need to attack. According to the historian Dimitry Quéloz, the French military theorist Gen. Hippolyte Langlois saw morale as "revolving around three main factors: confidence in the commander, the concept of 'race' and the offensive spirit."[8] These ideas were inextricably linked with fateful consequences. The "cult of the offensive," as the historian and analyst Azar Gat points out, demonstrated that a massive gap had emerged "between military doctrine, preached with an almost fanatic conviction, and the realities of war."[9] Thus, in terms of doctrine, the coordination of machine-gun fire, barbed wire, and field fortification came as a particularly vicious shock to the French Army, which suffered a million casualties in the first five months of the Great War. In defense of the French, it should be noted that their thinking had heavily influenced the Bulgarians regarding the attack and the use of denser formations, and they had been very successful in the first of the Balkan Wars. However, they had moved away from these ideas following their initial contact with the enemy.[10] Perhaps 1914 was too soon for the full implications to filter through, and justifiably the French could point to the Bulgarians' initial success as a better indication of the correctness of the general idea.

Much as in Russia, the French Army saw a need for heavier artillery; however, the introduction of a new quick-firing 155mm howitzer was mired in a debate regarding its role. The howitzer and heavy batteries were most closely associated with siege warfare and a lack of mobility, making them secondary in importance to the needs of the mobile offensive.[11] The army also had concerns regarding ammunition supply and the guns' mobility that eventually saw each corps being equipped with only six. This number was hardly enough to shift the enemy out of their fortifications, as the offensive demands of French doctrine would require in order for it to be successful.[12] In addition, in 1914 because French artillery was still expected to fire directly, it was used "in full view of the enemy and suffering fearful attrition in the process."[13] Thus, the French Army's artillery doctrine was skewed to the needs of its concept of the conduct of offensive operations and did not take full account of the tactical developments since 1877.

According to Howard, the German Army had escaped the worst of the fashion for all-out attack and preferred instead to pin down the enemy with fire before launching an attack from the flank. Howard saw this strategy as a response to the bloody attacks of 1870–1871.[14]

The 1908 *Felddienst Ordnung* (*Field Service Regulations*) provides a clear reflection of this idea and is worth quoting at length:

> *Lines of skirmishers* [italics in original] on the move in the open, will suffer severely from the fire of unshaken infantry at medium and even long ranges. Their losses will increase with the density of the skirmishing lines. Long and uninterrupted advances of dense skirmishing lines are therefore impossible under effective hostile fire, at short and medium ranges. A further advance can only be effected by working forward gradually, supported by fire from alternate flanks. At the closest range, the heavy losses which will ensue will rapidly decide the result of the combat.[15]

While having rather less offensive spirit than the French doctrine, the German observation still accepts that heavy casualties are very much a part of the process. In addition, the author is not trying to claim the Germans alone had all the right ideas, as the same regulations make clear when discussing cavalry. Formed bodies of cavalry were still expected to have a role in a fight and to be able successfully to charge infantry, machine guns, and artillery given the right conditions.[16] The French maneuvers of 1912 seemed to bear out this assertion when a charge of the French First Cavalry Division captured the commanding officer and headquarters staff of IX Corps, along with the corps's artillery and four airplanes.[17]

The Germans did have an advantage, albeit an accidental one, in their war plans: the emphasis on the Schlieffen plan, first put forward in 1905 to deal with the likelihood of simultaneous war on two fronts, meant that the German Army would need to tackle fortresses with alacrity if it was to meet its schedule of advance. To deal with the threat fortresses posed, the army received an unexpected bonus of heavy artillery, which was, of course, ideal for tackling an enemy who had dug in. This superiority was still evident at the battle of the Somme in 1916, with terrible consequences for the attackers.[18] Further, the Germans noted that the Balkan Wars demonstrated that even modern quick-firing artillery lacked power against troops who were in field fortification, for the relatively high velocity and flat trajectory of most field artillery made hitting a belowground target very difficult. Thus, large heavy howitzers were the ideal weapon for grappling with troops who were well fortified. Almost certainly this view was owed to the involvement of those German officers who had advised the Turkish forces, particularly the Ottoman artillery, which had performed so well at Tchataldja in the Balkan Wars. This influence caused the Germans to accelerate their heavy artillery and howitzer programs, and this decision provided a consequent advantage in the attack.[19] The equipment of the army with heavy guns complemented the earlier introduction of an "indirect laying instrument" along with a new regulation for its use, and "by 1894 indirect fire had become the rule rather than the exception."[20] This development had an attendant benefit: even an imperfect use of the technique would give the artillery the ability to damage troops in field fortifications.

A corresponding additional emphasis on using heavy artillery in conjunction with field artillery to target the enemy guns went into effect in 1912.[21] This combination too was significant, as it enabled the Germans to obtain more easily a local superiority in artillery that was beneficial in both the attack and the defense. In addition, and for largely the same reasons, the engineers had been equipped with the 7.58cm *minenwerfer* (mine launcher), which was an early form of trench mortar. Owing to the effectiveness of this weapon, the infantry acquired it by the end of 1914. Furthermore, the Germans had identified machine guns as weapons that should immediately be engaged by artillery before they were able to engage the infantry.[22] All these developments provided the Germans with an initial advantage through their greater ability to deal with fortification and defensive weaponry, in all its forms, than the Entente Powers of France, Great Britain, and Russia possessed. This advantage was amply demonstrated when, compared with the Japanese assaults at Port Arthur, the Germans took the Belgian fortresses of Liege and Namur in only a few days and without great loss of life. Much credit for this achievement should be given to the use of the Austrian 30.5cm mortar, which was motorized and could be used away from a rail line.

In the U.S. Army, the offensive was seen as the only way to achieve a decisive success. It was considered possible because the improvement in the technology of artillery had more than outweighed the improvement in the power of small arms and was held to favor the offensive. However, the U.S. Army's *Field Service Regulations* of 1910 recognized that "it is impossible to shoot an enemy out of a position. To avoid serious losses, the defender has only to lie down behind cover; but a resolute and simultaneous advance on the front and flank of a position, made after thorough preparation by and with the effective accompaniment of artillery and infantry fire, will generally be successful."[23] This passage recognizes the power of fortification but clearly does not see the problems posed by a well-fortified enemy. The regulation goes on to describe how infantry in the attack should maintain a firing line that is "as dense as possible" in order to maintain a superiority of fire.[24] Though it does cover maintaining superiority of fire over the enemy, this effort too, much as with the French doctrine, was greatly reliant on closing with the enemy and on the bravery of its troops. Maj. Gen. J. B. A. Bailey points out that in the wake of the Russo-Japanese War, experiments conducted with indirect fire had led to its incorporation in the *Drill Regulations for Field Artillery* of 1907; however, no further interest seems to have developed, owing to a lack of relevant experience and the funds needed for training.[25]

The British Army too placed a similar emphasis on the value of the offensive as the only means to bring about a decisive success, which was to come through superior numbers, skill, and moral courage. The regulations emphasized that the "superiority of fire" would make the final assault possible, but the overall logic was similar to that of its contemporaries. The regulations devoted an almost equal amount of space, however, to the issue of defense and repeatedly suggested using trenches.[26] Their inclusion does demonstrate that at least some of the lessons of the previous wars had been digested. Of course, this information could have stemmed legitimately from the nature of service in the British Army, with its long stints garrisoning colonies and providing security against much larger numbers of potential enemies. Even though the British had recognized the need for indirect fire during the Second Anglo-Boer War of 1899–

1902, progress was slow and often met with stiff resistance in the Royal Field Artillery. Thus, by 1914 the artillery officers' ideas were still dominated by their experience in colonial wars, where direct fire was the norm. The British also suffered a consequent shortage of howitzers when war started,[27] a shortage that contributed to some of the problems that followed in 1914–1916.

In Turkey, the Balkan Wars had left the army in a better position than the other major powers had regarding experience. It was able to complete the military reforms that had been ongoing in 1912, and they indirectly led to changes in the officer corps and a general improvement in its efficiency. The one area where the Turks were weak was that they were desperately short of modern equipment.[28] Yet, as they were to prove in 1915, they really knew how to fight, particularly when they were in fortified positions.

The thinking in Austria-Hungary also placed the emphasis on the attack, with morale seen as central to its success. Hew Strachan commented that Austrian commander in chief Gen. Franz Conrad von Hötzendorf, as "one of its most vociferous advocates," believed that he "who seized the initiative" would determine the victor.[29] However, this enthusiasm should not be interpreted as blind adherence to the infantry attack, as Lawrence Sondhaus notes that Conrad had recognized, following his visit to the battlefield at Plevna in 1889, the need for artillery to support infantry in the attack.[30] There were problems with its implementation. Though the Austro-Hungarian Army recognized that firepower was the main weapon in the attack of a defensive position, it was short of artillery.[31] Another problem was the smaller size of the Austro-Hungarian Army when compared to those of its main enemies. In addition, there was a great deal of mistrust of new ideas, and its artillerymen "often remained ignorantly conservative."[32] Nevertheless, they had produced the previously mentioned excellent 30.5cm mortar, so there was hope.

Conrad was also well aware that the tactics he put forward were likely to lead to heavy losses. He argued that they were acceptable as long as they were not "so great, that the morale of the attacking troops broke down before their goal."[33] This limit was not quantified, so we do not know what he meant by "so great." Given his interest in social Darwinism, it could well have been astronomical. These ideas tied in with his views on the use of the spade, where he was of the widely held opinion that once men were under fire and had taken cover, it was very difficult to get them going again.[34] When the infantry regulations were revised in 1911, they maintained Conrad's emphasis on the attack with the bayonet. Field fortification was further deemphasized, and the role of artillery and machine guns received very little attention.[35] Overall, the Austro-Hungarian ideas were not that dissimilar from those of other countries.

The importance of field fortification was reflected in the issuance of entrenching tools in most of the armies. Tools were issued at the rate of approximately one per soldier in Germany, Britain, Russia, Belgium, and Austria, but France entered the war with only thirty-four tools per company. The number had been about double that, but it had been reduced to lighten the load carried by the men. In 1914 the United States did not routinely equip its infantrymen with entrenching tools.[36] Italy and the United States at least had the advantage of entering the war later. However, the French emphasis on the attack left the infantry sorely in need of tools with which to dig in should they wish to hold the ground that they might have captured. As this idea was well understood at the time, the failure to so equip the men seems perverse.

On the whole, the offensive was seen as the key to winning wars, and despite a number of contradictions, the lessons of the previous forty years had provided evidence that supported many of the prevailing views regarding its use. The main problem was that the wars prior to the First World War were not sufficiently large enough in scale or length to provide the full lessons that the immense changes in scale, technique, and technology would bring. Thus, although many of the lessons may have turned out to be false, largely they appeared correct in the context of the time. Perhaps the military officers of the day simply learned the lessons too well.

Other Views of War

The counter to the ideas of the use of the offensive, along with the implications for the fighting of wars, came largely from Ivan

Bloch and others — Norman Angell and Lord Lytton being the most famous — who argued, broadly speaking, that modern war was impossible because of both its sheer economic cost and the new technological developments that had made it so deadly. Bloch went so far as to claim that the people who believed war was possible under modern conditions were "utopians," an accusation frequently thrown at him. It is important to understand that the point he was making about war did not relate to, in his words, "trumpery expeditions against semi-barbarous peoples." Rather he was referring to a war among the Great Powers, which had become, in his view, "impossible alike from a military, economic, and political point of view."[37] To support these bold claims, he amassed an immense amount of information, which he included in his writing.

The problem he faced was that inventions that made war deadlier — and there had been a prodigious leap forward in their numbers and their power — often were countered relatively quickly, making his claims largely redundant or, at the very least, reducing their veracity. Furthermore, he also often extrapolated incorrectly about the pace and route of the development of weapons. This miscalculation led to some rather dubious conclusions. For instance, he believed that the caliber of rifle rounds would keep decreasing from 7.62mm to 4mm and even smaller, thus allowing greater loads of ammunition to be carried, as well as providing the rifle with ever-increasing penetrative power.[38] The latter idea was rather simply argued: "As you contract the calibre of the gun you increase the force of its projectile. For instance, a rifle with a calibre of 6.5 mm. has 44 per cent. [sic] more penetrative power than the shot fired by an 8mm rifle."[39] This concept completely ignores any other factors that might come into play in terms of bullet design, including the weight of the round, its velocity, and so forth. Furthermore, this change did not happen; the reduction in caliber size stabilized around 7 millimeters. He pointed out that the small-bore modern bullet "finds no obstacle in earthworks such as would have turned aside the larger bullets."[40] As has been pointed out in this book, the army's answer was quite simple: dig deeper. He also claimed that the penetrative power of the modern bullet would kill several people as the bullet passed through each man in turn.[41] I suggest that the obvious solution to the issue had already largely been thought of: spread out and not follow behind anyone too closely.

Bloch made similar claims about the use of high-explosive shell, citing an estimate that a seventy-pound shell would "effectively destroy all life within a range of 200 meters of the point of the explosion." Simply put, that assertion was not true. He also assumed that the gunners could not survive long and would be picked off by infantry fire.[42] However, he ignored the range of modern artillery, which extended beyond the range of rifle fire, and failed to extrapolate that it too might further increase and be used indirectly. Indeed, the German Army had already started using artillery in that manner in the 1890s, which was before he published his main work. Again, simply put, his logic was wrong. Further, he does not seem to have thought that the gunners were intelligent enough, or perhaps frightened enough, to take cover, let alone construct some type of shield for protection. Previously these devices had taken the form of a pavis, which again had become relatively common in the Russo-Japanese War and afterward.

Bloch had much to say about the use of entrenchment, and some of that was spot on, particularly when he described the use of trenches and the virtual state of siege that would exist on the modern battlefield. Citing the example of the Russo-Turkish War of 1877–1878, he explained, "If war were to break out in Europe to-day, each combatant would find itself confronted, not by an isolated and improvised Plevna, but by carefully prepared and elaborately fortified networks of Plevnas."[43] Here at least he was rather prescient, though it must be remembered he had claimed that earthworks would not protect against the small-bore rifle fire of the near future. Thus, the comment about Plevnas must be taken with a pinch of salt, as it was somewhat contradictory.

The description he provided of the collapse of the economies and societies of the combatants is also appealing in hindsight, especially when looking at the fate of the vanquished. Given that the victors of the big wars of the previous fifty to sixty years had not undergone as dramatic an economic and social collapse as he had predicted, how realistic was his view? While it is true that the American South experienced a postwar collapse, France had lost an emperor, and Russia had a revolution (though with the latter two examples it could be argued that was quite normal, with or without major conflict), the Union had not dissolved in revolution. Nor had Germany in 1870–1871, Russia or Turkey in 1878, or Britain in 1902, and the Balkan states had not collapsed in economic or social terms. Perhaps Bloch can be forgiven for overplaying his argument, given his sincere desire to win his point. But it does not make him any more than partially correct, given that he expected the warring states' economies to collapse very quickly. His detractors quickly could point out this error, further undermining his other arguments.

Bloch's description of future war was convincing. The only problems came from the absolute nature of his points. He argued that the men would not be able to cross the "thousand paces" of ground that separated the two sides and that modern high explosives would destroy everything that might provide cover to them.[44] This claim was clearly not the case. Admittedly, heavy casualties were to be expected in any attempt, but that point was already understood. He also hinted at a matter he seemingly failed to take into account in his vision of the future of warfare—that is, the positive nature of the human element. He had bought into the not unpopular view that prosperous society had produced a modern man incapable of enduring the type of hardship war required.[45] When discussing the Russo-Turkish War of 1877–1878, he mentioned that the "endurance shown by the Russian soldiers in the passage of the Balkans in the winter of 1877–78 awakened the astonishment of strangers."[46] Surely, one of the most important points is that the human spirit and ability to endure enormous hardships allowed for individuals, and armies, to overcome the very limitations and hindrances Bloch dwelled upon. This human spirit was repeatedly demonstrated in his lifetime; later, incontrovertibly, in their repeated and frequently almost suicidal attacks during the Russo-Japanese War, the Japanese infantry aroused the admiration of many observers. The lesson of such spectacles was that superior élan and cohesion would carry the day despite the barriers put up by emerging technology.

In addition, humans eventually devised the technology that led to the end of the very deadlock Bloch had envisioned, through the invention of the airplane, tank, and poison gas, as well as the techniques needed to coordinate their use. In fact, some of these ideas were already being experimented with, to the extent that the issue of gas had been addressed at the Hague Conference in 1899. Though Bloch made a number of prescient points about the future of war, he also was wrong often and ignored historical evidence regarding the ability of humankind consistently to overcome the most difficult obstacles. However much we might have wanted what he said to be true, reality unfortunately provided a rather nasty smack in the face.

That his ideas largely were rejected can be explained partly by the failure of his argument. It certainly makes more sense than simply condemning the military for having an innate lack of curiosity or sheer unwillingness to change. Nor did the establishment ignore him; on the contrary, its willingness to engage with him, such as when he lectured at the Royal United Services Institute in London in 1901, gives the lie to that idea. After all, why bother to listen at all? Of course, the innate conservatism of his audience weighed against his ideas, and people quickly and aggressively pointed out even minor gaps in his logic. It is also true that many military men were worried about the loss of control over their troops that the need for dispersion threatened and correspondingly fought strongly against the idea. They were also all too aware that war was violent and deadly, but they were tasked with planning for a short victorious one, just as their political masters wanted. In addition, there was no guarantee that politicians would fund large-scale changes in equipment and training, and reorganizing the way an army fights and the equipment it uses is an expensive business. Logically the anti-Bloch argument had some practical legitimacy.

Perhaps, then, a combination of the conservatism of the military men of the day, the demands placed on them, and Bloch's inability to persuade them with his unreliable evidence led to his failure to convince his critics. Undoubtedly the fact that he was a pacifist and wanted to bring an end to war skewed some of his logic and only served to undermine his arguments. Then again, and given the evidence of the wars that took place after Bloch died, perhaps he was simply wrong in much of what he claimed. To this author that judgment would be too strong, but the question is a legitimate one to ask. The benefits of hindsight have somewhat clouded our view of the past, and by bringing in our modern mores and seeking an explanation for the horror of the Great War, perhaps we have given Bloch far too much credence in our quest.

Despite the arguments against the ideas of the offensive spirit and the rise of new technologies aiding the defense, the state of thinking of most of the Great Powers was remarkably similar, with a strong emphasis on the attack. New techniques too were coming to the fore, with indirect fire starting to be seen as an effective means to deal with the problems that modern field fortifications posed. It must be said that the full potential of indirect fire was not immediately realized, and without really much need for it tactically, relatively little import was given to its use. Ultimately, the lessons of previous wars were that the side that seized the initiative and fully pushed home attacks with élan, as well as to the last resource, often was the victor. Thus, the logic of prewar military thinking is perhaps understandable, especially when placed in context: in their past Europeans had overcome all kinds of obstacles to progress, and they had gone on almost completely to dominate the planet. This success understandably reinforced some of the social-Darwinian ideas of the time; of course, with only an extra bit of gumption, they could overcome some technical difficulties. For good or bad—mostly the latter—the Europeans relied on these ideas when confronting the circumstances of late 1914, circumstances that they were simply not sophisticated enough to handle.

7

Conclusions

During the thirty-seven years separating the start of the Russo-Turkish War and the beginning of the First World War, an immense change took place in the technology with which wars were fought and affected how and why field fortifications were used. The emphasis on their construction moved away from such imperatives as preventing desertion and became increasingly concerned with offering better protection for the men sheltering in them. The vast increase in firepower led to the increasing need to dig deeper down into the ground rather than continuing to pile the earth dug up in front of the position to be protected, as had been the previous practice. This evolution in the technique of construction was the most significant change in the theory and practice of field fortification as it signaled the transition from an old-style aboveground structure to one that was almost completely buried in the earth and became synonymous with the western front. Another significant development was the increasingly important relationship between fortification, barbed wire, and the machine gun. These elements came together and massively increased the power of the defensive, particularly when combined with defensive artillery support. This development in turn led to the greater need for more plentiful and heavier artillery support for the attacker.

Prior to the period covered by this book, one of the main reasons for using field fortification had been to prevent desertion. Although it was not a reason for its continued use, fortification still had that effect for the simple reason that the battlefield had become so dangerous that leaving a field fortification was likely to prove fatal. As larger and larger areas were covered by fortifications, because of the increasing range and power of artillery and the greater size of the armies, fewer and fewer opportunities existed to desert safely from an army in the field. Only when troops were away from the front lines did desertion once again become an easy option, particularly among the chaos of a retreating army. Further, the fear that men would not want to risk getting out of their fortification and that somehow this reluctance would affect their willingness to attack had proven unfounded, and this ideological barrier to their widespread utilization was removed. Soldiers repeatedly demonstrated that they were willing to move out of fortifications to attack, but normally they did not do so to desert. Logically, there was an explanation: desertion usually was a more individual act—though not always, as witnessed in the Russian Revolution of 1917—and a more general attack or retreat from a fortification was a collective one. Striking up the courage to expose oneself, as an individual, was certainly more difficult to do than when doing so as part of a more cohesive group. Thus, soldiers were willing to get out and attack as part of a group but were loath to move and desert as individuals. Though desertion from the frontline trenches of the Great War was not unheard of, it was not a large-scale problem. It was far easier to wait for an opportunity to present itself in the chaos of a retreat, or when in transition to a new posting, than to risk an almost certain lonely death trying to escape from a frontline trench.

Field fortification did make desertion physically more difficult, but it did not remove all of the reasons for wanting to do so. Therefore, determining whether the use of field fortification did provide a genuine benefit in preventing desertion during the entire period covered, including its use in peacetime, would be interesting. However, that effort would be a book in itself and thus beyond the scope of this one, though the topic does warrant further research.

Field fortification provided both physical and moral protection to troops throughout the period covered. Any type of fortification was almost certainly better than none, but as time went on it became increasingly important to dig in properly. With the improvements in artillery and infantry weapons, it was essential that troops were well protected. When field fortifications were dug properly, the protection that they provided was one of the main reasons for the change in warfare: armies increased their heavy reliance on artillery primarily to neutralize or kill well-protected defenders. The improved protection increased the amount of time and preparation needed for a successful assault, further giving the defenders more time to improve their positions, which in turn meant more and heavier guns were required to blast them out of their positions. Thus, this problem was cyclical.

As the amount of citizens who were serving as soldiers increased, a corresponding need to protect them also grew. Given the sheer size of armies of the period, some numbering in the millions, large groups of men who were essential to a modern economy were likely to serve and had to be properly protected. Though countries such as Turkey and Russia hardly can be claimed to be equivalent with some of the Western powers in that respect, they all still needed to preserve the morale and confidence of the men. Further, they also had to guarantee that these citizen soldiers and conscripts actually would stand and fight.

The physical and moral protection provided by fortification enhanced the fighting power of the troops through the increased confidence it provided to them. The enhancement of fighting power was important in its relation to poorer quality troops, especially with reservists; there were many examples of troops in all four conflicts standing their ground when fortified, when they might not have done so otherwise. The issue of reinforcing the fighting ability of reservists was an important one, because increasingly the armies of the world had turned to large conscript armies to fulfill their military requirements. These troops now more frequently saw action in wars, and all of the armies in the case studies, with the exception of Britain, were essentially conscript in nature. It was also understood that, in any conflict, large numbers of men likely would be called to the colors, and the best method of keeping them steady in action was to place them in fortifications. Further, many soldiers who had recently been called up had not had time for adequate training in order to withstand the rigors of combat, and field fortification provided a cheap and effective means of enhancing their ability to fight. Further, if they were well constructed, the fortifications physically could provide support for the weapons themselves, thus allowing them to be used in a steadier fashion and with a corresponding increase in accuracy. This factor was particularly beneficial for less-well-trained troops who might have had limited time to practice their rifle skills. The widespread introduction of the machine gun, which allowed small numbers of men to hold a position more effectively than ever before, also greatly enhanced their soldiers' fighting power.

The reinforcement of key tactical points on the battlefield was another theme that changed little in theory, but it also was enhanced with the use of machine guns. Redoubts frequently were used in this role, and they were particularly useful where the terrain did not afford a convenient geographic feature for the purpose. The skillful choice of a tactical point could quite easily allow a fortification as small as a single machine-gun position to dominate a large section of the battlefield. Using a well-chosen tactical point in this context further enhanced fighting power and provided new levels of efficiency of force. It also presaged the problems of the First World War, where well-placed defensive machine guns in a well-constructed strongpoint were able to stall an advance effectively. The use of a key tactical point in this fashion forced the attacker to move in a more predictable manner or over prepared ground and further enhanced the ability of the artillery to intervene on the behalf of the defending infantry, reinforcing the increasing dominance of artillery upon the battlefield.

The combination of protection and force multiplication assisted in providing secure lines of communication. As the size of the armies and the amount of supplies and material required for war fighting increased, the need to secure the lines of communication correspondingly grew too. Throughout the period, covered field fortification was used to secure bases of operations and lines of communications whether that was at Plevna in 1877, guarding the rail lines through the Boer Republics or into Manchuria, or the routine digging-in of the Serbs and Bulgarians as a secure jumping-off point for their next move forward during the Balkan Wars.

Dominating an area had been the previous role of permanent fortification, but increasingly fieldworks were used to accomplish this function. Their use permitted a much greater degree of flexibility, because they could be dug virtually anywhere. With the increasing size of armies, it was also more common for field fortification to cover long stretches of the front. Large areas of South Africa were divided up with long lines of blockhouses and wire in 1900–1902 to prevent the movement of Boer soldiers. The Russian Army in Manchuria dug in their troops over a seventy-five-mile-long front at Mukden, and the Ottomans on a thirty-six-mile-long front at Lule-Burgas. In an area where the transportation network was limited, this use of fortification made it very difficult to turn troops out of their fortification given the long distances involved. Further, any move away from rail lines led either to a slowing down in troop movement or to a complete halt, even after the widespread introduction of motorized transport, which the Central Powers — Austria-Hungary, Bulgaria, Germany, and the Ottoman Empire — severely lacked through most of the First World War. Troop movement was particularly hampered if large quantities of supplies or artillery were involved, which was likely given the increasing size of the major powers' armies. The growing use of field fortification only made this situation worse. Well-dug-in defenders required more time and effort to shift them, thus compounding the original problem. This issue became clear for all to see once the western front bogged down in trench warfare toward the end of 1914.

Prior to the Russo-Turkish War of 1877–1878 field fortification largely consisted of aboveground structures such as breastworks and redoubts. The shift from breastworks to trenches followed the increase in firepower. Initially the changes were made to provide better protection against the greater power of rifle fire, which did not greatly affect the construction of redoubts. Improvements in metallurgy and chemistry in the 1880s enhanced the power of artillery and led the troops to lower the profile of the entrenchments in order to avoid its worst effects. Thus, where the trenches seen at Plevna had been viewed as being both new and innovative enough to provoke comment, by the start of the Russo-Japanese War they were seen as being both normal and essential. Indeed, during the latter conflict observers were more likely to comment on the lack of properly dug trenches. By the time of the Balkan Wars, it certainly was the case that the attachés frequently only took note when properly dug trenches were absent. This record indicates that the trench had become the norm and its absence the oddity. Additionally, the lack of comment did not mean the theory or practice had stopped.[1]

Redoubts with only minor changes, through their sheer size, initially were able to withstand the substantial increase in firepower that occurred between 1877 and 1914. Over time, as a direct result of the increase in artillery firepower, they too were dug deeper into the ground, their profile lowered, and their tactical depth reduced. These changes occurred because the armies needed to reduce the redoubt's size in order to make it more difficult for the enemy both to see it and to hit it. Relying on the redoubt's sheer mass was no longer sufficient to safeguard the men defending it. The reduction in its tactical depth was a response to the expanded use of indirect fire during the Russo-Japanese War, and the change made the redoubt more difficult to hit. Again, as with the trenches, observers normally extensively commented on the redoubts only when they were not properly dug or when they fulfilled a particular purpose, such as providing a base for machine-gun fire. The use of top cover and splinter-proofs also followed a similar pattern. As the amount of shrapnel being fired rose and as rifle fire became more powerful, so the use of splinter-proof and top cover became more frequent and its absence more notable.

The use of concealment also became more important as the power and range of artillery grew. To guarantee that an attack or a defense could be conducted successfully, the infantry, machine guns, and particularly the artillery had to remain hidden for as long as possible. They had to withstand the bombardments of the enemy artillery intact so that they could effectively intervene in the decisive fight. The increasing need for concealment also affected the growing phenomenon of the empty battlefield. During the American Civil War, it had largely been a product of the more heavily forested terrain, but the concept of the empty battlefield increasingly came to be understood as rather different—that is, an open battle-field with the enemy hidden somewhere within the line of sight. It applied to both the attacker, who needed to be covered by artillery when approaching an enemy position, and the defender, who had to remain concealed for as long as possible. However, the need for concealment sometimes clashed with the emphasis on moral courage. Troops with bayonets fixed were more visible (presumably as light caught the bare metal) in open ground, thus making the final advance to close with the enemy that much more problematic.[2] Given that fixing bayonets was seen as essential to the attack, this exposure presented a conundrum. Furthermore, the use of airplanes over the battlefield provided another tool for observation that had to be countered by those on the ground, first to reduce the likelihood of being observed and second to reduce the effects of the enemy artillery fire, which was sure to follow observation.[3]

The emergence of the empty battlefield along with the longer ranges of infantry and artillery fire led to a greater need for improved optical devices. This necessity had become obvious during the Second Anglo-Boer War, where dispersed troops in dull colors often were difficult to see, especially given the lack of sufficient quantities of modern optics. The great expansion of the battle space and new methods of fighting required quantities of telescopes, binoculars, and range finders (another new invention).[4] To fulfill this need a whole industry had to be created, an effort that required government encouragement. Germany had a head start, being the center of the modern optics industry, and both Britain and France had to catch up. By 1914 British companies produced only 10 percent of the required prewar demands for optics, with the bulk of the devices being imported from Germany. The massive expansion of the army in 1914 required an exponential increase in the output of the British optics industry, even without the understandable loss of supply from German firms.[5]

The role and type of obstacles also changed during the period 1877–1914. During the Russo-Turkish War, typically an obstacle consisted of a ditch in front of an earthwork, though it was no longer particularly useful as it did not effectively delay the enemy under the fire of the defender. In the Russo-Japanese conflict, troops made extensive use of wire entanglements, which usually consisted of smooth telegraph wire that worked well, albeit not as effectively as barbed wire. With sufficient time and labor, the Russians constructed extensive rows of military pits, abatis, and wire entanglements, covering many miles, and they also made use of mines and fougasses. These obstacles had the advantage of delaying the attacker under the fire of the defender, so multiplying their effectiveness. However, with the exception of wire entanglements, they took time to construct, sometimes blocked the line of sight, required large amounts of labor, and were vulnerable to the effects of artillery fire. Meanwhile, the military attachés often noted both the near immunity of the wire to the effects of the enemy's artillery and the ease and speed with which it was possible to construct a simple wire obstacle. These factors had important implications, because defenders could quickly and easily construct an effective obstacle that was difficult to destroy; indeed, attackers physically had to cut down the wire itself almost certainly while under fire. As such the defender's use of barbed wire presented a stubborn and dangerous obstacle for an attacker to surmount. During the Balkan Wars the combination of field fortification, barbed-wire entanglements, and machine guns is what made the attack so difficult and pointed to one of the most intractable problems of the First World War.

The symbiotic relationship between barbed wire and machine guns, when incorporated with properly dug field fortification, created a tactical problem for the attack during the First World War—how to deal with the defensive machine guns. The solution in the Russo-Japanese and the Balkan Wars was to use ever larger and more powerful artillery and literally blast them out of their positions. This barrage would be followed by an infantry attacking with élan that had been indoctrinated to accept suffering heavy casualties. All this war fighting required greater numbers of more powerful artillery, firing more rounds, because the infantry was digging in more deeply and was better protected. The better dug in the infantry, the heavier the guns required to shift them, which provoked a corresponding counterresponse and so on and so forth.

Quick-firing guns consumed massive amounts of ammunition, and the need for heavier and more ferocious bombardments created problems too. Supplying all of this equipment and matériel to the relevant part of the front became difficult and consequently strained the transport network, which was already burdened with men, casualties, food, and other supplies. Thus, more effective digging techniques provoked a counterresponse, which in turn made maneuver more difficult owing to the sheer quantity of supplies and equipment needed. This complication, in turn, led troops to remain relatively static, allowing them time adequately to dig in and thus restart the cycle. This cycle was seen in the Russo-Japanese conflict as the Japanese advanced along the rail line to Mukden. It was also true of the Bulgarian advance into eastern Thrace during the Balkan Wars. There the Bulgarians were forced to culminate their advance outside the lines of Tchataldja through their inability to operate effectively at the end of their supply lines. Because they could not bring up and supply sufficient heavy artillery to neutralize the Ottoman guns, they could not make a successful assault on the position.[6]

There was also the exorbitant cost of all of this business. For example, by 1901 the average British soldier cost the taxpayer half again as much as he had cost in 1898, and he also required "one ton of bullets, costing £140, to incapacitate a single Boer farmer."[7] Now I do not know how these figures were calculated, but if correct they do indicate the rising cost of waging battle. The army required greater stocks of ammunition. The British Army in 1899 possessed a stock of 172 million rifle rounds, of which 21 million were earmarked for yearly practice. Of these rounds, a faulty design left around 66 million virtually unusable in South Africa.[8] The implications of this error are obvious, particularly given that the British were using more rifle ammunition than they could produce.[9] The size of the stockpile required to ensure an army going into action had sufficient ammunition was enormous. Ammunition also has a "best by" date after which it is less reliable. Thus, the cost of maintaining sufficient stocks of usable ammunition, particularly for the artillery, must have been astronomical. Therefore, is it any wonder that the armies involved in the First World War suffered severe shortages of it, on and off, through much of the first year of the war? Not many finance ministers could successfully justify massive amounts of government spending on items that might never be used and that had a limited shelf life.

The 1877–1914 period saw a transformation in warfare that was driven in part by the use of field fortification. The move to longer and longer lines of trenches, protecting the men and dominating the ground, presaged what occurred in the First World War. Further, the emergence of the combination of machine guns, barbed wire, and trenches went on to dominate the tactical landscape of the near future. That combination was largely responsible for the increase in the importance of the role of artillery, particularly heavy artillery, in both the attack and the defense of a position. Not only was it needed to blast the defenders out of their positions; it was also needed to help protect them against enemy artillery and infantry attack. With its increased power, fewer men safely could be placed in close proximity to each other, thereby weakening the fighting power of the defense. Increasingly machine guns and artillery were needed to make up for that deficiency, with the consequent knock-on effect already described. However, the cost and technical complexity of heavy guns precluded most countries from providing their armies with them in sufficient numbers to have a significant effect on the battlefield in 1914. As with the difficulties in justifying the cost of spending on ammunition stocks, unless an army could demonstrate a clear need for heavy guns, it was unlikely to get them.

Despite all of the improvements to the defense, the strategic aggressor was victorious in all of the wars studied. The tactical aggressor suffered mixed results in the Russo-Turkish War and the Boer War, though, indicating that the naysayers' ideas might have been correct. However, by 1914 this situation had reversed itself. The tactical aggressors frequently proved successful if they applied the new lessons of war fighting that most of the attachés from the previous conflicts took home: despite the increased power of the defensive, and strong arguments to the contrary, troops defending field fortifications could be overcome with skillful planning, execution, and moral courage, especially when these efforts were supported with plentiful heavy artillery. Quite understandably, that lesson — the offensive clearly was still possible, given enough skill, planning, and vigor — was carried through to the First World War.

At the beginning of the First World War, all the belligerent armies recognized that field fortification would play an important role in the conflict. However, it was impossible for them to predict that in the West, within a few months, continuous field fortification would cover an area from Switzerland to the North Sea — an unprecedented situation that brought immense difficulties for the combatants. The lessons of previous wars had indicated that the strategic, and often the tactical, aggressor would usually prove victorious. However, the extensive trench lines that the combatants quickly dug covered so much space that a breakthrough was not likely given the reigning tactics and technology and without a flank to turn. In the Russo-Japanese War, the answer had been simply to commit to an attack until the defender gave in. The problem for the armies of the First World War in the West was that they did not confront the same Russian Army that had fought in Manchuria under Kuropatkin.

On the one hand, as trench systems physically became deeper and more spread out over a greater geographical area to avoid the worst effects of heavier fire, so the difficulties for the attack were exacerbated as the distances that needed to be covered to achieve a breakthrough increased proportionately. On the other hand, this situation also promoted the application of better technology: the increased use of aircraft, the introduction of poison gas, the invention of tanks, the building of good roads, and the rise of reliable motorized transportation. Once these new technologies were properly integrated into the system of attack, the problem of dealing with heavily fortified defensive systems, though still immensely difficult, largely was solved. These developments, which occurred specifically to break through these new types of deep defensive systems, led ultimately to the blitzkrieg and modern forms of operational maneuver warfare.

The return to a more mobile form of warfare also somewhat reduced the shocking impact of the immense scale of casualties, as an attacker more often made tangible gains. This issue is reflected in the respective treatment of the military men of the two world wars: despite the immense casualty rates of both conflicts, many of the generals on all sides of the First World War were vilified, while many of the generals of the Second World War were almost deified. It is very difficult for people viewing the First World War, even with the benefit of a nearly hundred-year gap, to place its immense casualties into a rational context when the physical gains from many of the offensives were so limited, especially when compared with those of the famous campaigns of the Second World War. But it is worth pointing out that the Germans had a similar or higher casualty rate in France in 1940 and in Russia in 1941, in comparison to either side in the battles of the Somme or at Verdun.[10] It is also worth asking how decisive were the first war's battles when compared to those of the second war. Perhaps when examining the First World War, we need a new method for evaluating success. If attrition really were the key piece of this new form of warfare, then perhaps the historian William Philpott's recent analysis of the battle of the Somme is correct.[11] Despite the lack of ground taken, it was a victory for Britain and France. We must therefore open our minds to a different way of evaluating success. Mere maneuver is largely irrelevant unless it provides an army with a means to destroy its enemy more cost effectively. A bold stratagem might well look spectacular, but if it does not get an army closer to ending the war, it is largely useless. That determination is so even if the strategy does seem to be more artful than the brutal bare-knuckle fights that most of the wars in this book resemble.

As for today, what role does field fortification still play? The wars in Iraq and Afghanistan have demonstrated its continued valuable use. Coalition forces in both countries have used extensive field fortification for many of the reasons outlined in this book. Forward operating bases have allowed coalition forces in both countries to project power, protect their forces, enhance combat power, secure lines of supply, and dominate terrain. On their face the techniques may have changed somewhat, but the essence is the same. For example, although gabions are now frequently called HESCOs,[12] they are essentially the same thing. The modern version has the advantage of standardization, and the manufacturer gives some basic ideas for the bastions' use. They still provide protection from enemy fire and a physical barrier to prevent movement, and they can be used to control space. The main difference is that all of these applications are described on the company's website rather than in a field manual.[13]

Finally, the following is a question that my students at the U.S. Army Command and General Staff College frequently pose: given the casualties and seeming lack of imagination, were the generals of the period covered by this book and the 1914–1918 war stupid? The answer remains a definitive *no*.

Appendix: The American Civil War, 1861–1865

The American Civil War deserves special mention because it was the first conflict to involve the widespread use of battlefield fortification by both sides. The United States Military Academy at West Point had strongly emphasized engineering in its prewar curriculum, and one of the most important minds lecturing at the school was Professor Dennis Hart Mahan, who had written a number of books related to engineering and field fortification. Understandably, given his role as a professor at the academy, he influenced many officers who later fought in the Civil War. In addition, Union commander Maj. Gen. George B. McClellan had witnessed the fighting in the Crimea and had helped to write a report on it that was available to the U.S. Army prior to the war.

Field fortifications were constructed on the battlefield during the early campaigns of the Civil War, though the practice was not systematic until the Union's drive to Richmond in 1864. The bitter experience of the early fighting, which took place in a more Napoleonic style, generated changes. The reasons for using field fortification during the Civil War were typical of the theories of the time: to protect the troops, to provide fortified bases, and so forth.[1] Historian Earl Hess has argued that the frequent employment of field fortification "was the result of continuous contact between opposing armies." Both sides used them from the beginning of the war and before they began universally using rifled muskets. Indeed, troops often created fieldworks after the action had already taken place, most likely in reaction to the "shock of combat." Thus, when the two sides remained in close proximity to each other for days at a time, it was logical for them to entrench in some manner.[2] Given the nature of the often heavily wooded terrain, it was easy to be surprised, and field fortifications were a natural remedy against an unseen enemy attack. In contrast, with its greater proportion of agricultural land, the more open battlefields of western Europe had not created so much of an issue because the longer lines of sight made it difficult, if not impossible, for the opposing sides to stay in close proximity for long periods. Hence, fortification on the battlefields of Europe was less essential than in North America until the increased power of the breech-loading rifle and artillery fire made it so.

The use of the cover of night for attacks did occur during the Civil War, but it was not as common as it would become in the case studies examined. Nighttime activity was generally restricted to conducting raids and moving troops rather than to waging full-blown assaults. While some very successful night raids occurred, they were the exception rather than the rule. Repeated attempts were made to move troops at night, though more often than not they ended in confusion with only a limited amount of ground covered to show for the effort. Moving around in the vast American forests was difficult enough without the need to make matters worse, as Paddy Griffith pointed out in his *Battle Tactics of the American Civil War*.[3] There was also little need to attack at night, given that a properly prepared assault had a good chance of success.

The style of aboveground fortification that both sides used during the Civil War was typical of the style of field fortification of the period, and breastworks were easy and quick to build with the plentiful materials at hand.[4] In addition, without large numbers of breech-loading rifles and powerful artillery available, the troops did not yet have to dig down into the ground for protection; instead, they did so largely because of their officers' "ingrained, doctrinaire book learning."[5] Griffith is quite clear on this point and writes that McClellan and his successor, Maj. Gen. Henry W. Halleck, ordered the use of field fortification not because Confederate weaponry forced them to do so but because they believed it was the "scientific" way to fight.

Indeed, Halleck had studied under Professor Mahan and had published the influential book *Elements of Military Art and Science* in 1846.[6] He served as a senior commander in the western theater of the war before becoming general in chief of the Union armies in 1862, after McClellan's removal from that post. As two proponents of the art of fortification played a key role in charge of the U.S. Army for much of the war, their influence is understandable.

Again, later in the war, the infantry did not suddenly start digging in because of the improved power of rifle fire; rather, they did so out of "exaggerated fears, doctrinal orthodoxy, and war-weariness."[7] One would also imagine that they were still scared of needlessly getting shot.

The firepower available to Civil War infantry did not come close to what was available only a few short years later, as witnessed in the Franco-Prussian War of 1870–1871 and in the wars covered in this book. Griffith shows that effective infantry fire in the Civil War occurred at less than 150 yards and lacked the power to do much damage beyond that range. Only at very short ranges, on average 33 yards and fewer, was infantry fire particularly effective, and even then it was difficult to kill large numbers of men quickly.[8] When combined with the nature of the terrain (many battles taking place in areas of dense forest), long-range fire was the exception rather than the rule. In addition, the rate of fire was much lower with the muzzle-loading rifles that predominated during the war, and the work of firing was very physical, further limiting the men's ability to fire large numbers of rounds on anything like a regular basis. Men armed with modern breech-loading rifles did not face this problem, and particularly by the end of the nineteenth century, they did not normally have to deal with black powder either.[9] In addition, firing a breech-loading rifle was a much simpler affair, with only a few drill movements required rather than the previous seventeen or eighteen.[10] Given the lack of power and relatively slow rate of fire of muzzle-loading muskets and rifles, it is no wonder that troops did not need to dig deep down into the ground for protection when some logs covered with earth were more than likely adequate for the task.

What was true for infantry fire was also true for artillery fire of the period: effective range was short at 1,000 yards or less. Thus, the ranges for artillery and infantry were not too much different from those of the Napoleonic wars.[11] Given that European battlefields of the late nineteenth century often were physically more open than American ones were, and that modern breech-loading rifles and artillery could fire both farther and faster than their Civil War equivalents could, it is not surprising that the wars fought later in the nineteenth century witnessed the evolution of a different technical structure for field fortifications—that is, belowground fortifications as opposed to breastworks. Though the conflict was important, the American Civil War did not see the style changes to the construction of field fortifications that first became evident during the Russo-Turkish War of 1877–1878. This fact is borne out in Hess's follow-up book on field fortification, *Trench Warfare under Grant and Lee: Field Fortifications in the Overland Campaign*. In this book, he points out that his use of the term "trench warfare" differs from that used to describe the combat in the First World War. In addition, he specifies that his use of the word "trench" relates to "campaigning that was centered on the presence of significant earthworks."[12] Thus, he does not deal with the important technical change examined in this book, that is, the transition from above- to belowground fortification. Further, his descriptions of field fortification are almost exclusively of aboveground breastworks rather than belowground trenches.[13]

The use of field fortifications during the American Civil War appears to have had little initial impact on the major European powers, as Jay Luvaas points out in his work *The Military Legacy of the Civil War: The European Inheritance*. The study of Prussia's wars in 1864, 1866, and 1870–1871 took precedence over examining the Civil War.[14] The Franco-Prussian War of 1870–1871 witnessed a more traditional use of field fortification that was not as systematic as it had been in the last year or so of the American Civil War. Fortifications were dug to enable the siege of Paris and to supplement the defense of French fortresses, and they were only occasionally used on the battlefield. Only later was the study of the American

Civil War treated more seriously, after British military historian and thinker G. F. R. Henderson published his *The Campaign of Fredericksburg* in 1886 and *Stonewall Jackson and the American Civil War* in 1898.[15] Even then, continental armed forces largely still neglected the issue of field fortification, because the prevailing maxim of attack, not defense, did not combine well with the concern that field fortification would sap the troops' offensive spirit.[16]

Despite the pertinent lessons for the future conduct of warfare that emerged during the Civil War, the weapon technology and the style of construction used for fortification then show that it was the last of the old-style wars, and as such it did not warrant a full examination in this book. Further, even if the field fortification techniques and the weapon technology of the Civil War had been more modern, the conflict did not have a major impact on European thinking about warfare until decades later.

Glossary

Abatis: an obstacle consisting of felled trees and large tree limbs set out with their sharpened branches pointing toward the enemy.

Banquette: the step inside the parapet allowing a defender to stand and fire over the parapet while being protected.

Barbette: a raised platform on the interior of a parapet allowing the artillery to fire over the top of the parapet.

Bastion: a field fortification consisting of two faces and two flanks, constructed to allow the whole **escarp** to be seen.

Blindage: a cover erected to prevent the enemy from seeing into a **trench**.

Blockhouse: a small fort or strongpoint, typically positioned in isolation, used to supplement the defense of a key location against an enemy who does not possess artillery.

Bomb-proof: a fortification with a roof sufficiently strong to withstand the blast of high explosives.

Breastwork: a field fortification about chest high, constructed with earth dug up and thrown in front of, or behind, the trench to form a raised parapet. This is essentially an aboveground structure.

Burgher: another name for a Boer.

Caltrop: a spiked piece of metal designed so that when it is thrown onto the ground one spike is always facing up. It is used to puncture a hole in the foot of a person or animal. It is often made of metal nails.

Caponier: a covered work across, and defending, a ditch.

Cheval-de-frise (plural, chevaux-de-frise): a freestanding obstacle consisting of a beam with four sets of protruding spikes.

Covered way: a passage sheltered from enemy fire by digging the walkway deeper and providing a parapet.

Defilade: the protection of a position from observation and gunfire.

Demi-lune (also ravelin): an outwork with the trace of a **redan**.

Drift: a South African word for a ford.

Enceinte: the first continuous line of parapet in a fieldwork that encloses the ground fortified.

Enfilade: a position on the flank of an opponent where fire can be directed along the longest axis of the unit being targeted. Enfilading fire has the potential to hit all targets in a line at the same time. It can be especially devastating.

Entrenchment: a modified form of **breastwork** that presents a lower profile to the enemy.

Epaulement: a simple earthen embankment designed to provide shelter from enemy fire and usually placed on the flanks of a parapet.

Escarp: the sloped inner wall of a ditch between the fortification and the enemy.

Fascine: a bundle of sticks or brushwood used as a means quickly to fill a ditch.

Fougasse: an explosive mine placed in the ground, facing its blast toward the likely direction of an approaching enemy. The explosion would shower the attacker with shrapnel, earth, and stones.

Gabion: usually an open cylinder made from wire netting, iron bands, or interwoven strips of wood that can be filled with earth and used to provide cover or revet for the side of an earthwork. Typically, today, a HESCO Concertainer™ or such would be used for this purpose.

Glacis: a long, gentle slope forming part of the parapet and allowing a clear field of fire for the defenders.

Gorge: the main entrance to a **bastion** or a **redoubt**.

Head cover: literally, cover for the heads of troops in field fortifications.

Kopje: a Boer word for a small hill.

Laager: a Boer word for an improvised shelter, typically formed of circled wagons with the people and their animals sheltering inside it. The term is also sometimes used to describe an improvised military-style camp.

Loophole: a hole designed to allow the defenders to fire from a covered position behind a parapet or a wall.

Lunette: a detached fortification open at the gorge and possessing two faces that form a salient angle, as well as having two flanks.

Military pit (also Trou-de-loup): a deep hole, four to eight feet wide and deep, with sharpened stakes at the bottom.

Nek: a Boer word for a mountain pass.

Nullah: a dry ravine.

Orillon: an ear-shaped work projecting from the side of a bastion and designed to protect the flanks against enfilading fire.

Palisade: a barrier made of tree trunks or wooden stakes. It was sometimes used to form a wall of a temporary fort.

Parados: a mound of earth to the rear of a fortified position, designed to protect against an attack from the rear.

Pavis: a large shield for protecting the body from missile fire.

Quincunx: a pattern that resembles the dotted five on a playing die, with one dot in each corner and one in the middle of the square.

Ravelin: see **demi-lune**.

Redan: a fortification that consists of two faces forming a salient angle.

Redoubt: an enclosed fieldwork.

Retrenchment: a fortified line dug within a larger work.

Revetment: a structure that holds the earth of a fortification at an angle greater than the soil would otherwise stand. It is usually constructed using stone, wood, sandbags, and such.

Sangar: a small **breastwork**, usually constructed entirely above-ground. Often built from rocks but can consist of sandbags and other materials. Usually used in areas of very hard ground or where there is little depth to the soil.

Schanze: a Boer word for a field fortification. It is often used to describe **sangars** and small trenches.

Splinter-proof: a structure strong enough to withstand the impact of shrapnel. It could be added to existing fortifications for additional protection.

Terreplein: the clear space inside an enclosed work. It was also used to describe a space behind the parapet for artillery.

Top cover: cover for the top of a trench or other space open vertically, which provided protection from shrapnel, or, if deep enough, high-explosive shell.

Traverse: raised mounds of earth used to defilade the interior space of a field fortification.

Trench: an infantry position that is almost entirely belowground and presents almost no profile to the enemy.

Notes

Chapter 1. The Theory of Field Fortification, 1740–1914

1. For an excellent overview of warfare, see Michael Howard, *War in European History* (Oxford, UK: Oxford University Press, 1993).

2. J. F. C. Fuller, *Armament and History* (London: Eyre & Spottiswoode, 1946), 112–13.

3. Henry Barnard, *Military Schools and Courses of Instruction in the Science and Art of War, in France, Prussia, Austria, Russia, Sweden, Switzerland, Sardinia, England, and the United States* (New York: E. Steiger, 1872; Greenwood Press, 1969).

4. While waiting for some books at the École Militaire, the author counted the titles published on fortification that the library held. I found that writing on field fortification exploded in the 1870s and 1880s and quickly subsided thereafter. For example, from the 1830s to the 1860s there were seven titles dealing with the topic. In the 1870s alone there were fifteen, and in the 1880s, nineteen more. What's more, in the 1860s sixteen titles were listed for fortification as a whole, of which two related to field fortification. In the 1870s that ratio had changed to forty-six and fifteen, and in the 1880s, fifty-one and nineteen, respectively. Although unscientific, this review demonstrates the point that people of the era were interested in the topic.

5. J. B. A. Bailey, *Field Artillery and Firepower* (Annapolis, MD: Naval Institute Press, 2004), 209–12. Indirect fire is a technique by which artillery can shoot at a target that is not in the direct line of sight of the firing gun. This method requires that the gunners know where both they and their projected targets are. It also requires some means of effective communication to allow the person observing the target and requesting the artillery fire to coordinate his actions with the gunners themselves so that the artillery shells will land on the target rather than elsewhere.

6. Nicolas-Joseph Cugnot, *La Fortification de Campagne Théorique et Pratique* (Paris: C. A. Jombert, 1769), v.

7. Sébastien Le Prestre de Vauban, *The New Method of Fortification*, trans. W. Allingham (London: W. Freeman, 1702), 61.

8. Dennis Hart Mahan, *A Treatise on Field Fortification, Containing Instructions on the Methods of Laying Out, Constructing, Defending, and Attacking Intrenchments, with the General Outlines also of the Arrangement, the Attack and Defence of Permanent Fortifications* (New York: John Wiley, 1852), 1.

9. Gustave J. Fiebeger, *A Textbook on Field Fortification* (New York: John Wiley & Sons, 1913), 1–3. Gustave Fiebeger sometimes is written as Gustav Fiebeger.

10. Jay Luvaas, *The Military Legacy of the Civil War: The European Inheritance* (Lawrence: University Press of Kansas, 1988), 226–33. See also the appendix in this volume for a more thorough review of the place that the American Civil War holds in the progression of field fortification theory and practice.

11. For a full discussion of this issue, see Bailey, *Field Artillery*, 206–40.

12. Maj. Gen. B. P. Hughes, *Firepower: Weapons Effectiveness on the Battlefield, 1630–1850* (New York: Sarpedon, 1997), 61.

13. A more detailed description of explosives can be found in Manuel Eissler, *A Handbook of Modern Explosives: A Practical Treatise on the Manufacture and use of Dynamite* (London: Crosby, Lockwood and Son, 1890).

14. Fiebeger, *Text-book on Field Fortification*, 6.

15. Ibid., 4–6.

16. Maj. Gen. H. D. Hutchinson, *Field Fortification: Notes on the Text-Books* (London: Gale & Polden Ltd., 1904), 24.

17. These issues and the technology concerned are more fully discussed in Hew Strachan, *European Armies and the Conduct of War* (London: Routledge, 1991), 119; and Bailey, *Field Artillery*, 206–40.

18. Capt. James Woodruff, *Applied Principles of Field Fortification for Line Officers* (Leavenworth, KS: Ketcheson Printing, 1909), 100.

19. War Office, General Staff, *Military Engineering, Part 1—Field Defences* (London: His Majesty's Stationery Office [HMSO], 1908), 86.

20. A. H. Kovrigin, "Firing at Breast-Works of Snow with the Berdan Rifle," *Journal of the United States Cavalry Association* 4, no. 13 (June 1891): 161–65.

21. Hans Delbrück, *The Dawn of Modern Warfare*, vol. 4, *History of the Art of War*, trans. Walter J. Renfroe Jr. (Lincoln: University of Nebraska Press, 1990), 251.

22. F. J. Hudleston, *Gentleman Johnny Burgoyne* (Indianapolis: Bobbs-Merrill, 1927), 25–26.

23. J. A. H. de Guibert, *Essai Général de Tactique*, vol. 1 (Liege: Chez C. Plomteux, 1773), xii.

24. Jay Luvaas, ed., *Frederick the Great on the Art of War* (New York: Free Press, 1966), 114.

25. Louis Andre de la Maime, le Chevalier de Clairac, *The Field Engineer, with Observations and Remarks on Each Chapter*, trans. John Muller (London: John Millan, 1750), 78.

26. Paddy Griffith, *The Art of War in Revolutionary France, 1789–1802* (London: Greenhill Books, 1998), 134.

27. Luvaas, *Military Legacy*, 179.

28. MacGregor Knox and Williamson Murray, eds., *The Dynamics of Military Revolution, 1300–2050* (New York: Cambridge University Press, 2008), 90.

29. *Feldbefestigungsvorschrift*, February 1908, Militärbevollmächtigte und Militär Adjoints 1860–1918 (5/6), 724, Österreicherisches, Kriegsarchiv, Vienna (hereafter "OeStA/KA").

30. Hughes, *Firepower*, 136.

31. Carl von Clausewitz, *Principles of War*, in *Roots of Strategy, Book 2: 3 Military Classics*, ed. and trans. Hans W. Gatzke (Mechanicsburg, PA: Stackpole Books, 1987), 319.

32. Carl von Clausewitz, *On War*, trans. Michael Howard and Peter Paret (London: David Campbell Publishers Ltd., 1993), 427–28.

33. Mahan, *Treatise on Field Fortification*, vii–viii.

34. Alexis Henri Brialmont, *Hasty Intrenchments*, trans. Charles A. Empson (London: Henry S. King, 1872), 15.

35. William Kemmis, *The Attack of Entrenchments by Artillery* (Woolwich, UK: Royal Artillery Institution, 1880), 1.

36. Ministère de la Guerre, *Instruction Pratique sur les Travaux de Campagne à l'Usage des Troupes d'Infanterie* (Paris: Librairie Militaire Berger-Levrault, 1906, updated 1911), 8.

37. Griffith, *Art of War*, 212.

38. *Correspondance de Napoléon Ier*, 15, no. 12,111, quoted in J. F. C. Fuller, *The Conduct of War, 1789–1961* (New York: Da Capo, 1992), 52.

39. *Correspondance de Napoléon Ier*, 5, no. 4,083, quoted in ibid., 52.

40. Clausewitz, *Principles of War*, 341.

41. Ibid., 357.

42. H. Yule, *Fortification for Officers of the Army and Students of Military History, with Illustrations and Notes* (London: William Blackwood and Sons, 1851), 1–2.

43. Mahan, *Treatise on Field Fortification*, vi–vii.

44. Brialmont, *Hasty Intrenchments*, 1.

45. E. D. C. O'Brien, *Fortification* (London: Cassell, Petter & Galpin, 1875), 11.

46. H. Turner, *Field Fortification with Examples and Exercises* (London: Swan Sonnenschein, 1892), 13.

47. Ministère de la Guerre, *Instruction Pratique*, 8.

48. Yule, *Fortification*, 60–61.

49. D. Chandler, *The Campaigns of Napoleon* (New York: Macmillan, 1973), 790–810.

50. War Office, General Staff, *Instruction in Field Engineering, Field Defences*, vol. 1, part 1 (London: HMSO, 1877), 1.

51. Albrecht von Boguslawski, *Tactical Deductions from the War of 1870–1871* (Minneapolis: Absinthe Press, 1996), 98–100.

52. Henry Schaw, "Field Works from a Tactical Point of View," *Professional Papers of the Corps of Royal Engineers* 1 (1877): 25.

53. Delbrück, *The Dawn of Modern Warfare*, 297. (See also Brialmont, *Hasty Intrenchments*, 3; Yule, *Fortification*, 60; and Charles B. Brackenbury, *Field Works, Their Technical Construction and Tactical Application* [London: Kegan Paul, Trench, & Co., 1888], 111.)

54. Howard, *War in European History*, 71. Also see H. Dietrich von Bülow, *The Spirit of the Modern System of War*, trans. Gen. Charles de Malorti de Martemont (London: Egerton's Military Library, 1825).

55. Bülow, *Spirit of the Modern System*, 65. General de Malortie wrote a long analysis of Bülow's work as a guide to understanding it.

56. Quoted in Jay Luvaas, ed., *Napoleon on the Art of War* (New York: Touchstone, 2001), 111.

57. Quoted in ibid., 101. (Original taken from: Napoleon to Dejean, 3 September 1806, *Correspondance de Napoléon Ier* 13, no. 10,726, 131.)

58. Clausewitz, *Principles of War*, 362.

59. Brialmont, *Hasty Intrenchments*, 7. All three locations are on or are flanking the route of march for the French move toward Magenta.

60. W. Birkbeck Wood and James Edmonds, *A History of the Civil War in the United States, 1861–1865* (New York: G. P. Putnam's Sons, 1905), 527.

61. Felix Patrikieff and Harry Shukman, *Railways and the Russo-Japanese War* (New York: Routledge, 2007), 34 and 53.

62. O. G. S. Crawford, "Some Linear Earthworks in the Danube Basin," *The Geographical Journal* 116, no. 4/6 (1950): 218–20. (Some of these earthworks were still in existence when the article was written.)

63. Marshal Maurice de Saxe, *New System of Fortification*, trans. C. Vallancey (Dublin: Richard James, 1757), 115.

64. Thomas Raphael Phillips, ed., *Roots of Strategy: A Collection of Military Classics* (London: John Lane, 1943), 135.

65. Clairac, *The Field Engineer*, 1–2.

66. O'Brien, *Fortification*, 49–50.

67. Ibid., 12.

68. Clausewitz, *On War*, 647.

Chapter 2. The Russo-Turkish War and Plevna

1. Maureen O'Connor, "The Vision of Soldiers: Britain, France, Germany and the United States Observe the Russo-Turkish War," *War in History* 4, no. 3 (1997): 264.

2. John Henry Verinder Crowe, *An Epitome of the Russo-Turkish War, 1877–78* (London: Royal Artillery Institution, 1904), 17.

3. John Formby, *The First Two Battles of Plevna* (London: William Clowes & Sons Limited, 1910), 36.

4. Special Correspondent of *The Times*, 30 April 1877, cited in WO106/5, National Archives, Kew Gardens, London.

5. Bruce W. Menning, *Bayonets before Bullets: The Imperial Russian Army, 1861–1914* (Bloomington: Indiana University Press, 1992), 38–44.

6. The German military mission did not begin until 1882. Edward Erickson, *Defeat in Detail: The Ottoman Army in the Balkans, 1912–1913* (Westport, CT: Praeger, 2003), 11.

7. Francis Vinton Greene, *Report of the Russian Army and Its Campaigns in Turkey in 1877–1878* (New York: D. Appleton, 1879), 423.

8. J. Bornecque, *Rôle de la Fortification dans la Dernière Guerre d'Orient* (Paris: Librarie Militaire de J. Dumaine, 1881), 340–47. The defensive-offensive is where an attacker moves into a position (ideally fortified) to force his enemy

to counterattack him. Thus, he uses the offensive for defensive purposes. To invest a place is to besiege it.

9. R. Hamnett, Country Pasture/Forage Resource Profiles, "Bulgaria," Food and Agriculture Organization of the United Nations, November 2002–October 2006, http://www.fao.org/ag/Agp/agpc/doc/Counprof/Bulgaria/bulgaria.htm (accessed 20 May 2009).

10. Bornecque, *Rôle de la Fortification*, 164–71. See also Greene, *Report of the Russian Army*, 423–26.

11. Mouzaffer Pacha and Talaat Bey, *Défense de Plevna, d'après les Documents Officiels et Privés Réunis sous la Direction du Osman pacha par Mouzaffer pacha et Talaat bey*, 2 vols. (Paris: Librarie Militaire de L. Baudoin, 1889), 29–34.

12. Greene, *Report of the Russian Army*, 424.

13. Map based on Frederick Maurice, *The Russo-Turkish War, 1877: A Strategical Sketch* (London: Swan Sonnenschein, 1905).

14. Menning, *Bayonets before Bullets*, 53. (See also Capt. H. M. Hozier, ed., *The Russo-Turkish War: Including an Account of the Rise and Decline of Ottoman Power and the History of the Eastern Question*, 5 vols. [London: William Mackenzie, 1878]; and FO 881/3701 [Report on military operations in Europe] and FO881/3702 [Report on military operation in Asia], National Archives, London, for a more comprehensive overview of the whole Russo-Turkish War.)

15. Hozier, *Russo-Turkish War*, 560.

16. Letter from Colonel Wellesley to Lord Derby, 27 July 1877, FO65/985, National Archives, London.

17. Charles S. Ryan, *Under the Red Crescent: Adventures of an English Surgeon with the Turkish Army at Plevna and Ezeroum, 1877–1878* (London: John Murray, 1897), 152.

18. Quoted in a letter from Colonel Wellesley to Lord Derby, 29 October 1877, FO65/985.

19. Letter from Colonel Wellesley to Lord Derby, 21 September 1877, FO65/985.

20. Christian von Sarauw, *Der Russisch-Türkische Krieg 1877 bis 1878: Auf Grundlage der Veröffentlichten Officiellen Russischen Rapporte* (Leipzig: Verlag von Bernhard Schlicke, 1879), 115–28.

21. Report of Col. L. Gaillard, quoted in 7 N 1496, no. 166, 18 September 1877, 14, Service historique de la Défense, Château de Vincennes, Paris.

22. W. A. H. Hare, Report on the war in Asia, FO881/3702, 19–28. Also see Greene, *Report of the Russian Army*, 377–418. Hare's report is split between FO881/3701 and FO 881/3702. (It is a good source of information on the fighting in Asia, which is otherwise largely ignored.) The exact date is not always consistently given, but 25 April is most likely.

23. Greene, *Report of the Russian Army*, 385.

24. Ibid., 377–83.

25. Ibid., 386.

26. Ibid., 391–96.

27. Report of Consul Zohrab to Lord Derby, Erzeroum, 5 November 1877, WO106/2, National Archives, London.

28. Report of Russian consul provided to Col. W. Lennox and forwarded, Erzeroum, 27 March 1877, WO106/1, National Archives, London.

29. Hare, Report on the war in Asia, FO 881/3701, 68. A *muchir* was an Ottoman rank similar to governor, and the irregulars were the ill-famed Bashi-Bazouks (irregular auxiliaries) who supported the Ottomans.

30. This is the same Dr. Ryan who authored *Under the Red Crescent*. J. Drew Gay, *Plevna, the Sultan, and the Porte* (London: Chatto and Windus, 1878), 146–47.

31. Report of Col. L. Gaillard, quoted in 7 N 1496, no. 166, 18 September 1877, 14.

32. Greene, *Report of the Russian Army*, 234.

33. Frederick Wellesley, *With the Russians in Peace and War: Recollections of a Military Attaché* (London: Eveleigh Nash, 1905), 244.

34. H. Brunker, *Story of the Russo-Turkish War, 1877–78 (in Europe)* (London: Forster Groom, 1911), 83 (extract from a letter of General Todleben of the Russian Engineers to General Brialmont of the Belgian Engineers dated 18 January 1878).

35. Cornelius Clery, *Minor Tactics* (London: Kegan Paul, Trench, 1883), 335.

36. Sarauw, *Der Russisch-Türkische Krieg*, 115.

37. Reports of Col. L. Gaillard, quoted in 7 N 1496, no. 166, 21 July 1877, Service historique.

38. Formby, *First Two Battles of Plevna*, 26.

39. Brunker, *Story of the Russo-Turkish War*, 67.

40. No first name or official title was listed in his reports. Report from Höhneysen, 11 September 1877, Evidenzbüro des Generalstab (5/8), Karton 3364, OeStA/KA.

41. Letter from Colonel Wellesley to Lord Derby, 21 September 1877, FO65/985.

42. Report from Höhneysen, 20 October 1877, Evidenzbüro des Generalstab (5/8), Karton 3364.

43. Pacha and Talaat, *Défense de Plevna*, 128.

44. "Report of Lt.-Gen. Skobeleff to Lt.-Gen. Prince Imeretinsky, 15 September 1877," *The Royal Engineers Journal*, 1878, 102.

45. Report of Lieutenant General Skobeleff to Lt. Gen. Prince Imeretinsky, September 1877, as found in Lt. Gen. Sir R. Harrison, "The Use of Field Works in War," *The United Service Magazine* 787 (June 1894): 111–27.

46. Hippolyte Langlois, *Lessons from Two Recent Wars* (London: HMSO, 1909), 36.

47. The *Redifs* (reserves) formed the second reserve of the Ottoman Army. This is sometimes referred to as the *landwehr*. The Redifs were usually made up of the men who had finished their period of service with the regular army (*Nizam*) and who had already served in the first reserve (*Ikhtiat*). After service in the Redifs, they moved to the last line of reserves (*Mustahfiz*) to finish their service.

48. This is almost certainly the same Col. Dr. Johannes Zohrab who served as a superintendent at the Bursa Medical School in Turkey. Report of Consul Zohrab to Sir H. Elliot, Erzeroum, 5 November 1876, WO106/1.

49. Report of Colonel Lennox to Lord Derby, Shumla, 5 June 1877, WO106/2. Also note that the staff had to do the engineering work, as the Ottoman Army had few engineers.

50. Ibid.

51. Letter from Consul W. Kirby Green to Lord Derby, Scutari, 10 March 1877, WO106/1.

52. Report of Lennox to Derby.

53. Archibald Forbes and J. A. MacGahan, *The War Correspondence of the "Daily News" 1877* (London: Macmillan, 1878), 360 (from a report by J. MacGahan, 19 September 1877).

54. Formby, *First Two Battles of Plevna*, 30.

55. Henry F. Thuillier, *The Principles of Land Defence and Their Application to the Condition of To-day* (London: Longmans, Green, 1902), 148.

56. Pacha and Talaat, *Défense de Plevna*, 44.

57. Greene, *Report of the Russian Army*, 423; and Bornecque, *Rôle de la Fortification*, 340–47.

58. Formby, *First Two Battles of Plevna*, 2.

59. Valentine Baker Pacha, *War in Bulgaria: A Narrative of Personal Experiences* (London: Sampson Low, Marston, Searle and Rivington, 1879), 359.

60. Greene, *Report of the Russian Army*, 278.

61. Brunker, *Story of the Russo-Turkish War*, 80.

62. Crowe, *Epitome of the Russo-Turkish War*, 12.

63. Report from Consul Zohrab to Lord Derby, 22 December 1876, Erzeroum, WO106/1.

64. Formby, *First Two Battles of Plevna*, 2.

65. Brunker, *Story of the Russo-Turkish War*, 13.

66. Maurice, *Russo-Turkish War*, 47. The continued existence of Roman fortifications in the Balkans is briefly covered in Crawford, "Some Linear Earthworks."

67. Brackenbury, *Field Works*, 25–26. Brackenbury mentions the use of top cover in field fortifications at Sebastopol, yet the author cannot find mention of its widespread use there in protecting ordinary soldiers of the line, as was the case at Plevna.

68. Maurice, *Russo-Turkish War*, 117–18.

69. Wellesley, *With the Russians*, 254.

70. Hozier, *Russo-Turkish War*, 586–87.

71. "Notes by a Russian Engineer on the Theatre of War in European Turkey," trans. Capt. J. W. Savage, *Professional Papers of the Corps of Royal Engineers* 9 (1883): 13.

72. Greene, *Report of the Russian Army*, 399–402.

73. To Colonel Wellesley from Foreign Office, 24 October 1877, FO65/985.

74. This is taken from the file Return of the Officers of Royal Engineers,

dated 21 February 1877, by Deputy Adjutant General, Royal Engineers, J. Grant. Found in Parliamentary Papers 1877 (72), Army (officers employed in Turkey), National Archives, London.

75. Special correspondent of the *London Times*, Times, 30 April 1877, FO 106/5.

76. Menning, *Bayonets before Bullets*, 7.

77. Anton Springer, *Der Russisch-türkische Krieg, 1877–1878, in Europa* (Vienna: Verlag von Carl Konegen, 1891), 3:328.

78. Maurice, *Russo-Turkish War*, 287–88.

79. Greene, *Report of the Russian Army*, 417.

80. Report of General de Courcy, attaché militaire, 28 June 1877, 7 N 1496.

81. Maurice, *Russo-Turkish War*, 243.

Chapter 3. The Second Anglo-Boer War

1. This war was the second of two wars with the Boers. The first had taken place in 1880–1881 after the Transvaal declared its independence from Britain. After a short war the British agreed to a conciliatory peace, as it was obvious they would not be able to force the Boers to concede without expending considerable effort. The British Army had suffered a number of defeats, including a humiliating reversal at the battle of Majuba Hill (27 February 1881). These losses set up a desire for revenge, and the discovery of valuable mineral deposits in the Boer republics placed the two sides on course for another struggle.

2. The war dragged on for many months, and ultimately, the casualties and steady erosion of Boer resources and will led them to the peace table.

3. Units used the open order formation, which allowed more space between the men, to reduce their vulnerability to enemy fire. Essentially the men were spread out rather than bunched together.

4. Adjutant General's Office, *Reports on Military Operations in South Africa and China*, (War Department) Reel NNM-75, no. 43, 22–23, National Archives, College Park, Maryland (hereafter "U.S. Reports").

5. Ibid., 21–22, 43, 54, 191–92, and 202. Both Slocum and Capt. Carl Reichmann, the two U.S. Army attachés in South Africa, commented on this situation. Lieutenant Nix later died of his wounds. Almost certainly, Lt. M. J. Nix was an officer in the Koninklijk Nederlands-Indisch Leger (KNIL), which is sometimes translated as the Royal Netherlands Indian Army or Royal Netherlands East Indies Army.

6. Letter from Col. Ivor Herbert to the Austrian attaché Capt. Robert Trimmel, 9 January 1900. Offizielle Berichte des Hauptmann des Generalstabs-Korps Robert Trimmel über den Burenkrieg, AT-OeStA/KA AhOB GSt. EvB Akten 999. Hereafter "EvB Akten 999."

7. Letter from Brig. Gen. J. W. Murray to Col. Ivor Herbert, 7 January 1900, EvB Akten 999.

8. U.S. Reports, 196. Reichmann had better access after the date of this statement. Captain Reichmann was also an attaché during the Russo-Japanese War, and the experience provided him an excellent perspective on the changes occurring in warfare at that time.

9. Frederic Unger, *With "Bobs" and Krüger: Experiences and Observations of an American War Correspondent in the Field with Both Armies* (Philadelphia: Henry T. Coates, 1901), 75.

10. Bartle Frere, "On Temperate South Africa," *Proceedings of the Royal Geographical Society and Monthly Record of Geography* 3, no. 1 (January 1881): 1–19.

11. Ibid.

12. Britain had seized Cape Colony similarly in 1806 from the Dutch. It was from here that most of the Boers left on their Great Trek of the 1830s to the east and northeast. Natal was a British colony that had been seized from the Boers in 1843.

13. Bill Nasson, *The South African War, 1899–1902* (London: Arnold, 1999), 111.

14. Ibid., 115–16.

15. Ibid., 118–19.

16. Frederick Maurice, *History of the War in South Africa: 1899–1902* (1906; reprint, Uckfield, UK: Naval and Military Press, 2004), 1:246–51. This collection is the British official history of the war. The problem of identifying enemy positions would occur repeatedly during the conflict, and it is one of the key changes in warfare. Previously, the ranges at which combat took place and the use of black powder meant that usually the men had to be able to see at least a part of the enemy army, especially the troops engaged. The fighting in the Boer War demonstrated that this dynamic had forever changed.

17. Methuen's plan was poor and essentially consisted of moving forward to cross the river, following an inadequate reconnaissance of suspected Boer positions.

18. The setbacks of "Black Week" included the British defeat at Stormberg on 10 December, the defeat at Magersfontein on 11 December, and the defeat at Colenso on 15 December.

19. At Stormberg, Major General Gatacre failed adequately to reconnoiter the likely Boer positions, he did not allow his men to rest after an exhausting day and night approach, and thus they blundered into an ambush. This debacle was followed by a terrible lack of communication, which isolated several hundred British troops, who ultimately had to surrender.

20. Again, the lack of effective reconnaissance was egregious. The plan also had no clear main effort. Thus, attacking head-on into Boer positions without concentrating his force and gaining a clear picture of the Boers' location was simply suicidal. It was particularly so, given what had already eminently been demonstrated about defensive firepower from prepared positions.

21. Maurice, *History of the War*, 377.

22. Louis Botha, "General Botha's Own Report on the Battle of Colenso," ed. and trans. C. J. Barnard, South African Military History Society's *Military History Journal* 1, no. 7 (December 1970), http://samilitaryhistory.org/vol017cc .html (accessed 14 August 2011). General Botha gives the figure of 3,000 Boers, but it is not clear if this number includes the forces across the Tugela. Furthermore, accounting for the number of Boers at any given battle is problematic given that the men were apt to drift in and out of their units as they saw fit.

23. Maurice, *History of the War*, 551–53. After the battle there was an exchange of heliograph communications between General Buller and Lt. Gen. George White, commander of the besieged forces at Ladysmith. (A heliograph was a method of communication in which troops reflected sunlight with a mirror to transmit messages over long distances.) General Buller advised White that he would not be able to relieve him anytime soon and that White should fire off his remaining ammunition until he had none left and seek the best terms possible once Buller had established fresh defensive positions for his own force. The transcript of the heliograph transmissions can be found in Maurice's *History of the War*. Maj. Gen. George McClellan was an American general who fought in the American Civil War and often displayed a bizarre grasp of mathematics when estimating enemy troops numbers. It was not uncommon for him to estimate his enemy's force to be two or three times larger than it actually was.

24. Ibid., 380–81. Nasson states that it was two days after Colenso, but the official history is quite clear. Nasson, *The South African War*, 135.

25. Ibid., 597. The British official history gives British casualties of 1,733 for the several days of fighting leading up to the actual battle of Spion Kop. It is reasonable to assume most of them occurred during the battle itself. By way of comparison, the Boers suffered around 300 casualties. The word "kop" is still frequently used to describe the steeply sloped terrace inside a soccer stadium.

26. These fortifications are described in detail later in this chapter.

27. Maurice, *History of the War*, 68–79.

28. Christiaan de Wet, *Three Years' War* (New York: Charles Scribner's Sons, 1903), 18.

29. U.S. Reports, 233. Reichmann was discussing the retreat from Middleburg in late July and early August 1900.

30. Though it is outside the scope of this book to go into detail, there does seem to be a connection with the use of field fortification to prevent desertion and its use to secure prisoners of war or civilians caught up in a conflict—that is, using field fortification to prevent the escape of individuals whose containment is deemed necessary for the war effort. The British practice of rounding up Boer families into concentration camps and of housing prisoners of war, often secured in temporary barbed-wire enclosures, fits this interpretation. The ready availability of barbed wire meant that such camps could be established relatively quickly and cost effectively. Of course, housing prisoners of war in this fashion was not new, but the use of concentration camps had only been seen previously during the Spanish-American War of 1898. It indicated that the use of field fortification to prevent desertion (escape) could equally be applied to captured opponents and civilians.

31. Captain Trimmel noted that British artillery fire often began at 6,000 meters, and by 4,000 to 5,000 meters from the enemy, the troops had to deploy. He also noted that rifle fire often was opened at 2,000–3,000 yards (he mixed distance measurements in the original). What effect firing at this range was supposed to have is not clear, although it could well have prompted the Boers to return fire, thus increasing the chance of spotting them. EvB Akten 999.

32. I would rather not bore the reader with too much detail about this technical subject. However, simply put, a typical bullet fired from a Martini-Henry weighed 400 grains (grains being the standard unit of measure), and it generated about 1,800 foot-pounds (ft-lbs) of energy. A typical bullet from a Boer Mauser weighed about 200 grains and generated about 4,000 ft-lbs of energy. That is, it had more than twice the hitting power.

33. Both sides had large amounts of black-powder munitions, which must have proven somewhat problematic until sufficient stocks of more modern weapons and munitions were available. As late as August 1900, French attaché Col. Jules Charles du Pontavice du Heussey (sometimes listed as "de Heussey") noted the use of large amounts of black-powder artillery ammunition by the British. See his correspondence dated 31 August 1900, 7 N 1219, Service Historique de la Défense, Paris.

34. De Wet, *Three Years' War*, 41–42. A *schanze* was a fighting position. In this context it was a sangar, but elsewhere the word is used to describe a trench.

35. Deneys Reitz, *Commando: A Boer Journal of the Boer War* (New York: Sarpedon, 1970), 63–85.

36. Ibid., 61. The choice of racial epithets reflects the rather typical Boer disdain for black Africans.

37. Robert Trimmel, *Eindrücke und Beobachtungen aus dem Boerenkriege* (Vienna: Verlag von L. W. Seidel & Sohn, k. u. k. Hof-Buchhändler, 1901), 11.

38. Henry F. Mackern, *Side-Lights on the March: The Experience of an American Journalist in South Africa* (London: John Murray, 1901), 145. See also *Report of His Majesty's Commissioners Appointed to Inquire into the Military Preparations and Other Matters Connected to the War in South Africa Compiled by the Royal Commission on the War in South Africa* (London: HMSO, 1903), 48–49.

39. Alexander Horace C. Kearsey, *War Record of the York and Lancaster Regiment* (London: George Bells and Sons, 1903), 188.

40. De Wet, *Three Years' War*, 202.

41. The nature of Boer society, where many families lived out on the veld in small groups of farms, meant that they were highly self-reliant for their own food and protection. Typically, males knew how to use a rifle, a skill learned from an early age, and were often good shots. Given that wild game provided an important source of nutrition, the men were frequently good hunters. This prowess translated well to military use. They also were familiar with the use of camouflage, both to stalk game and as a combat multiplier against their African native enemies, who frequently greatly outnumbered them. In addition, they routinely used field fortification both for physical protection and as a force multiplier for many of the same reasons. Most Boers were good horsemen who used their horses to great effect in achieving great tactical and operational mobility. In this role, usually they functioned as mounted infantry, dismounting and seeking cover to fight (a tactic that the British were forced to mimic). Moreover, they often had an excellent feel for terrain, facilitating their choice of good fighting positions that would provide great cover and opportunities for ambush and observation of the surrounding country.

42. Frederick H. Howland, *The Chase of De Wet and Later Phases of the Boer War as Seen by an American Correspondent* (Providence, RI: Preston and Rounds, 1901), 176–77.

43. De Wet, *Three Years' War*, 44–45.

44. U.S. Reports, 234–37.

45. Kearsey, *War Record*, 185.

46. Lt. Col. R. M. Holden, "The Blockhouse System in South Africa," *Journal of the Royal United Services Institute* 46, no. 290 (1902): 479–89.

47. De Wet, *Three Years' War*, 77–81.

48. Ibid., 143.

49. Kearsey, *War Record*, 177–80.

50. U.S. Reports, 48.

51. Ibid., 192. Captain Reichmann implies that the British force was quite large, without providing a figure.

52. Ibid., 11.

53. Kearsey, *War Record*, 189.

54. Jan Christiaan Smuts, *The Boer War: Official Dispatches from Generals De La Rey, Smuts, and Others* (Philadelphia: George H. Buchanan and Company, 1902), 15.

55. E. P. C. Girouard, *History of the Railways during the War in South Africa, 1899–1902* (London: HMSO, 1903), 131–41.

56. Holden, "Blockhouse System," 479–89.

57. Field Marshal Lord Carver, *The Boer War* (London: Pan Books, 2000), 146–47. See also Thomas Packenham, *The Boer War* (New York: Avon Books, 1979), 417.

58. Kearsey, *War Record*, 183–84.

59. Girouard, *History of the Railways*, 77.

60. De Wet, *Three Years' War*, 41.

61. Report of Colonel du Pontavice, 2 January 1900. 7 N 1219, Correspondence non Officielle du Colonel Du Pontavice.

62. Report of Colonel du Pontavice, 18 January 1900. 7 N 1219.

63. J. F. C. Fuller, *The Last of the Gentlemen's Wars: A Subaltern's Journal of the War in South Africa, 1899–1902* (London: Faber and Faber Limited, 1937), 107–8.

64. De Wet, *Three Years' War*, 260.

65. Ibid., 260–66.

66. Ibid. He gives examples on pages 286–88 and 299.

67. Ibid., 135.

68. Ibid., 288.

69. Ibid., 201.

70. Smuts, *The Boer War*, 10–11. This material was from the August–September 1901 report.

71. Ibid., 11.

72. Kearsey, *War Record*, 182.

73. Girouard, *History of the Railways*, 80.

74. Count Adalbert Sternberg, *My Experiences of the Boer War* (London: Longmans, Green, 1901), 110.

75. De Wet, *Three Years' War*, 27–28.

76. Fuller, *Last of the Gentlemen's Wars*, 89. Helio is short for heliograph.

77. De Wet, *Three Years' War*, 102.

78. U.S. Reports, 31.

79. The Carl Zeiss Company developed the first prism binoculars in 1894. They provided a much clearer image and greater magnification than had previous models. The mass manufacture of high-quality optical instruments provided the means to spot targets more effectively at much greater ranges than previously had been feasible.

80. Sternberg, *My Experiences*, 112–13.

81. A puggaree is a cloth band wrapped around the crown of a hat. From an extract from Molony's diary, found in Carver, *Boer War*, 141–42.

82. Maurice, *History of the War*, 251.

83. U.S. Reports, 32–33.

84. Ibid., 35.

85. Ibid., 82–84.

86. David S. Miller, *A Captain of the Gordons: Service Experiences, 1900–1909*, ed. Margaret Miller and Helen Russell Miller (London: Sampson, Low, Marston, 1913), 102–4.

87. Sternberg, *My Experiences*, 120–21.

88. Captain Trimmel, AT-OeStA/KA, Nachgelassene Aufzeichnungen B/385.

89. U.S. Reports, 76.

90. French attaché Lieutenant Colonel Albert d'Amade, 21 February 1901. in 7 N 1219, Correspondence non Officielle du Colonel Du Pontavice.

91. Ibid.

92. Reitz, *Commando*, 75.

93. Sternberg, *My Experiences*, 205–6.

94. Observation balloons provided an effective means for observation and were used throughout the First World War. During the Second Anglo-Boer War, the British used balloons as a platform for observation where they could not find suitably high ground or where they required greater height to see clearly.

95. U.S. Reports, 31. See also Unger, *With "Bobs" and Krüger*, 35.

96. Unger, *With "Bobs" and Krüger*, 125. See also U.S. Reports, 37.

97. Gefechts-Thatigkeit, EvB Akten 999.

98. Holden, "The Blockhouse System," 479–89. Native peoples in the area of conflict were often used for labor, and some Boers seem to have brought the odd African servant with them. In addition, the British recruited quite a few local Africans to serve as soldiers guarding the lines of blockhouses, thus freeing up white soldiers for duty elsewhere. In addition, both sides often very poorly treated the native peoples and frequently left them to fend for themselves when their care was deemed detrimental to the military mission.

99. Fuller, *Last of the Gentlemen's Wars*, 108–10. Local farms were sometimes fortified and included in a line, if they were in a good location. When an alarm was heard, invariably the local blockhouses opened fire, and this action could easily carry down the line. Fuller mentions one occasion when firing spread to

about 120 blockhouses! His description of blockhouse construction matches others' accounts. See also Kearsey, *War Record*, 180–82; and Holden, "Blockhouse System," 479–89.

100. Kearsey, *War Record*, 180.

101. Richard Tomlinson, "Britain's Last Castles: Masonry Blockhouses of the South African War, 1899–1902," *The South African Military History Society's Military History Journal* 10, no. 6 (December 1997), http://samilitaryhistory.org/vol106rt .html (accessed 2 August 2010). Figures vary from 5,000 to 8,000 blockhouses. It is unlikely that an exact number is available, given the often haphazard nature of the addition of blockhouses to already fortified points. It is not clear if these structures were counted separately and thus may explain the large disparity in numbers.

102. Girouard, *History of the Railways*, 80.

103. Kearsey, *War Record*, 185.

104. Fuller, *Last of the Gentlemen's Wars*, 83–85.

105. Ibid., 91. A typical British regiment of the period would have roughly 400–600 soldiers.

106. Brackenbury, *Field Works*, 25–26.

107. Kearsey, *War Record*, 189.

108. Fuller, *Last of the Gentlemen's Wars*, 111–12.

109. Shell shock, nervous exhaustion, battle fatigue, and other phrases have all been used at various times to describe what we now call post-traumatic stress disorder.

110. Reitz, *Commando*, 63–64.

111. Sternberg, *My Experiences*, xxii. Henderson was commenting in the introduction to Sternberg's book. The British cavalry adapted and started to resemble the Boers, in that they often functioned as mounted infantry. In addition, the sheer mobility of the Boers forced the British to mount their infantry in order to try to maneuver sufficiently quickly to catch fast-moving groups of Boers. These mounted infantry also provided valuable service in patrolling between blockhouse lines. After the war, British cavalry retrained to fight on foot, as well as on horseback, and proved their worth in reconnaissance in 1914 (often performing better than their German counterparts did in that role).

112. *Report of His Majesty's Commissioners*, 86.

113. Captain Trimmel commented that British shrapnel fire suffered from fuses that did not work properly, either not exploding at all or deonating incorrectly. EvB Akten 999.

114. Fuller, *Last of the Gentlemen's Wars*, 48.

115. U.S. Reports, 31. See also Unger, *With "Bobs" and Krüger*, 125.

Chapter 4. The Russo-Japanese War

1. Lieutenant Colonel Yoda, "Modern Tendencies in Strategy and Tactics as Shown in Campaigns in the Far East," *The Russo-Japanese War Research Society*, February 1904–September 1905, originally from the *Kuikosha Kiji* (*Officers Club Journal*) 352 (December 1906), trans. Capt. E. F. Calthrop, R.F.A., and published

in *Journal of the Royal United Studies Institute* 51, http://www.russojapanesewar
.com/mod-tend.html (accessed 20 May 2009).

2. Ibid.

3. Menning, *Bayonets before Bullets*, 87–90.

4. Menning refers to them as the regulation of 1881 or the infantry tactical regulations. Ibid., 136.

5. Ibid., 134–51.

6. Bailey, *Field Artillery and Firepower*, 209.

7. Journal de marche du Colonel Lombard, 20 July 1904, 7 N 1701, Service Historique de la Défense, Paris.

8. These histories included War Department, Office of the Chief of Staff, *Reports of Military Observers Attached to the Armies in Manchuria during the Russo-Japanese War*, 5 parts (Washington: Government Printing Office, 1906–1907), hereafter "USOR"; and *Official History of the Russo Japanese War* (London: HMSO, 1906–1910). Also see Historical Section of the German General Staff, *The Russo-Japanese War*, trans. K. Donat (London: Hugh Rees, 1908).

9. Letter to Général Sylvestre from P. Mitschenko, general aide-de-camp of the Tsar, 14 February 1905, 7 N 1516, Rapports du Général Sylvestre, Service Historique de la Défense, Paris. (Lieutenant Burtin was killed in action while serving with the 1er Regiment de Cosaques de Verchneoudinsky. While not an official attaché, he had sent a number of detailed letters, reporting on the war, to fellow French officers during his time with the Russian Army.)

10. Report of Capt. Carl Reichman, RG 165, Box 126 (entry 310), 17, Records of the War Department and Special Staffs Intelligence Corps.

11. Report on the treatment of correspondents, WO 106/6336, National Archives, London.

12. *USOR*, part 3, 108. (Maj. Joseph Kuhn of the U.S. Corps of Engineers noted this difference in his report on field fortifications, 108–15.)

13. R. Stewart, "Manchuria: The Land and Its Economy," *Economic Geography* 8, no. 2 (1932): 134–60.

14. A. de C. Sowerby, "The Exploration of Manchuria," *The Geographical Journal* 54, no. 2 (1919): 73–89.

15. R. Turley, "Some Notes on the River System of the Upper Liao, Manchuria," *The Geographical Journal* 25, no. 3 (1905): 297–300.

16. Rapports du Général Sylvestre, 1 December 1904, 7 N 1517.

17. A. Glasfurd, *Sketches of Manchurian Battle-fields with a Verbal Description of Southern Manchuria: An Aid to the Study of the Russo-Japanese War* (London: Hugh Rees, 1910), 2.

18. Ibid., 2. (Also see Capt. Carl Reichmann's comments in *USOR*, part 1, 262.)

19. Ibid., 3.

20. *USOR*, part 3, 111.

21. R. M. Connaughton, *The War of the Rising Sun and Tumbling Bear* (London: Routledge, 1988), 55.

22. Menning, *Bayonets before Bullets*, 157. For an overview of the whole war,

see Connaughton, *War of the Rising Sun*; and Denis Warner and Peggy Warner, *The Tide at Sunrise: A History of the Russo-Japanese War, 1904–5* (London: Angus and Robertson, 1975).

23. *USOR*, part 1, 134–35.

24. Report of Lt. Col. A. L. Haldane, 18 July 1904, *Reports from British Officers Attached to the Japanese Forces in the Field*, 1:60. Held in WO33/1518, National Archives, London (hereafter "*BORJ*").

25. Ibid., 75. Despite this valiant defense against tremendous odds, Colonel Tretyakov and his men were upbraided by their commanding officer—Gen. Anatole Stoessel—who had abandoned them to their fate. Tragically typical of much of the Russian war effort, General Stoessel received a medal for his troubles.

26. Gen. Alexei Kuropatkin, *The Russian Army and the Japanese War*, trans. Capt. A. B. Lindsay (New York: E. P. Dutton, 1909), 1:256.

27. Report of Lieutenant Colonel Haldane, 14 September 1904, *BORJ*, 1:89.

28. Connaughton, *War of the Rising Sun*, 137. See also Kuropatkin, *Russian Army*, 2:41.

29. Ibid., 136. Therefore, perhaps it is not surprising that General Kuropatkin glosses over this fact in his account of the war. Kuropatkin, *Russian Army*, 2:39–40.

30. Report of Capt. B. Vincent, 4 July 1904, *BORJ*, 1:153–60. Also, the report of Lt. Gen. Sir Ian Hamilton, *BORJ*, 1:142–53.

31. Kuropatkin, *Russian Army*, 2:40–43.

32. Rapports du Général Sylvestre, 31 August 1904, 7 N 1516.

33. Kuropatkin, *Russian Army*, 2:230–31.

34. Ibid., 1:242.

35. Connaughton, *War of the Rising Sun*, 187.

36. Ibid., 205–26.

37. A. von Schwartz, *Influence of the Experience of the Siege of Port Arthur upon the Construction of Modern Fortresses*, trans. Second (Military Information) Division General Staff, War Department (Washington: Government Printing Office, 1908), 29–37. This work has an excellent overview of the fortifications at Port Arthur.

38. See E. Ashmead-Bartlett, *Port Arthur: The Siege and Capitulation* (London: William Blackwood and Sons, 1906). Also see B. W. Nörregaard, *Die Belagerung von Port Arthur* (Leipzig: Theodor Weicher, 1912); and W. Richmond Smith, *The Siege and Fall of Port Arthur* (London: Eveleigh Nash, 1905).

39. Warner and Warner, *Tide at Sunrise*, 435–48.

40. Connaughton, *War of the Rising Sun*, 273.

41. Ibid.; and Warner and Warner, *Tide at Sunrise*, 400–401.

42. The tsar had appointed Admiral Alexeiev viceroy to the Far East, and the chain of command in the theater of war became extremely confused. Admiral Alexeiev regularly interfered in the conduct of the campaign. It was a welcome relief for Kuropatkin when Alexeiev was recalled to Russia, though this move did not prevent his political machinations in St. Petersburg.

43. Connaughton, *War of the Rising Sun*, 278–79.

44. Ibid., 279–81.

45. Ibid., 280.

46. This description was said about both sets of troops in combat. *Reports from British Officers Attached to the Russian Forces in the Field,* 3:239. Held in WO33/1522, National Archives, London (hereafter "*BORR*").

47. Naoko Shimazu, "The Myths of the 'Patriotic Soldier': Japanese Attitudes towards Death in the Russo-Japanese War," *War and Society* 19, no. 2 (October 2001).

48. Note by Lt. Gen. Sir C. J. Burnett, Headquarters, Third Army, 9 August 1905, *BORJ,* 2:660–61. Held in WO33/1520, National Archives, London.

49. Report of Lt. Gen. Sir Ian Hamilton, 5 September 1904, *BORJ,* 1:316.

50. Report of Colonel Waters, March 1904, *BORR,* 2:239. Perhaps this situation is why he mentioned on page 171 of the same report that the exercise of Russian martial law was "much less harsh than might be expected."

51. Kuropatkin, *Russian Army,* 2:73–77.

52. Ibid., 19.

53. Warner and Warner, *Tide at Sunrise,* 460. Also Connaughton, *War of the Rising Sun,* 259.

54. Kuropatkin, *Russian Army,* 2:173.

55. The report of Colonel Hoff gives the numbers of officers reported missing as lower than the numbers killed: 26 officers killed at the battle of the Yalu as opposed to 6 missing; he reports the number of men lost at the Yalu as 564 killed and 679 missing. During the war these figures retained a similar ratio until the battle of Mukden when he reported 233 officers were killed and 282 went missing along with 7,638 men killed and 28,156 missing. *USOR,* part 2, 115–16.

56. Report of Maj. Charles Lynch, *USOR,* part 4, 399.

57. Report of Lieutenant Colonel Haldane, 14 September 1904, *BORJ,* 1:86.

58. *USOR,* part 1, 262.

59. Report of Lieutenant General Hamilton, 25 July 1904, *BORJ,* 1:150–51.

60. Ibid., 158.

61. *USOR,* part 1, 84. Captain Morrison wrote a guide, published in 1914, titled *Training Infantry.* Morrison was also a key figure in the education of Gen. George C. Marshall.

62. Chinese labor had prepared the quite formidable fortifications protecting Liaoyang well in advance of the battle itself.

63. *USOR,* part 1, 42. (See also Maj. Joseph Kuhn's report in part 3, 31. It mentions that high explosives formed a fourth to a third of the Japanese shells fired.)

64. *USOR,* part 1, 34–35.

65. Report of Colonel Tulloch, 1 October 1904, *BORJ,* 2:626.

66. Report of Captain Vincent, 12 November 1904, *BORJ,* 1:381.

67. Ibid., 397.

68. Journal de marche du Colonel Lombard, 21, 7 N 1701.

69. Frederick Palmer, *With Kuroki in Manchuria* (London: Methuen, 1904), 120.

70. Report of Lieutenant Colonel Agar, January 1906, *BORJ*, 2:639.

71. Report of Capt. Carl Reichman, RG165, Box 126 (entry 310), 22.

72. Report of Colonel Tulloch, 1 October 1904, *BORJ*, 2:627.

73. *USOR*, part 1, 80.

74. Ibid., 95.

75. *USOR*, part 3, 110.

76. Report of Captain Robertson, 19 June 1905, *BORJ*, 2:213.

77. Report of Oberleutnant Hoess, *Kais 15 Japanische Division*, Evidenzbüro des Generalstab (5/8) 3405, OeStA/KA.

78. Report of Colonel Tulloch, 1 October 1904, *BORJ*, 2:624.

79. *USOR*, part 3, 108.

80. Remarks by Lt. Gen. Sir W. Nicholson, 1 October 1904, *BORJ*, 2:627–28.

81. *USOR*, part 1, 37.

82. Ibid., 114.

83. Ibid., 134.

84. Report of Captain Robertson, 10 February 1905, *BORJ*, 2:19.

85. Report on the Liaotung Peninsula operations of the Third Japanese Army, Lt. G. R. Fortescue, RG 165, Box 124, Records of the War Department and Special Staffs Intelligence Corps.

86. Ibid. Also see Report of Lieutenant Colonel Haldane, 18 July 1904, *BORJ*, 1:60–76.

87. Ibid.

88. *USOR*, part 1, 9.

89. Ibid.

90. This style had more in common with that seen in figure 2.1 than it does with constructions in figures 4.3 and 4.4.

91. Reports of Capt. J. B. Jardine, 12 and 15 July 1904, *BORR*, 1:135–41.

92. Report of Col. W. Apsley Smith, 10 September 1904, *BORR*, 1:78.

93. *USOR*, part 3, 109–10. Kuhn went on to describe the redoubt shown in figure 4.3 as possessing "the best profile and trace of any seen during the war."

94. Ibid., 110.

95. This network is in all essence a modern defensive system of fortified positions, similar to those found in the later stages of the First World War.

96. *USOR*, part 1, 135.

97. Ibid., 79.

98. Ibid., 25. This observation refers to Russian troops breaking under shell fire (26 August 1904) despite being in field fortifications and is briefly described later in this chapter.

99. *USOR*, part 1, 134. (Maj. Joseph Kuhn of the U.S. Army Corps of Engineers noted that the Russians did not make any attempt to conceal their trenches before the battle of Liaoyang. See pp. 108–9.)

100. Ibid., 262.

101. Report of Lieutenant Colonel Hume, 18 February 1905, *BORR*, 1:642.

102. *USOR*, part 3, 109.

103. Report of Captain Jardine, 3 February 1905, *BORR*, 1:656.

104. Report of Lieutenant Colonel Hume, 5 September 1904, *BORR*, 1:360. Outside of Liaoyang, Hume noted that the Russians had constructed proper entrenchments despite the difficult soil; however, Chinese laborers had constructed many of these positions.

105. *USOR*, part 1, 80–81.

106. Report of Captain Vincent, 1 November 1904, *BORR*. 1:586.

107. Rapports du Général Sylvestre, 19 January 1905, 7 N 1518.

108. Report of Captain Vincent, 1 November 1904, *BORR*, 1:591.

109. *USOR*, part 3, 111.

110. Ibid., 110–15.

111. *USOR*, part 4, 190–91.

112. *USOR*, part 1, 81–82.

113. *USOR*, part 3, 113.

114. Report of Lieutenant Colonel Hume, 13 May 1904, *BORJ*, 1:18.

115. Report of Lt. Gen. Sir Ian Hamilton, 13 May 1904, *BORJ*, 1:44–45.

116. *Observations sur l'Artillerie dans la Guerre Russo-Japonais*, Enseignements de la guerre, 10, 7 N 1532, Service Historique de la Défense, Paris.

117. "Machine Gun Tactics," *Journal of the United States Cavalry Association*, trans. M. S. E. Harry Bell, 22 (May 1912): 1140–46.

118. *USOR*, part 1, 32.

119. Ibid., 46.

120. *USOR*, part 5, 98–99.

121. *USOR*, part 1, 43.

122. Report of Lieutenant Colonel Haldane, 4 September 1904, *BORJ*, 1:226.

123. Translated copy of a Japanese officer's report on the Battle of Liaoyang. Evidenzbüro des Generalstab (5/8) 3403, OeStA/KA.

124. Bericht des Hauptmann v. Dáni, no. 132, 18 October 1905, *Panzer für Infanterie und Pionniere*, Evidenzbüro des Generalstab (5/8) 3402, OeStA/KA.

125. Rapports du Général Sylvestre, 31 August 1904, 7 N 1516.

126. *USOR*, part 1, 82.

127. *USOR*, part 3, 33–34.

128. Ibid., 28–35.

129. Report of Lt. Gen. Sir Ian Hamilton, 12 November 1904, *BORJ*, 1:327.

130. Report of Lieutenant Colonel Haldane, 14 September 1904, *BORJ*, 1:91.

131. *USOR*, part 1, 82–83, 90. Captain Morrison provided a more detailed description of the effects of mines during the battle of Liaoyang. A total of ten mines exploded as the Japanese infantry moved through a fortified position, but apart from soldiers being covered in dirt, no one was injured, though much confusion resulted. See also Rapports du Général Sylvestre, 14 September 1905, 7 N 1516.

132. *USOR*, part 3, 113–14. At the Shoushanpu position the Russians had constructed military pits that were four miles long and four rows deep.

133. Rapports du Général Sylvestre, 9 July 1904, 7 N 1516.

134. *USOR*, part 1, 25.

135. Ibid., 25–28.

136. *USOR*, part 3, 107–8.

137. *Observations sur l'Artillerie*, Enseignements de la guerre, 7 N 1532, 24.

138. Rapports du Général Sylvestre, 31 August 1904, 7 N 1516, 22.

139. *USOR*, part 1, 53–55.

140. Maj. Charles Lynch, who compiled a medical report on the war for the U.S. government (*USOR*, part 4, 193–94), contradicts this idea. He noted that bayonet and sword wounds were relatively rare, with only one sword wound being seen. Even allowing that such "close battle" injuries were much more likely to be fatal because of the nature of hand-to-hand fighting, his comments are worth bearing in mind when set against the statistics. Col. Valery Harvard, a U.S. assistant surgeon-general, wrote in his report that only 0.3 percent of casualties were caused by bayonets. See *USOR*, part 3, 33.

141. *USOR*, part 1, 81.

142. *USOR*, part 5, 102.

143. *USOR*, part 3, 114.

144. The U.S. Army addressed this issue in General Orders No. 42, War Department, 1913. War Department, Annual Reports Fiscal Year Ended June 30, 1913. *Report of the Chief of Engineers U.S. Army, 1913*, Part 1 (Washington: Government Printing Office, 1913), 25.

145. *USOR*, part 1, 112.

Chapter 5. The Balkan Wars

1. Richard Hall, *The Balkan Wars, 1912–1913: Prelude to the First World War* (London: Routledge, 2002), 15.

2. Ibid., 15–19. Also see Hellenic Army General Staff, *A Concise History of the Balkan Wars* (Athens: Army History Directorate Publication, 1998), 7; and Alexander Vachkov, *The Balkan Wars, 1912–1913* (Sofia, Bulgaria: Angela Publishing, 2005), 93–95. The Military Resources of Bulgaria in FO881/10110X (National Archives, London) gives the figure of 400,000 for the Bulgarian Army, including the militia.

3. Erickson, *Defeat in Detail*, 11–15.

4. Ibid., 12.

5. Hew Strachan, *The First World War*, vol. 1, *To Arms* (Oxford: Oxford University Press, 2003), 681.

6. Erickson, *Defeat in Detail*, 59.

7. Ibid., 13. U.S. military attaché Maj. Monroe McFarland reported that the Serbians removed sixteen 4.7" guns from the fortress of Nis and gave them to the field army to make up for this shortfall. Major McFarland, 31 December 1913, M1024, Reel 131.

8. Ibid., 51–67.

9. The European exceptions were Denmark and the Balkan allies. Attachés representing Argentina and Japan were present too. British attaché Lieutenant Colonel Lyon also reported that more than a hundred attachés and correspondents traveled with the Bulgarians, and this number might explain the difficulty of controlling reporting on the war. Lieutenant Colonel Lyon (Sofia)

to Sir Henry Bax-Ironside, 17 December 1912, FO881/10278, National Archives, London.

10. Major Taylor, 5 March 1913, M1024, Reel 131, Correspondence of the War College Division and Related General Staff Offices, 1903–1919, National Archives, College Park, Maryland. At the time of writing, the correct reel numbers are listed as being 127 and 128 in the National Archives' catalogue. In addition, reel 130 was also labeled as reel 131.

11. Major McFarland spent the month of January 1913 with the Serbian Army. Lt. Sherman Miles requested his reports on 31 May 1913, M1024, Reel 131.

12. Sir F. Elliot (British ambassador in Athens) to Sir Edward Grey, 31 July 1913, FO881/10442, National Archives, London. See also Lieutenant Colonel Lyon (Sofia) to Sir Henry Bax-Ironside, 17 December 1912, FO881/10278. A Hungarian, Major Tanczos, is mentioned by the former Austro-Hungarian foreign service officer Joseph Goričar as being involved in spying in the Balkans in the same time frame. See Joseph Goričar, *The Inside Story of the Anglo-German Intrigue: Or How the World War Was Brought About* (Garden City, NY: Doubleday, 1920), 27.

13. Hall, *Balkan Wars*, 134.

14. D. G. Hogarth, "The Balkan Peninsula," *The Geographical Journal* 41, no. 4 (April 1913): 324–36.

15. Noel Buxton, "Balkan Geography and Balkan Railways," *The Geographical Journal* 32, no. 3 (September 1908): 217–34. The abundant rocks in the soil were also commented on in reports of Lt. Sherman Miles, 28 February 1913, M1024, Reel 131.

16. Buxton, "Balkan Geography," 217–34.

17. B. Nr. 1900 res. Vom 23 December 1912, Evidenzbüro des Generalstab (5/8) 3462 Situation am Balkan Tagesbericht Okt–Dez, 1912, OeStA/KA.

18. Hogarth, "Balkan Peninsula," 324–36.

19. Lieutenant Miles, 28 February 1913, M1024, Reel 131. (Lt. Sherman Miles was the son of Lt. Gen. Nelson Appleton Miles and grandson of Gen. William T. Sherman.) This view is confirmed by V. N. Polyanski, "The Siege of Adrianople," *Injenerni Jurnal*, September 1913, contained in *The Royal Engineers Journal* 19 (January–June 1914): 410–28.

20. Hall, *Balkan Wars*, 55–57.

21. Ibid., 14–15.

22. Ibid., 14.

23. Ibid., 23.

24. Erickson, *Defeat in Detail*, 64.

25. Hall, Balkan Wars, 24–25. Erickson disputes this view, but it is outside the scope of this book to cover the full argument. See *Defeat in Detail*, 84.

26. Ibid.

27. A translation of an article from the "Koelnische Zeitung," [*sic*] Cologne 208 (22 February 1913). Contained in Maj. J. Taylor, 28 February 1913, M1024, Reel 131.

28. Hall, *Balkan Wars*, 26.

29. Ibid., 16–19. See also Sir Edward Grey (secretary of foreign affairs) from Sir Gerard Lowther (British ambassador in Constantinople), 26 October 1912, FO195/2437, National Archives, London. The communication plays down the scale of the rout.

30. Lt. Sherman Miles, 28 February 1913, M1024, Reel 131.

31. Erickson, *Defeat in Detail*, 102–21.

32. Maj. J. Taylor, 20 May 1913, M1024, Reel 131.

33. Sir Gerard Lowther to Sir Edward Grey, 20 November 1912, FO881/10263, National Archives, London.

34. Hall, *Balkan Wars*, 52–58. See also Sir Gerard Lowther, 26 October 1912, FO195/2437.

35. Ibid., 47–49.

36. Ibid., 59–63.

37. Ibid., 63.

38. From a Turkish account contained in Maj. J. Taylor, 8 May 1913, M1024, Reel 131.

39. Ernest Christian Helmreich, *The Diplomacy of the Balkan War, 1912–1913* (New York: Russell & Russell, 1969), 268.

40. Maj. J. Taylor, 5 March 1913, M1024, Reel 131.

41. Hall, *Balkan Wars*, 80–83.

42. Ibid., 87.

43. Lieutenant Miles, 3 July 1913, M1024, Reel 131.

44. Extracts from French newspaper articles found in a report of Major Taylor, 8 April 1913, M1024, Reel 131.

45. Colonel Piarron de Mondésir had previously served as a professor teaching the course on fortifications at the l'École Supérieure de Guerre. Col. Jean Frédéric Lucien Piarron de Mondésir, *Siege et Prise d'Adrianople* (Paris: Librairie Chapelot, 1914), 202.

46. Ibid., 198–99.

47. Hellenic Army General Staff, *A Concise History*, 179–99.

48. Hall, *Balkan Wars*, 91–95.

49. Helmreich, *Diplomacy of the Balkan War*, 196.

50. Ibid., 231–309.

51. Die Befestigungen von Scutari und die militärische Situation vor Scutari Marz 1913, Evidenzbüro des Generalstab (5/8) 3464 Einzelschriften über dem Balkan. OeStA/KA.

52. Hall, *Balkan Wars*, 94–95.

53. Ibid., 107. Also Helmreich, *Diplomacy of the Balkan War*, 341–67.

54. Hall, *Balkan Wars*, 109–17.

55. Ibid., 117–19.

56. Lt. Sherman Miles, 28 February 1913, M1024, Reel 131.

57. Vice Consul Greig (in Monastir) to Sir Gerard Lowther, 29 October 1912, FO881/10278.

58. Consul Maj. L. L. R. Samson (in Adrianople) to Sir Gerard Lowther, 31 December 1912, FO881/10410, National Archives, London.

59. Ibid., 2 February 1913, FO881/10410.

60. Hall, *Balkan Wars*, 83.

61. Major Yanikieff, The 4th Division at Karagac, 7 N 1191, Service Historique de la Défense, Paris.

62. Major McFarlane, Report on the Servian Army [*sic*], M1024, Reel 131.

63. Lieutenant Miles, 4 July 1914, M1024, Reel 131.

64. Lieutenant Colonel Fournier, 23–24 October 1912, 7 N 1568, Service Historique de la Défense, Paris.

65. Major Taylor, 19 March 1913, M1024, Reel 131.

66. Capt. G. Bellenger and Col. J. F. L. Piarron de Mondésir, "Notes on the Employment of Artillery in the Balkan Wars," *The Royal Engineers Journal* 19 (January–June 1914): 109–13.

67. Major McFarlane, Report on the Servian Army, M1024, Reel 131.

68. Yanikieff, 4th Division at Karagac, 7 N 1191.

69. Lt. Col. E. Tyrrell, 21 November 1912, FO 881/10278.

70. Lt. Col. G. W. Tyrrell to Sir G. Lowther, 18 February 1913, FO 881/10296, National Archives, London. Though this report is by "G. W. Tyrrell," it is almost certainly the same officer listed in the preceding note, as the reports originate from a "Lt. Col. Tyrrell" in the same place (a "G. E. Tyrrell" is also given). As the letter *E* is next to *W* on a standard typewriter, a simple error is the likely cause.

71. Major McFarlane, Report on the Servian Army, M1024, Reel 131.

72. Bellenger and Mondésir, "Notes on the Employment," 109–13.

73. Major Taylor, 20 May 1913, M1024, Reel 131.

74. Ibid., 3 June 1913, M1024, Reel 131.

75. Interview with Lieutenant Colonel Alexandroff of the Bulgarian Army, in report of Lieutenant Miles, 4 April 1914, M1024, Reel 131.

76. Norman Morrow, "The Employment of Artillery in the Balkan and in the Present European War," *Field Artillery Journal*, April–June 1915, 316–36.

77. Consul Samson (in Adrianople) to Sir G. Lowther, 31 December 1912, FO881/10410.

78. Sir Henry Bax-Ironside (military attaché in Sofia) to Sir Edward Grey, 12 November 1912, FO881/10263.

79. Sir Gerard Lowther to Sir Edward Grey, 23 November 1912, FO881/10263.

80. Major Taylor, 22 May 1913, M1024, Reel 131.

81. Lieutenant Antoniat, Campagne des Armées Bulgares en Thrace Octobre–Novembre 1912, 7 N 1193, Service Historique de la Défense, Paris.

82. Account of a Turkish officer from Janina, Major Taylor, 7 May 1913, M1024, Reel 131.

83. Ibid. See also Consul Samson (in Adrianople) to Sir Gerard Lowther, 31 December 1912, FO881/10410.

84. Yanikieff, 4th Division at Karagac, 7 N 1191. This was certainly the case in previous wars also.

85. Interviews with Bulgarian officers contained in Lieutenant Miles, 5 April 1914, M1024, Reel 131.

86. Ibid.

87. Ibid.

88. Lieutenant Miles, 3 July 1913, M1024, Reel 131.

89. Consul Samson (in Adrianople) to Sir Gerard Lowther, 31 December 1912, FO881/10410. See also Lieutenant Miles, 3 July 1913, M1024, Reel 131. The same was true at Janina. See the account of a Turkish officer from Janina, Major Taylor, 7 May 1913, M1024, Reel 131.

90. Lieutenant Miles, 3 July 1913, M1024, Reel 131.

91. Yanikieff, 4th Division at Karagac, 7 N 1191.

92. Lieutenant Colonel Fournier, 30 August 1913, 7 N 1568.

93. Lieutenant Miles, 3 July 1913, M1024, Reel 131.

94. Eob.Nr. 3900, October 1913, Evidenzbüro des Generalstab (5/8) 3480 Tagesberichte vom Balkankrieg von Janner–April 1913, OeStA/KA.

95. Lieutenant Colonel Fournier, 27 May 1913, 7 N 1568.

96. Polyanski, "Siege of Adrianople," 410–26.

97. Ibid.

98. Zu T. No.1133. Evidenzbüro des Generalstab (5/8) 3462.

99. Major Taylor, 5 March 1913, M1024, Reel 131.

100. Ibid., 20 May 1913, M1024, Reel 131.

101. Esquisse d'un Projet d'Opérations de l'Armée Bulgare, 7 N 1193.

102. Vice Consul C. A. Greig (in Monastir) to Sir Gerard Lowther, 2 November 1912, FO 881/10278. In the same report, Javid Pasha was also reported to have taken measures to shore up the morale of his forces. The implication given was that fortification played a role in doing so, but its veracity is not clear.

103. Both areas are close to the border with Bulgaria, and clearly fortifications were being constructed with a possible war with Bulgaria in mind. Report on Serbia, 9 June 1913, Evidenzbüro des Generalstab (5/8) 3482 Tagesberichte vom Balkankrieg von Mai–Oktober 1913, OeStA/KA.

104. Commandant Devignes, 24 June 1913, 7 N 1336, Service Historique de la Défense, Paris.

105. Rapport attaché militaire français, Sophia [Sofia], 23 March 1913, 7 N 1191.

106. Lieutenant Miles, 28 February 1913, M1024, Reel 131.

107. Ibid.

108. Ibid.

109. Ibid.

110. Yanikieff, 4th Division at Karagac, 7 N 1191.

111. Lieutenant Colonel de Matharel, 10 April 1913, 7 N 1191.

112. Major Taylor, 20 May 1913, M1024, Reel 131.

113. Obersten [sic] Pomianowski, 23 November 1912, Evidenzbüro des Generalstab (5/8) 3462.

114. Lieutenant Antoniat, Rapport no. 2 relatif aux opérations de la Campagne de Thrace, 1912, 7 N 1193.

115. Pomianowski, 23 November 1912, Evidenzbüro des Generalstab (5/8) 3462.

116. Ibid.

117. Memorandum by Lieutenant Colonel Tyrrell, 21 November 1912, FO881/10278.

118. "Some Notes on Fieldworks," *The Royal Engineers Journal* 19 (January–June 1914): 109–13.

119. Interviews with Bulgarian officers contained in a report of Lieutenant Miles, 5 April 1914, M1024, Reel 131.

120. Hauptmann des Generalstabkorps Gustav Hubka, 12 November 1912, Evidenzbüro des Generalstab (5/8) 3462.

121. Account of a Turkish officer from Janina, Major Taylor, 7 May 1913, M1024, Reel 131.

122. Lieutenant Miles, 3 July 1913, M1024, Reel 131.

123. Ibid.

124. 2nd Lt. Donald Armstrong, trans., "The Fortifications of Adrianople," *Journal of the United States Artillery* 41, no. 3 (1914): 337–44.

125. Die Befestigungen von Scutari und die militärische Situation vor Scutari Marz 1913, Evidenzbüro des Generalstab (5/8) 3464.

126. Lieutenant Miles, 3 July 1913, M1024, Reel 131.

127. Die Befestigungen von Scutari, Evidenzbüro des Generalstab (5/8) 3464.

128. Lieutenant Miles, 3 July 1913, M1024, Reel 131.

129. Extracts from French newspaper articles found in Major Taylor, 8 April 1913, M1024, Reel 131.

130. Lieutenant Miles, 3 July 1913, M1024, Reel 131.

131. Ibid.

132. Instructions of a Serbian Gen. P. Bojovic, 16 May 1913, Evidenzbüro des Generalstab (5/8) 3482.

133. Reichenau, Lt-Gen. von, "Tactical Lessons of the War in the Balkans," *The Royal Engineers Journal* 19 (January–June 1914): 185–88. Extracts of original taken from Militär-Wochenblatt, 30 September 1913.

134. Lieutenant Miles, 3 July 1913, M1024, Reel 131.

135. Account of a Turkish officer from Janina, whose article was collected by Major Taylor, 7 May 1913, M1024, Reel 131.

136. Lieutenant Miles, 3 July 1913, M1024, Reel 131.

137. Sir Gerard Lowther to Sir Edward Grey, 1 February 1913, FO881/10348, National Archives, London.

138. Interview with Colonel Papadopoff of the Bulgarian Army, report of Lieutenant Miles, 4 April 1914, M1024, Reel 131.

139. Lieutenant Miles, 3 July 1913, M1024, Reel 131.

140. Interview with Lieutenant Colonel Alexandroff.

141. Both models of 12cm howitzer saw a decline in usage, presumably because the sieges at Adrianople, Janina, and Scutari had ended. The numbers of rounds that these guns used also were quite low in comparison to the other pieces. Res. Nr. 182, Band 1, Karton 8, Belgrad Akten aus den Jahren 1907–1914, OeStA/KA.

142. Ibid.

143. In *Field Artillery and Firepower* (p. 232), Bailey gave the figure of 87,000 rounds of artillery per month for the Russian Army in Manchuria. Given the

large size of that army compared with the Bulgarian Army, rates of usage had increased dramatically.

144. Interview with Lieutenant Colonel Alexandroff.

145. Res.Nr. 182, Band 1, Karton 8, Belgrad Akten aus den Jahren 1907–1914.

146. Res.Nr. 366, Band 60, "G"-Akten von 1912–13, OeStA/KA.

147. Lieutenant Colonel Fournier, 30 August 1913, 7 N 1568.

148. Acting Vice Consul Harris (in the Dardanelles) to Consul General Eyres, 8 March 1913, FO881/10348.

149. Erickson, *Defeat in Detail*, 329. See also Hall, *Balkan Wars*, 135–36.

150. Acting consul general James Morgan (in Salonika) to Mr Marling, 29 July 1913, FO881/10442.

151. Acting consul general James Morgan (in Salonika) to Sir Edward Grey, 6 July 1913, FO881/10437, National Archives, London.

Chapter 6. The State of Military Thinking in 1914

1. Ivan S. Bloch, *The Future of War in Its Technical, Economic, and Political Relations: Is War Now Impossible?* (London: Grant Richards, 1899; Aldershot, UK: Ashgate, 2001).

2. Menning, *Bayonets before Bullets*, 256–69.

3. Major Generaz, "Tactical Connection between Infantry and Artillery during the Battle of Liao-Yang," *Field Artillery Journal*, July–September 1914, 366–89.

4. War Office, General Staff, *Report on Foreign Manoeuvres in 1912* (Uckfield, UK: The Naval and Military Press, 2008) (reprint of original 1912 edition), 100.

5. Menning, *Bayonets before Bullets*, 258–69; and "New Russian Guns," *Field Artillery Journal* 2, no. 1 (January–March 1912): 112–15.

6. Bailey, *Field Artillery and Firepower*, 213.

7. Michael Howard, *The Lessons of History* (New Haven, CT: Yale University Press, 1991), 98–99.

8. Dimitry Quéloz, *De la Manoeuvre Napoléonienne à l'Offensive à Outrance: La tactique générale de l'Armée Française, 1871–1914* (Paris: Institut de Stratégie Comparée, 2009), 127.

9. Azar Gat, *A History of Military Thought: From the Enlightenment to the Cold War* (Oxford, UK: Oxford University Press, 2001), 382.

10. Captain Mindoff (Bulgarian Army), "Movement of Infantry in the Zone of Artillery and Infantry Fire," *Infantry Journal* 11 (July 1914–June 1915): 258–63.

11. George Nestler Trioche, "French Artillery: The Heavy Field Batteries," *Field Artillery Journal*, January–March 1915, 74–82.

12. David Herrmann, *The Arming of Europe and the Making of the First World War* (Princeton, NJ: Princeton University Press, 1997), 91.

13. Bailey, *Field Artillery and Firepower*, 235.

14. Howard, *Lessons of History*, 99.

15. *Felddienst Ordnung*, trans. General Staff, War Office (Berlin: E. S. Mittler & Son, 1908; republished as *Field Service Regulations of the German Army* [London: HMSO, 1909]), 177–78.

16. Ibid., 179–80.

17. War Office, General Staff, *Report on Foreign Manoeuvres*, 8.

18. Hew Strachan, "The Battle of the Somme and British Strategy," *Journal of Strategic Studies* 21, no. 1 (March 1998): 79–85.

19. Bailey, *Field Artillery and Firepower*, 230.

20. Ibid., 211.

21. Capt. J. Pesseaud, "Present Tendencies in Germany Regarding the Use of Heavy Artillery," *Field Artillery Journal*, April–June 1914, 304–11.

22. Major General Richter, "Retrospect of the Development of the German Field and Siege Artillery in the Past Twenty-Five Years," *Field Artillery Journal*, January–March 1915, 83–141.

23. War Department, *Field Service Regulations: U.S. Army 1910* (Washington: Government Printing Office, 1910), sections 250–72.

24. Ibid.

25. Bailey, *Field Artillery and Firepower*, 238.

26. War Office, General Staff, *Field Service Regulations* (London: HMSO, 1909), 107–29.

27. Bailey, *Field Artillery and Firepower*, 209–24.

28. Strachan, *First World War*, 680–93.

29. Ibid., 285.

30. L. Sondhaus, *Franz Conrad von Hötzendorf: Architect of the Apocalypse* (Boston: Humanity Press, 2000), 41.

31. From an unpublished report on the attack and defense of field fortification, *Die Feldbefestigungsvorschrift*, sections 2–3. Found in 724 Operations Büro. OeStA/KA.

32. Bailey, *Field Artillery and Firepower*, 213.

33. Franz Conrad von Hötzendorf, *Zum Studium der Taktik* (Vienna: Commissions-verlag von L. W. Seidel & Sohn, 1891), 200.

34. Ibid., 115.

35. Sondhaus, *Franz Conrad von Hötzendorf*, 103.

36. E. Lavisse, *Field Equipment of the European Foot Soldier, 1900–1914*, trans. Edward Lawton (Nashville: The Battery Press, 1994).

37. Bloch, *Future of War*, ix–xi.

38. Ibid., 5.

39. Ibid., xxii. See also page 4 of the same work, where he takes experimental weapons and wrongly assumes that they will both function effectively and be introduced.

40. Ibid., xix–xxii.

41. Ibid., xxii.

42. Ibid., xxv–xxvi.

43. Ibid., xxxviii.

44. Bloch, *Future of War*, 49.

45. Tim Travers, "Technology, Tactics, and Morale: Jean de Bloch, the Boer War, and British Military Theory, 1900–1914," *The Journal of Modern History* 51, no. 2 Technology and War (1979): 264–86.

46. Bloch, *Future of War*, 52.

Chapter 7. Conclusions

1. Indeed, at the start of the First World War, trenches had become deeper and had their parapet lowered based on the experiences of the fighting. The depth of a trench might be six feet, with a parapet of only one foot in height. See figure 1.6, where the depth is five feet, and the height of the parapet is eighteen inches.

2. War Office, General Staff, *Report on Foreign Manoeuvres*, 92.

3. War Office, General Staff, *Notes from the Front: Collated by the General Staff 1914* (London: HMSO, 1914; reprint, Uckfield, UK: The Naval and Military Press, 2008), 9.

4. Ray MacLeod and Kay MacLeod, "Government and the Optical Industry in Britain, 1914–1918," in *War and Economic Development: Essays in Memory of David Joslin*, ed. J. M. Winter (Cambridge, UK: Cambridge University Press, 1975), 168. See notes 25 and 26 on that page.

5. Ibid., 170–74.

6. The Bulgarians were short of heavy artillery and had trouble finding enough heavy pieces for the siege of Adrianople, let alone the storming of the lines at Tchataldja.

7. Clive Trebilcock, "War and the Failure of Industrial Mobilisation: 1899 and 1914," in Winter, *War and Economic Development*, 141.

8. Royal Commission on the War in South Africa, *Report of His Majesty's Commissioners*, 86. The Mark IV expanding bullet had proved defective, and all of the stocks sent to South Africa were withdrawn.

9. See chapter 3.

10. The author bases his claim on the casualty rates per day for the respective campaigns. Exact numbers are difficult to obtain, and comparisons will invariably bring criticism, but it is worth asking the question. British casualties on the Somme were approximately 400,000 to 450,000 over a period of about 140 days. Compared with the (roughly) 150,000 German casualties in 1940 (42 days), and those of 775,000 in 1941 (170+ days), they do not look anywhere near as bad (though they are still horrific).

11. See William Philpott, *Bloody Victory: The Sacrifice on the Somme and the Making of the Twentieth Century* (London: Little, Brown, 2009).

12. Typically, when soldiers talk about HESCOs, they are really discussing the use of a HESCO Concertainer (a trademarked name).

13. HESCO Bastion Ltd., "We Are HESCO," http://www.hesco.com/index .asp (accessed 17 April 2012).

Appendix: The American Civil War, 1861–1865

1. Earl Hess, *Field Armies and Fortifications in the Civil War: The Eastern Campaign, 1861–1864* (Chapel Hill: University of North Carolina Press, 2005), 309.

2. Ibid., 312.

3. Paddy Griffith, *Battle Tactics of the American Civil War* (Marlborough, UK: The Crowood Press, 1996), 157–58.

4. Hess, *Field Armies and Fortifications*, 181, 226, 228, 236.

5. Griffith, *Battle Tactics*, 127.

6. Four of the fifteen chapters in Halleck's book relate to the use of fortification. See Henry Wager Halleck, *Elements of Military Art and Science* (1846; reprint, Westport, CT: Greenwood, 1971).

7. Griffith, *Battle Tactics*, 127.

8. Ibid., 145–50.

9. The author can attest to this, as he has fired a number of historical firearms, from seventeenth-century matchlocks and eighteenth-century flintlock muskets through to modern rifles. In addition, he takes regularly organized classes, where students shoot firearms dating from 1400 to the present period. Muzzle-loading firearms are physically more difficult to load. They also throw out clouds of smoke, which get into the eyes and lungs of the firer, often causing discomfort, and obscure the target. In addition, prolonged firing gums up the barrel, making the loading process all the more difficult.

10. Griffith, *Battle Tactics*, 85.

11. Ibid., 169.

12. Earl Hess, *Trench Warfare under Grant and Lee: Field Fortifications in the Overland Campaign* (Chapel Hill: University of North Carolina Press, 2007), xvii.

13. Ibid., 214. In Hess's conclusions relating to trench warfare, one of the first two quotes describes the use of breastworks. It was originally taken from Wilbur Fisk's letter to the Green Mountain Freeman, July 11, 1864, and is found in Wilbur Fisk, *Hard Marching Every Day: The Civil War Letters of Private Wilbur Fisk, 1861–1865*, edited by Emil Rosenblatt and Ruth Rosenblatt (Lawrence: University Press of Kansas, 1992), 237.

14. Luvaas, *Military Legacy of the Civil War*, 226–28.

15. Ibid., 170–203.

16. Luvaas, *Military Legacy of the Civil War*, 179.

Bibliography

Unpublished Primary Documents

NATIONAL ARCHIVES, KEW GARDENS, LONDON

Russo-Turkish War, 1877–1878

WO106/1, Attaché reports: Russo-Turkish War and the Ottoman Empire
WO106/2, Attaché reports: Russo-Turkish War and the Ottoman Empire
WO106/5, Press cuttings, January–May 1877
FO65/985, Reports of military attaché, Colonel Wellesley
FO881/3701, Report on military operations in Europe
FO881/3701X, Report on military operations in Asia
FO881/3702, Report on military operations in Asia
Parliamentary Papers 1877 (72), Return of the Officers of Royal Engineers,
    dated 21 February 1877

Russo-Japanese War, 1904–1905

WO106/6336, Rules for correspondents

Balkan Wars, 1912–1913

FO195/2436, Balkans War correspondence
FO195/2437, Balkans War correspondence
FO881/10110X, Military resources of Bulgaria, part 2, 1912
FO881/10224, Correspondence on the Turkish War, part 1
FO881/10263, Further correspondence on the Turkish War, part 2
FO881/10278, Further correspondence on the Turkish War, part 3
FO881/10292, Further correspondence on the Turkish War, part 4
FO881/10296, Further correspondence on the Turkish War, part 5
FO881/10348, Further correspondence on the Turkish War, part 6
FO881/10410, Further correspondence on the Turkish War, part 7
FO881/10418, Further correspondence on the Turkish War, part 8
FO881/10431, Further correspondence on the Turkish War, part 9
FO881/10437, Further correspondence on the Turkish War, part 10
FO881/10442, Further correspondence on the Turkish War, part 11
FO881/10443, Further correspondence on the Turkish War, part 12

SERVICE HISTORIQUE DE LA DÉFENSE,
CHÂTEAU DE VINCENNES, PARIS

Russo-Turkish War, 1877–1878

7 N 1496, Guerre Russo-Turque: Rapports du Colonel Gaillard et du Général Coucy

Second Anglo-Boer War, 1899–1902

7 N 1219, Correspondance non Officielle du Colonel Du Pontavice

Russo-Japanese War, 1904–1905

7 N 1516, Rapports du Général Sylvestre, chef de la mission militaire
7 N 1517, Rapports du Général Sylvestre, chef de la mission militaire
7 N 1518, Rapports du Général Sylvestre, chef de la mission militaire
7 N 1532, Enseignements de la guerre
7 N 1533, Enseignements de la guerre
7 N 1534, Enseignements de la guerre
7 N 1701, Journal de marche du Colonel Lombard
7 N 1702, Journal de marche du Colonel Lombard

Balkan Wars, 1912–1913

7 N 1191, Rapports de l'attaché militaire Français Bulgarie
7 N 1192, Rapports de l'attaché militaire Français Bulgarie
7 N 1193, Rapports de l'attaché militaire Français Bulgarie
7 N 1336, Rapports de l'attaché militaire Français la Grèce
7 N 1568, Rapports de l'attaché militaire Français la Serbie

HELD BY THE ÖSTERREICHERISCHES STAATSARCHIV,
KRIEGSARCHIV, VIENNA (OESTA/KA)

Russo-Turkish War, 1877–1878

AT-OeStA/KA AhOB GSt
Evidenzbüro des Generalstab (5/8)
3364 Trüppenstarke und Dislokation der türkischer Armee

Second Anglo-Boer War, 1899–1902

AT-OeStA/KA
Nachgelassene Aufzeichnungen B/385
AT-OeStA/KA AhOB GSt
EvB Akten 999 Offizielle Berichte des Hauptmann des Generalstabs-Korps
    Robert Trimmel über den Burenkrieg
EvB Akten 999 Gefechts-Thatigkeit

Russo-Japanese War, 1904–1905

AT-OeStA/KA AhOB GSt
Evidenzbüro des Generalstab (5/8)
3402 Russisch-Japanische Krieg Berichte

3403 Russisch-Japanische Krieg Berichte
3404 Russisch-Japanische Krieg Ubersetzüng
3405 Russisch-Japanische Krieg Tagebücher
3406 Russisch-Japanische Krieg Lichtbilder

Balkan Wars, 1912–1913

AT-OeStA/KA AhOB GSt Militärattachés
Militärbevollmächtigte und Militär Adjoints, 1860–1918 (5/6)
Band 1, Karton 8, Belgrad Akten aus den Jahren, 1907–14
Band 60, "G"-Akten von 1912–13
724 Operations Büro
AT-OeStA/KA AhOB GSt Evidenzbüro des Generalstab (5/8)
3462 Situation am Balkan Tagesbericht Okt–Dez, 1912
3464 Einzelschriften über dem Balkan
3480 Tagesberichte vom Balkankrieg von Janner–April 1913
3482 Tagesberichte vom Balkankrieg von Mai–Oktober 1913

NATIONAL ARCHIVES, COLLEGE PARK, MARYLAND

Second Anglo-Boer War, 1899–1902

NNM-75 Reports on Military Operations in South Africa and China

Russo-Japanese War, 1904–1905

These records supplement the *Reports of Military Observers Attached to the Armies in Manchuria* during the Russo-Japanese War listed below.
RG 165, Box 124, Records of the War Department and Special Staffs Intelligence Corps
RG 165, Box 125, Records of the War Department and Special Staffs Intelligence Corps
RG 165, Box 126, Records of the War Department and Special Staffs Intelligence Corps
RG 165, Box 127, Records of the War Department and Special Staffs Intelligence Corps
RG 165, Box 129, Records of the War Department and Special Staffs Intelligence Corps

Balkan Wars, 1912–1913

RG 165, M1024, Correspondence of the War College Division and Related General Staff Offices, 1903–1919

Published Works

PRIMARY DOCUMENTS

Second Anglo-Boer War, 1899–1902

Trimmel, Robert. *Eindrücke und Beobachtungen aus dem Boerenkriege*. Vienna: Verlag von L. W. Seidel & Sohn, k. u. k. Hof-Buchhändler, 1901.

Report of His Majesty's Commissioners Appointed to Inquire into the Military Preparations and Other Matters Connected to the War in South Africa Compiled by the Royal Commission on the War in South Africa. London: His Majesty's Stationery Office (HMSO), 1903.

Russo-Japanese War, 1904–1905

National Archives, Kew Gardens, London
WO33/1518, The Russo-Japanese War, official reports, volume 1
WO33/1519, Plates for volume 1
WO33/1520, The Russo-Japanese War, volume 2
WO33/1521, Plates for volume 2
WO33/1522, The Russo-Japanese War, volume 3
WO33/1523, Plates for volume 3

Reports Published by the U.S. Government Printing Office

War Department, Office of the Chief of Staff. *Reports of Military Observers Attached to the Armies in Manchuria during the Russo-Japanese War.* 5 parts. Washington: Government Printing Office, 1906–1907.
War Department, Annual Reports Fiscal Year Ended June 30, 1913. *Report of the Chief of Engineers U.S. Army, 1913.* 3 parts. Washington: Government Printing Office, 1913.

PRIMARY SOURCES

Ashmead-Bartlett, E. *Port Arthur: The Siege and Capitulation.* London: William Blackwood and Sons, 1906.
Baker Pacha, Valentine. *War in Bulgaria: A Narrative of Personal Experiences.* London: Sampson Low, Marston, Searle and Rivington, 1879.
Bülow, H. Dietrich von. *The Spirit of the Modern System of War.* Translated by Gen. Charles Malorti de Martemont. London: Egerton's Military Library, 1825.
de Wet, Christiaan. *Three Years' War.* New York: Charles Scribner's Sons, 1903.
Forbes, Archibald, and J. A. MacGahan. *The War Correspondence of the "Daily News" 1877.* London: Macmillan, 1878.
Fuller, J. F. C. *The Last of the Gentlemen's Wars: A Subaltern's Journal of the War in South Africa, 1899–1902.* London: Faber and Faber Limited, 1937.
Gay, J. Drew. *Plevna, the Sultan, and the Porte.* London: Chatto and Windus, 1878.
Glasfurd, A. *Sketches of Manchurian Battle-fields with a Verbal Description of Southern Manchuria: An Aid to the Study of the Russo-Japanese War.* London: Hugh Rees, 1910.
Greene, Francis Vinton. *Report of the Russian Army and Its Campaigns in Turkey in 1877–1878.* New York: D. Appleton, 1879.
———. *Report of the Russian Army and Its Campaigns in Turkey in 1877–1878, Atlas.* New York: D. Appleton and Company, 1879.
Howland, Frederick H. *The Chase of De Wet and Later Phases of the Boer War as Seen by an American Correspondent.* Providence, RI: Preston and Rounds, 1901.

Kearsey, Alexander Horace C. *War Record of the York and Lancaster Regiment*. London: George Bells and Sons, 1903.

Kuropatkin, Gen. Alexei. *The Russian Army and the Japanese War*. Translated by Capt. A. B. Lindsay. New York: E. P. Dutton, 1909.

Mackern, Henry F. *Side-Lights on the March: The Experience of an American Journalist in South Africa*. London: John Murray, 1901.

Miller, David S. *A Captain of the Gordons: Service Experiences, 1900–1909*. Edited by Margaret Miller and Helen Russell Miller. London: Sampson, Low, Marston, 1913.

Nörregaard, B. W. *Die Belagerung von Port Arthur*. Leipzig: Theodor Weicher, 1912.

Pacha, Mouzaffer, and Talaat Bey. *Défense de Plevna, d'après les Documents Officiels et Privés Réunis sous la Direction du Osman pacha par Mouzaffer pacha et Talaat bey*. 2 vols. Paris: Librarie Militaire de L. Baudoin, 1889.

Palmer, Frederick. *With Kuroki in Manchuria*. London: Methuen, 1904.

Reitz, Deneys. *Commando: A Boer Journal of the Boer War*. New York: Sarpedon, 1970.

Richmond Smith, W. *The Siege and Fall of Port Arthur*. London: Eveleigh Nash, 1905.

Ryan, Charles S. *Under the Red Crescent: Adventures of an English Surgeon with the Turkish Army at Plevna and Erzeroum, 1877–1878*. London: John Murray, 1897.

Sternberg, Count Adalbert. *My Experiences of the Boer War*. London: Longmans, Green, 1901.

Unger, Frederic William. *With "Bobs" and Krüger: Experiences and Observations of an American War Correspondent in the Field with Both Armies*. Philadelphia: Henry T. Coates, 1901.

Wellesley, Frederick. *With the Russians in Peace and War: Recollections of a Military Attaché*. London: Eveleigh Nash, 1905.

TECHNICAL WORKS

Boguslawski, Albrecht von. *Tactical Deductions from the War of 1870–1871*. Minneapolis: Absinthe Press, 1996.

Brackenbury, Charles B. *Field Works, Their Technical Construction and Tactical Application*. London: Kegan Paul, Trench, & Co., 1888.

Brialmont, Alexis Henri. *Hasty Intrenchments*. Translated by Charles A. Empson. London: Henry S. King, 1872.

———. *Manuel de Fortification de Campagne*. Bruxelles: E. Guyot, 1879.

Clairac, Louis Andre de la Mamie le Chevalier de. *The Field Engineer, with Observations and Remarks on Each Chapter*. Translated by John Muller. London: John Millan, 1750.

Clausewitz, Carl von. *On War*. Translated by Michael Howard and Peter Paret. London: David Campbell Publishers Ltd., 1993.

———. *Principles of War*, in *Roots of Strategy Book 2: 3 Military Classics*. Edited and translated by Hans W. Gatzke. Mechanicsburg, PA: Stackpole Books, 1987.

Clery, Cornelius. *Minor Tactics*. London: Kegan Paul, Trench, 1883.

Conrad von Hötzendorf, Franz. *Zum Studium der Taktik*. Vienna: Commissions-verlag von L. W. Seidel & Sohn, 1891.

Cugnot, Nicolas-Joseph. *La Fortification de Campagne Théorique et Pratique*. Paris: C. A. Jombert, 1769.

de Guibert, J. A. H. *Essai Général de Tactique*. Vol. 1. Liege: Chez C. Plomteux, 1773.

Eissler, Manuel. *A Handbook of Modern Explosives: A Practical Treatise on the Manufacture and Use of Dynamite*. London: Crosby, Lockwood and Son, 1890.

Felddienst Ordnung, 1908. Translated by the General Staff, War Office. Republished as *Field Service Regulations of the German Army*. London: HMSO, 1909. Originally published by E. S. Mittler & Son, Berlin, in 1908.

Fiebeger, Gustave J. *A Text-book on Field Fortification*. New York: John Wiley & Sons, 1913.

Hutchinson, Maj. Gen. H. D. *Field Fortification: Notes on the Text-Books*. London: Gale & Polden Ltd., 1904.

Kemmis, William. *The Attack of Entrenchments by Artillery*. Woolwich: Royal Artillery Institution, 1880.

Lavisse, E. *Field Equipment of the European Foot Soldier, 1900–1914*. 1902. Translated by Edward Lawton. Nashville: The Battery Press, 1994.

Mahan, Dennis Hart. *A Treatise on Field Fortification, Containing Instructions on the Methods of Laying Out, Constructing, Defending, and Attacking Intrenchments, with the General Outlines also of the Arrangement, the Attack and Defence of Permanent Fortifications*. New York: John Wiley, 1852.

Ministère de la Guerre. *Instruction Pratique sur les Travaux de Campagne à l'Usage des Troupes d'Infanterie*. Paris: Librairie Militaire Berger-Levrault, 1906. Updated, 1911.

O'Brien, E. D. C. *Fortification*. London: Cassell, Petter & Galpin, 1875.

Saxe, Marshal. *New System of Fortification*. Translated by C. Vallancey. Dublin: Richard James, 1757.

Schwartz, A., von. *Influence of the Experience of the Siege of Port Arthur upon the Construction of Modern Fortresses*. Translated by the Second (Military Information) Division, General Staff, War Department. Washington: Government Printing Office, 1908.

Thuillier, Henry F. *The Principles of Land Defence and Their Application to the Condition of To-day*. London: Longmans, Green, 1902.

Turner, H. *Field Fortification with Examples and Exercises*. London: Swan Sonnenschein, 1892.

Vauban, Sébastien, le Prestre de. *The New Method of Fortification*. Translated by W. Allingham. London: W. Freeman, 1702.

War Department. *Field Service Regulations: U.S. Army, 1910*. Washington: Government Printing Office, 1910.

War Office, General Staff. *Armies of the Balkan States, 1914–1918*. London: Imperial War Museum, 1996.

———. *Field Service Regulations*. London: HMSO, 1909.

———. *Handbook of the German Army, 1912* (Amended to August 1914). London: Imperial War Museum, 2002.

————. *Instruction in Field Engineering, Field Defences*. Vol. 1, Part 1. London: HMSO, 1877.

————. *Instruction in Military Engineering: Part 1 — Field Defences*. London: HMSO, 1902.

————. *Manual of Field Engineering*. London: HMSO, 1911.

————. *Military Engineering: Part 1 — Field Defences*. London: HMSO, 1908.

————. *Notes from the Front: Collated by the General Staff 1914*. Uckfield, UK: Naval and Military Press, 2008. First published 1914 by HMSO.

————. *Report on Foreign Manoeuvres in 1912*. Uckfield, UK: The Naval and Military Press, 1912, reprint of original.

Woodruff, Capt. James. *Applied Principles of Field Fortification for Line Officers*. Leavenworth, KS: Ketcheson Printing, 1909.

Yule, H. *Fortification for Officers of the Army and Students of Military History, with Illustrations and Notes*. London: William Blackwood and Sons, 1851.

SECONDARY SOURCES

Bailey, J. B. A. *Field Artillery and Firepower*. Annapolis, MD: Naval Institute Press, 2004.

Barnard, H. *Military Schools and Courses of Instructions in the Science and Art of War, in France, Prussia, Austria, Russia, Sweden, Switzerland, Sardinia, England, and the United States*. New York: E. Steiger, 1872. Reprinted and edited by Col. T. Griess and J. Luvaas. New York: Greenwood Press, 1969.

Bloch, Ivan S. *The Future of War in Its Technical, Economic, and Political Relations: Is War Now Impossible?* London: Grant Richards, 1899. Reprint, Aldershot, UK: Ashgate, 2001.

Bornecque, J. *Rôle de la Fortification dans la Dernière Guerre d'Orient*. Paris: Librarie Militaire de J. Dumaine, 1881.

Brunker, H. *Story of the Russo-Turkish War, 1877–78* (in Europe). London: Forster Groom, 1911.

Carver, Field Marshal Lord. *The Boer War*. London: Pan Books, 2000.

Chandler, D. G. *The Campaigns of Napoleon*. New York: Macmillan, 1973.

Connaughton, R. M. *The War of the Rising Sun and Tumbling Bear*. London: Routledge, 1988.

Crowe, John Henry Verinder. *An Epitome of the Russo-Turkish War, 1877–78*. London: Royal Artillery Institution, 1904.

Delbrück, Hans. *The Dawn of Modern Warfare*. Translated by Walter J. Renfroe, Jr. Vol. 4, *History of the Art of War*. Lincoln: University of Nebraska Press, 1990.

Erickson, Edward. *Defeat in Detail: The Ottoman Army in the Balkans, 1912–1913*. Westport, CT: Praeger, 2003.

Fisk, Wilbur. *Hard Marching Every Day: The Civil War Letters of Private Wilbur Fisk, 1861–1865*. Edited by Emil Rosenblatt and Ruth Rosenblatt. Lawrence: University Press of Kansas, 1992.

Formby, J. *The First Two Battles of Plevna*. London: William Clowes & Sons Limited, 1910.

Fuller, J. F. C. *Armament and History*. London: Erye and Spottiswoode, 1946.

———. *The Conduct of War, 1789–1961*. New York: Da Capo Press, 1992.

Gat, Azar. *A History of Military Thought: From the Enlightenment to the Cold War*. Oxford, UK: Oxford University Press, 2001.

Girouard, E. P. C. *History of the Railways during the War in South Africa, 1899–1902*. London: HMSO, 1903.

Goričar, Joseph. *The Inside Story of the Anglo-German Intrigue: Or How the World War Was Brought About*. Garden City, NY: Doubleday, 1920.

Griffith, Paddy. *The Art of War in Revolutionary France, 1789–1802*. London: Greenhill Books, 1998.

———. *Battle Tactics of the American Civil War*. Marlborough, UK: The Crowood Press, 1996.

Hall, R. *The Balkan Wars, 1912–1913: Prelude to the First World War*. London: Routledge, 2002.

Halleck, Henry Wager. *Elements of Military Art and Science*. Westport, CT: Greenwood Press, 1971. Reprint of 1846 edition.

Hellenic Army General Staff. *A Concise History of the Balkan Wars*. Athens: Army History Directorate Publication, 1998.

Helmreich, E. C. *The Diplomacy of the Balkan War, 1912–1913*. New York: Russell & Russell, 1969.

Herrmann, David. *The Arming of Europe and the Making of the First World War*. Princeton, NJ: Princeton University Press, 1997.

Hess, E. *Field Armies and Fortifications in the Civil War: The Eastern Campaigns, 1861–1864*. Chapel Hill: University of North Carolina Press, 2005.

———. *Trench Warfare under Grant and Lee: Field Fortifications in the Overland Campaign*. Chapel Hill: University of North Carolina Press, 2007.

Howard, Michael. *Lessons of History*. New Haven, CT: Yale University Press, 1991.

———. *War in European History*. Oxford, UK: Oxford University Press, 1993.

Hozier, Capt. H. M., ed. *The Russo-Turkish War: Including an Account of the Rise and Decline of Ottoman Power and the History of the Eastern Question*. 5 vols. London: William Mackenzie, 1878.

Hudleston, F. J. *Gentleman Johnny Burgoyne*. Indianapolis: Bobbs-Merrill, 1927.

Hughes, Maj. Gen. B. P. *Firepower: Weapons Effectiveness on the Battlefield, 1630–1850*. New York: Sarpedon, 1997.

Knox, MacGregor, and Williamson Murray, eds. *The Dynamics of Military Revolution, 1300–2050*. New York: Cambridge University Press, 2008.

Langlois, Hippolyte. *Lessons from Two Recent Wars*. London: HMSO, 1909.

Luvaas, Jay, ed. *Frederick the Great on the Art of War*. New York: Free Press, 1966.

———. *The Military Legacy of the Civil War: The European Inheritance*. Lawrence: University Press of Kansas, 1988.

———, ed. *Napoleon on the Art of War*. New York: Touchstone, 2001.

Maurice, Maj. Gen. Sir Frederick. *History of the War in South Africa: 1899–1902*. 4 vols. 1906. Reprint, Uckfield, UK: Naval and Military Press, 2004.

———. *The Russo-Turkish War, 1877: A Strategical Sketch*. London: Swan Sonnenschein, 1905.

Menning, Bruce W. *Bayonets before Bullets: The Imperial Russian Army, 1861–1914*. Bloomington: Indiana University Press, 1992.

Nasson, Bill. *The South African War, 1899–1902*. London: Arnold, 1999.

Packenham, Thomas. *The Boer War*. New York: Avon Books, 1979.

Patrikeeff, Felix, and Harry Shukman. *Railways and the Russo-Japanese War: Transporting War*. New York: Routledge, 2007.

Phillips, Thomas Raphael, ed. *Roots of Strategy: A Collection of Military Classics*. London: John Lane, 1943.

Philpott, William. *Bloody Victory: The Sacrifice on the Somme and the Making of the Twentieth Century*. London: Little, Brown, 2009.

Piarron de Mondésir, Col. Jean Frédéric Lucien. *Siège et Prise d'Adrianopole*. Paris: Librairie Chapelot, 1914.

Quéloz, Dimitry. *De la Manoeuvre Napoléonienne à l'Offensive à Outrance: La tactique générale de l'Armée Française, 1871–1914*. Paris: Institut de Stratégie Comparée, 2009.

Sarauw, Christian von. *Der Russisch-Türkische Krieg 1877 bis 1878: Auf Grundlage der Veröffentlichten Officiellen Russischen Rapporte*. Leipzig: Verlag von Bernhard Schlicke, 1879.

Smuts, Jan Christiaan. *The Boer War: Official Dispatches from Generals De La Rey, Smuts, and Others*. Philadelphia: George H. Buchanan and Company, 1902.

Sondhaus, L. *Franz Conrad von Hötzendorf: Architect of the Apocalypse*. Boston: Humanity Press, 2000.

Springer, Anton. *Der Russisch-türkische Krieg, 1877–1878, in Europa*. Vienna: Verlag von Carl Konegen, 1891.

Strachan, Hew. *European Armies and the Conduct of War*. London: Routledge, 1991.

———. *The First World War*. Vol. 1, *To Arms*. Oxford, UK: Oxford University Press, 2003.

Vachkov, A. *The Balkan Wars, 1912–1913*. Sofia, Bulgaria: Angela Publishing, 2005.

Warner, Denis, and Peggy Warner. *The Tide at Sunrise: A History of the Russo-Japanese War, 1904–5*. London: Angus and Robertson, 1975.

Winter, J. M., ed. *War and Economic Development: Essays in Memory of David Joslin*. Cambridge, UK: Cambridge University Press, 1975.

Wood, W. Birkbeck, and James Edmonds. *A History of the Civil War in the United States, 1861–1865*. New York: G. P. Putnam's Sons, 1905.

ARTICLES

Bellenger, Capt. G., and Piarron de Mondésir, Col. J. F. L. "Notes on the Employment of Artillery in the Balkan Wars." *The Royal Engineers Journal* 19 (January–June 1914): 109–13.

Buxton, N. "Balkan Geography and Balkan Railways." *The Geographical Journal* 32, no. 3 (September 1908): 217–34.

Crawford, O. G. S. "Some Linear Earthworks in the Danube Basin." *The Geographical Journal* 116, no. 4/6 (1950).

Field Artillery Journal. "New Russian Guns." 2, no. 1 (January–March 1912): 112–15.

Frere, Bartle. "On Temperate South Africa." *Proceedings of the Royal Geographical Society and Monthly Record of Geography* 3, no. 1 (January 1881): 1–19.

Generaz, Major. "Tactical Connection between Infantry and Artillery during the Battle of Liao-Yang." *Field Artillery Journal*, July–September 1914, 366–89.

Harrison, Lt. Gen. Sir R. "The Use of Field Works in War." *The United Service Magazine* 787 (June 1894): 111–27.

Hogarth, D. G. "The Balkan Peninsula." *The Geographical Journal* 41, no. 4 (April 1913): 324–36.

Holden, Lt. Col. R. M. "The Blockhouse System in South Africa." *Journal of the Royal United Services Institute* 46, no. 290 (1902): 479–89.

Journal of the United States Artillery. "The Fortifications of Adrianople." Translated by 2nd Lt. Donald Armstrong. 41, no. 3 (1914): 337–44.

Journal of the United States Cavalry Association. "Machine Gun Tactics." Translated by M. S. E. Harry Bell. 22 (May 1912): 1140–46.

Kovrigin, A. H. "Firing at Breast-Works of Snow with the Berdan Rifle." *Journal of the United States Cavalry Association* 4, no. 13 (June 1891): 161–65.

MacLeod, Ray, and Kay MacLeod. "Government and the Optical Industry in Britain, 1914–1918." In Winter, *War and Economic Development*.

Mindoff, Captain (Bulgarian Army). "Movement of Infantry in the Zone of Artillery and Infantry Fire." *Infantry Journal* 11 (July 1914–June 1915): 258–63.

Morrow, Norman P. "The Employment of Artillery in the Balkan and in the Present European War." *Field Artillery Journal*, April–June 1915, 316–36.

O'Connor, Maureen. "The Vision of Soldiers: Britain, France, Germany and the United States Observe the Russo-Turkish War." *War in History* 4, no. 3 (1997).

Pesseaud, Capt. J. "Present Tendencies in Germany Regarding the Use of Heavy Artillery." *Field Artillery Journal*, April–June 1914, 304–11.

Polyanski, V. "The Siege of Adrianople." Extract from *Injenerni Jurnal*, September 1913. In *The Royal Engineers Journal* 19 (January–June 1914): 410–26.

Professional Papers of the Corps of Royal Engineers. "Notes by a Russian Engineer on the Theatre of War in European Turkey." Translated by Capt. J. W. Savage. 9 (1883).

Reichenau, Lieutenant General von. "Tactical Lessons of the War in the Balkans." *The Royal Engineers Journal* 19 (January–June 1914): 185–88. Extracts of original taken from Militär-Wochenblatt, 30 September 1913.

Richter, Major General. "Retrospect of the Development of the German Field and Siege Artillery in the Past Twenty-Five Years." *Field Artillery Journal*, January–March 1915, 83–141.

The Royal Engineers Journal. "Report of Lt.-Gen. Skobeleff to Lt.-Gen. Prince Imeretinsky, 15 September 1877." 1878.

———. "Some Notes on Fieldworks." 19 (January–June 1914): 109–13.

Schaw, Henry. "Field Works from a Tactical Point of View." *Professional Papers of the Corps of Royal Engineers* 1 (1877).

Shimazu, Naoko. "The Myths of the 'Patriotic Soldier': Japanese Attitudes towards Death in the Russo-Japanese War." *War and Society* 19, no. 2 (October 2001).

Skobeleff, General. (From "Revue Militaire de L'Etranger," February 2, 1878). Translated by G. Plunkett. *Professional Papers of the Corps of Royal Engineers* 2 (1878): 91–104.

Sowerby, A de C. "The Exploration of Manchuria." *The Geographical Journal* 54, no. 2 (1919): 73–89.

Stewart, R. "Manchuria: The Land and Its Economy." *Economic Geography* 8, no. 2 (1932): 134–60.

Strachan, Hew. "The Battle of the Somme and British Strategy." *Journal of Strategic Studies* 21, no. 1 (March 1998): 79–85.

Travers, Tim. "Technology, Tactics, and Morale: Jean de Bloch, the Boer War, and British Military Theory, 1900–1914." *The Journal of Modern History* 51, no. 2 Technology and War (1979): 264–86.

Trioche, George Nestler. "French Artillery: The Heavy Field Batteries." *Field Artillery Journal*, January–March 1915, 74–82.

Trebilcock, Clive. "War and the Failure of Industrial Mobilisation: 1899 and 1914." In Winter, *War and Economic Development*.

Turley, R. "Some Notes on the River System of the Upper Liao, Manchuria." *The Geographical Journal* 25, no. 3 (1905): 297–300.

JOURNALS

Field Artillery Journal
Infantry Journal
Journal of Modern History
Journal of the Royal Artillery
The Journal of the Royal United Services Institution
Journal of the United States Artillery
Journal of the United States Cavalry Association
Professional Papers of the Corps of Royal Engineers
The Royal Engineers Journal
Special Supplement to the Professional Papers of the Royal Engineers
War in History

ONLINE SOURCES

Botha, Louis. "General Botha's Own Report on the Battle of Colenso." Edited and translated C. J. Barnard. South African Military History Society's *Military History Journal* 1, no. 7 (December 1970). http://samilitaryhistory.org/vol017cc.html. Accessed 14 August 2011.

Hamnett, R. Country Pasture/Forage Resource Profiles. "Bulgaria." Food and Agriculture Organization of the United Nations, November 2002–October 2006. http://www.fao.org/ag/Agp/agpc/doc/Counprof/Bulgaria/Bulgaria.htm. Accessed 20 May 2009.

HESCO Bastion Ltd. "We Are HESCO." http://www.hesco.com/index.asp. Accessed 17 April 2012.

Tomlinson, Richard. "Britain's Last Castles: Masonry Blockhouses of the South African War, 1899–1902." *The South African Military History Society's Military His-*

tory Journal 10, no. 6 (December 1997). http://samilitaryhistory.org/vol106rt .html. Accessed 2 August 2010.

Yoda, Lieutenant Colonel. "Modern Tendencies in Strategy and Tactics as Shown in Campaigns in the Far East." *The Russo-Japanese War Research Society.* February 1904–September 1905. Originally from the Kuikosha Kiji (Officers Club Journal) 352 (December 1906). Translated by Capt. E. F. Calthrop, R.F.A. Published in *The Journal of the Royal United Studies Institute* 51. http:// www.russojapanesewar.com/mod-tend.html. Accessed 20 May 2009.

Index

Greig, C. A. (British vice consul), 183–97
ground. *See* soil
guerrilla, 82, 86, 89–90, 104

Haldane, Lt. Col. A. L. (British attaché), 138, 148, 163
Halleck, Maj. Gen. Henry W., 240–41, 277
Hamid II, Abdul, 171
Hamilton, Lt. Gen. Sir Ian (British attaché), 81, 139, 161
Harbin, 127, 135
Hare, Lt. W. A. H. (British attaché), 58, 253
head cover, 113, 131, 150, 158, 160, 185, 200, 202, 205, 246
Henderson, G. F. R., 121, 243, 262
high angle fire (indirect), 4, 10, 93, 114, 124, 162, 168–69, 187–88, 212, 215–17, 220, 223, 230, 249. *See also* artillery, and bombardment
high explosive, 11, 13, 18, 127,140, 142, 152, 165–66, 205–7, 220, 248; ineffective fuses, 121, 206; melinite, 13; poudre B, 13, 111. *See also* shrapnel
Hoess, Oberleutnant (Austrian attaché), 146
Hoff, Col. John (American attaché), 136, 265
Höhneysen, (no first name) (Austrian attaché), 61–62
Holden, Lt. Col. R. M., 97, 101, 114, 117
Howland, Frederick (American journalist), 96
Hubka, Hauptmann Gustav (Austrian attaché), 201
Hume, Lt. Col. C. V. (British attaché), 157, 160–61, 267
Hutchinson, Maj. Gen. Henry, 17, 30

Imeretinsky, Prince Alexander, 62
indirect fire. *See* high angle fire
Industrial Revolution (industrial, industrialized war), 2–3, 20, 34, 45, 100, 122–23, 147, 167, 207, 231.

See also optics and Bessemer steel process
Inkerman, battle of (1854), 39
Italo-Turkish War (1911–1912), 45

Janina (Ioánnina), siege of (1912–1913), 37, 174, 178–79, 181, 184, 190, 194–95, 202, 205, 209, 273
Japanese Army, 5, 39, 123–69, 208–9, 212, 215, 221, 233, 265, 267–68
Jardine, Capt. J. B. (British attaché), 150, 157
Johannesburg, 85–86, 91
Jomini, Baron, 53
journalist. *See* Gay, J. Drew; Howland, Frederick; MacGahan, Januarius; Mackern, Henry; McCormick, Frederick; Palmer, Frederick; Unger, Frederic. *See also* attaché, consul, and observer

Kaoliang, 126–27, 144, 157, 161, 163, 165. *See also* concealment
Kars, (Turkey), 7, 37, 53–58, 70, 76, 79, 124
Kaulbars, Gen. Alexander, 158
Kazankoj, 199
Kearsey, Lt. Alexander (British officer), 94, 97–102, 106
Kemmis, Maj. William, 27
Kilkis-Lahanas, battle of (1913), 174, 182
Kimberley, town and siege of (1899–1900), 85–89, 91
Kirkkilise (Kirklareli), battle of (1912), 176–77, 183, 197, 209
Kitchener, Lord, 97–98, 122
Kosovo, 174, 178
Kresna defile, 198
Krischin, 49–50
Kruger, Paul (Boer President), 100, 106
Kuhn, Maj. Joseph (American attaché), 145–46, 152, 159–60, 162, 166, 168, 263, 265–66
Kumanovo, battle of (1912), 174, 178, 183, 185, 190, 195, 209

About the Author

Nicholas Murray received a doctorate in history from the University of Oxford. He is an associate professor at the U.S. Army Command and Staff College, where he teaches military history. His specialty is the evolution of warfare prior to 1914. He is a proponent of using the traditional military teaching technique of Tactical Exercises Without Troops as a tool to better understand military decision making.

Murray is the editor of a book on the French experience in counterinsurgency warfare, and he has written articles on fortification and the Russo-Turkish War of 1877–1878, as well several articles on professional military education. He lives in Lawrence, Kansas.